Portrait in Grey

To the memory of my teachers

Reginald William Sorensen (1891–1971)
Jane Cattell-Jones (1891–1983)

John Punshon was Quaker Studies Tutor in
the 1980s at Woodbrooke Quaker Study
Centre, Birmingham, and until retirement
Professor at Earlham School of Religion,
the Quaker seminary in Richmond,
Indiana. He is widely travelled among
Friends, and his books include this general
Quaker history, *Portrait in Grey*, and
Encounter with Silence, an introduction
to Quaker worship. His Swarthmore
Lecture for 1990, *Testimony and Tradition*,
examined the nature of the Quaker
testimonies, and his latest book, *Reasons
for Hope* (2001) is an assessment of the
present state of Evangelical Quakerism.
Though now back in England, he remains
a recorded minister in Indiana Yearly
Meeting.

Portrait in Grey

A SHORT HISTORY OF THE QUAKERS

John Punshon

QUAKERbooks

First published May 1984, reprinted with revisions 1986.
Second edition published September 2006 by Quaker
Books

© John Punshon 1984, 2006.

www.quaker.org.uk

ISBN 0 85245 399 X

The cover image is a watercolour by Evelyn Ashby
of Godalming meeting house, 1939. © Library of the
Religious Society of Friends, London

Cover design: Hoop Associates
Book design and typesetting: Golden Cockerel Press

Contents

Foreword to the Second Edition

THE QUAKERS ARE AN INTERESTING IF NOT A PUZZLING phenomenon. They worship in silence but publish a continuous stream of books and pamphlets largely about themselves. They are few in number yet you find them everywhere, often in places of considerable influence. They are fearless social reformers and have a very good head for business, some of their leading families being among the richest in England at the time of the Industrial Revolution. They proclaim a great message, yet do it in curiously muted tones. They have never celebrated sacraments nor borne arms. They have never refused to recognise women as ministers and their status as Christians is unquestioned, except by free-thinking members of their own community. They recognise a bond of unity among themselves, but have never appropriated the title of 'church', preferring to call themselves a 'society' only. The basis of the unity they feel with one another is not doctrine but an attitude which gave rise to one of their earlier names – Friends of Truth.

Quakers are serious people. Rightly so, for their vocation is a serious business. You do not seek to defeat the forces of prejudice, ignorance and cruelty in society unless you are in deadly earnest. Though there is a special off-beat Quaker humour, the belly laugh is not one of their gifts. This makes them introspective – defining the proper 'Quakerly' attitude to a multitude of matters is their greatest sport. Seeking to avoid spiritual pride they view with suspicion the use of language, history and theology in any way that might fetter the personal quest for truth of any of their members. They much prefer to travel hopefully than to arrive.

To outsiders, they are frequently annoying. Their kindly, calm and tolerant religion is difficult to convey in words. Those who seek to experience it by worshipping with them tend to end up by becoming Quakers. They seldom answer questions about their faith directly. Some are deeply mystical and have much in common with adherents of other faiths with whom they seem more at home; some are so deeply

9

rooted in biblical faith as to be fundamentalists – one yearly meeting in America going so far as to refuse to recognise all the rest. They are a world-wide fraternity, yet have no central authority. They are so small in numbers that in some countries all the Quakers know all the other Quakers. There are Anglo-Saxon Quakers, Masai Quakers, Mexican Quakers, Eskimo Quakers, Chinese Quakers, Nepali, Indonesian and Navajo Indian Quakers. A bewildered onlooker might ask, where is the unity in this mass of people as varied as the human race itself?

Part of the answer lies in the Quaker tradition, the story of what the Friends have done and said and written, what they have stood for, and even died for, since they arose as a people in seventeenth-century England. There are perhaps three parts to this story. It begins with the rise of London Yearly Meeting, 'the mother church of Quakerism'. The focus then shifts to the story of Friends in America, with William Penn almost at the beginning and the election of two Quaker presidents, Herbert Hoover and Richard Nixon, when we reach the twentieth century. The third phase of the story involves the spread of Quakerism round the world, thanks largely to missionary endeavour from the evangelical yearly meetings in the United States.

This book was written over twenty years ago now, and since that time a number of significant additions to our knowledge of the Quaker movement have been made. Theological and historical work have both continued vigorously, and the internal questions that animate the Quaker body have changed in some measure. I have stuck nevertheless to this overall plan because it seems the simplest thing to do. The time will come when incremental change will render some of my sections obsolete, but the successor volume will appear, I think, when Friends relinquish the current historical orthodoxy, that Quakerism is best seen as a variant of Puritanism, and a new overall interpretation of Quaker history takes the field.

As I said in the original Foreword twenty years ago, I was aiming for an impossible combination of brevity and comprehensiveness, and what I wrote would be open to criticism at many points, notably its balance, its selection of material, and the stances it took. A longer book would have been written differently, the logical holes closed or concealed, the dubious judgements cut out and the overstatements toned down. Fortunately, not too many of these things have been noticed in the present volume, and I am both astonished and gratified that people still find it useful. So it has been a privilege to prepare a second edition.

The previous text is reproduced almost entirely but I have added several new passages, notably a section on George Fox's trip to America, a new account of the demography of the early Friends, and a fuller treatment of Friends and the Second Great Awakening. The last chapter has been reworked to take account of my own recent reflections, and I have decided to end by a consideration of the possible future of religion in Europe and North America generally rather than of the Society of Friends specifically.

When I look at the list of people who were of great help to me when I originally wrote *Portrait in Grey*, I see that some of them have been called to their rest, while others are still only a phone call away. These folks are: my wife and family, Hugh Barbour, Clifford Barnard, Tom Bodine, Wilmer Cooper, Hugh Doncaster, Howard Gregg, Herbert Hadley, David J. Hall, Ted Milligan, Neville Newhouse, Geoffrey F. Nuttall, Joseph Pickvance, Elizabeth Watson, George Watson, and Arthur G. Olver. I am grateful, too, to Peter Daniels for overseeing the production of this second edition. My perspectives have changed and been enriched over the years, and for this I am grateful to all my friends and academic colleagues with whom I have carried on a wonderful (and continuing) conversation. I owe a special debt of gratitude to my students at Woodbrooke and Earlham School of Religion, and also at George Fox University, which I have been privileged to visit on many occasions. Above all, I am grateful to the Warwickshire Monthly Meeting evening class where I first presented the ideas and personalities who appear in this book about a quarter of a century ago. They gave the book its shape, and determined the way I have taught Quaker studies ever since. My final thanks go to all those Friends who have found *Portrait in Grey* helpful over the years and whose encouragement has been a blessing.

John Punshon
Milton Keynes

1 November 2005

The Roots of Quakerism in the Reformation

I N THEIR OWN ESTIMATION, THE ENGLISH PEOPLE ARE ORDINARY, law-abiding and undemonstrative. They like dogs and children, the countryside, plain food, and talking about the weather. They play tedious games such as dominoes, cribbage and cricket, and drink a lot of beer and tea. Their well known talent for self-government is little more than an obstinate disrespect for any government at all, and they have a deep suspicion of preachers, politicians and intellectuals. Secretly, though, as anyone knows who has studied their history, they are nothing of the sort. They are poetic, war-like and religious. They would grumblingly (but with secret pride) accept the achievements of Shakespeare or Wordsworth. They would gladly (but sheepishly) accept as deserved the great reputations of the Dukes of Marlborough and Wellington. But only shifty embarrassment would follow the suggestion that both their Catholic and Protestant pasts have permanently enriched Western Christianity.

Yet, such is the case. It was under the former dispensation that Pelagius threw down what was a challenge to Augustine but a lifeline to many modern Christians; that Boniface was called to be the Apostle to the Germans; that the Italian Anselm became the greatest mind to adorn the see of Canterbury, and that in the later Middle Ages prosperous towns and quiet villages nourished a profound school of Christian mysticism. At the Reformation, the Church of England could not wholly let go of the past, and its world-wide communion now bears witness to the possibility of the reunion of all Christians. Puritanism, though, in its widest sense, gave classical form to Protestantism in the

Anglo-Saxon world, perhaps giving an irresistible impulse to democratic sentiments, literature and revival alike in the persons of Milton, Bunyan and Wesley. The Quakers are an integral part of this story, and, though they have now spread all over the world, they were originally as English as a wet summer Sunday, and it is in England that any telling of their story must begin.

Seventeenth-Century Society

Seventeenth-century England was in crisis. The opening of the period saw the installation of the new Stuart dynasty in the person of King James I (and VI of Scotland). The middle years saw the ultimate dislocation of civil war. The closing years brought a political settlement in the 'Glorious' revolution of 1688 which forms the basis of the modern British Constitution. The nation was still crossing over the slender bridge which separates the Middle Ages from recognisably modern times. There was an uncertainty of direction in some; a revolutionary confidence in destiny in others. Some displayed a caution that hankered after a lost security; others possessed a sublime confidence born of misreading the signs of the times. Apart from entrepreneurs and placemen, probably nobody got what he wanted. Compromises abounded, and the conflicts of the century bred in the succeeding generations a cynicism about politics and a contempt for religious idealism.

Paradoxically, it is out of this apparently unpromising milieu that England gave birth to parliamentary democracy and religious toleration. In addition, it also nourished two of the most respected national institutions – the Royal Society and the Religious Society of Friends. It is a baffling and exciting period, and to understand the emergence of the Quakers we must understand what the seventeenth-century turmoil was about.

With the benefit of hindsight, we can see that England was well set on the process of growth that was to mature into the Industrial Revolution. There are no figures to compare with our modern statistical information, but it seems likely that the population had doubled in the century before 1650 to a level of about five million. Life expectancy was low, but provided you reached the middle thirties, you had a fair chance of reaching a ripe old age. Infant mortality was high and all classes were vulnerable to a much wider range of disease and disability. The proportion of active and productive people in the population was probably considerably higher than it is today. Nine people in every ten lived in the country and London, the largest city in Europe outside Constantinople, far outstripped its English rivals in size. Manchester and Birmingham were little more than villages. Towns such as Bristol, Norwich, York, Coventry and Newcastle-upon-Tyne were the centres of what urban population there was.

So the economy had an agricultural base, but a very diverse one with considerable regional variations. There was a complicated marketing system and inland trade did not suffer the system of internal tolls and customs that were often encountered on the Continent. Contrary to the popular view, there was considerable specialisation and innovation in farming techniques. There was a steady and undramatic trend towards the enclosure of waste and forest land, and towards the consolidation of smallholdings and the ancient open fields into intensively farmed estates. This often created social tensions and was achieved by the dispossession or forcible buying out of smaller farmers. Significant developments were taking place in this countryside of enclosed capitalist estates, open fields, moors, commons and forests.

As the pressures of increasing population came to be felt, a market economy was beginning to develop. Communications improved along with farming methods and rural unemployment was on the increase. Contrary to the popular view, the small nuclear family was the norm rather than the extended family network, and it was rare, rather than usual, for more than a couple of generations to continue to live in one place. Underemployment meant that many men were seasonal and part-time farm workers, and a sizeable pool of under-utilised labour emerged, often available for the 'outwork' that preceded the factory system. Cottage trades and crafts were carried on and the products sold to merchants. These often supplied the equipment, collected the goods, occasionally finished them and then undertook the marketing at home, in Europe, or in the burgeoning trade with the East and the colonies in America.

Technical change and increasing output was also a feature of manufacturing industry at the time, notably in coal, iron and woollen goods. It is probably going too far to suggest that there was an 'industrial revolution' in the seventeenth century, but the origins of the greater Industrial Revolution, with which we are familiar, appear above the surface of history at this point, and they are part of the turbulent story of the period. There is no need to accept a thoroughgoing theory of economics as the engine of history to take account of its influence.

In the fifty years before the outbreak of the Civil War in 1642 there were some very bad harvests and three severe crises in trade.

Behind all these developments in late Tudor and early Stuart times there was one stark fact: the English economy was coming to terms with one of the most severe and prolonged price inflations in its history. Fortunes were made and lost in land. Many of the smaller farmers found their holdings enclosed by more powerful neighbours, and many of the small gentry, who had let land on long leases at low rents, were ruined. Equally, those in a position to speculate were able either to farm for the market themselves or else to increase their own wealth by letting out estates at high rents. Financiers and professional men such as lawyers were favourably affected by these developments, and among the merchant classes economic power was becoming concentrated in fewer and fewer hands.

For the rest, there were rising prices and hunger. England was characterised by poverty, unemployment and vagrancy. There were elegant Jacobean mansions and deer parks. There were also many paupers' graves on the cold north side of the churchyard. For the insecure or the dispossessed, there were many possible responses: emigration, crime, political sycophancy or the aggressive pursuit of wealth. But these are personal solutions. In an age when politics and religion were intimately connected, men who sought the common good looked to the social causes of their difficulties. The circumstances of the age were a recipe for trouble, and in due course trouble materialised.

It came on two fronts, in ways that were intimately connected, though the separation of church and state in a modern secular democracy predisposes us to think of them separately. At that time the machinery of state and the machinery of the church were two aspects of one power structure, and the Quakers and other dissenters were to find that if you took on one, you took on the other too. At the head stood a divinely ordained monarch, who was considered to be God's vicegerent in matters spiritual and temporal. The church sat in Parliament in the persons of the bishops, who had their own courts. These exercised a wide jurisdiction including the censorship of morals, blasphemy, adultery, intestacy, the proof of wills, and a range of matters relating to questions of illegitimacy and the validity or annulment of marriages.

Much of the royal power was exercised outside Parliament under the 'Prerogative'. The King in Council acted through a number of bodies. Among them was the Privy Council, which reached deep down into society by appointing and supervising the Justices of the Peace, district officials – usually smaller landowners – responsible for the lower criminal courts and what we would now call 'local government'. In tandem with the Privy Council was the infamous Court of Star Chamber, a secretive and authoritarian tribunal that took responsibility for public order and crimes against the state. Part of the Privy Council was constituted as the High Commission, which exercised the Crown's authority over the church. When the seeds of Quakerism were germinating in the rich soil of Puritanism, it was the implacable hostility of this body that did so much to persuade the dissidents that the state church was beyond redemption or reform.

When James I was petitioned to introduce a Presbyterian form of church government in 1604 he is reputed to have remarked, 'No bishop, no King'. So there was a double jeopardy: to oppose the church was also to oppose the state and that could not be tolerated. In the days of the Cold War, President Eisenhower spoke of the 'industrial–military complex', then considered by many to have excessive influence on the policymaking of the superpowers. At that time there was an 'administrative–ecclesiastical complex', a leviathan which the religious and political reformers of the seventeenth century set out to slay. It was in the heart of this struggle that the Quaker movement came into being.

Partial Reformation

The nub of the religious problem lay in the peculiar nature of the English Reformation. The break with Rome had been anything but clear-cut. Henry VIII (1509–47) broke the constitutional and financial ties with the Papacy, neutralised the incipient Lutheran party in England and had himself constituted 'Supreme Head of the Church'. In the reign of his adolescent son Edward VI (1547–53) the church was steered in a strongly Protestant direction but went into sharp reverse when Edward's half-sister, Mary (1553–8), restored the Roman allegiance with such severity that her name has become a by-word for repression and cruelty. She soon died, however, and matters settled down during the long reign of her half-sister, Elizabeth (1558–1603). The last Tudor certainly made England a firmly Protestant nation, but at the expense of fudging the issue of which brand of Protestantism it was to have. 'The wolves out of Geneva', as the new Queen called them, the refugees from Mary's persecution, flocked back to positions in Elizabeth's church from their

17

lairs in the mercantile cities of Europe expecting a thoroughly reformed church to be Calvinist in theology and Presbyterian in organisation. It was not what they found, and thus began the Puritan movement that would ultimately wage a civil war, abolish bishops, execute a king and establish a republic. The Presbyterians, the Congregationalists (or Independents) and the Baptists were its legitimate offspring, its love-child was the Society of Friends.

The early Quakers bequeathed a vast literature of tracts, pamphlets, letters, records and journals to subsequent generations, and from this material it is possible to build up a clear picture of what they were saying. Nevertheless, any theory of their origins must be subject to considerable qualification. Sometimes they appear in the Puritan mould. At other times they bear the imprint of spiritual movements in Continental Europe. Sometimes they appear to reflect the genius of their founder, George Fox (1624–1691). Often they just look like a group of people who have joyfully come to the same discovery of religious faith.

Here we shall not attempt an assessment of these things. Rather we shall attempt to show the richness and diversity of the influences working upon them, and hence the solid foundation on which they built their church. In turn we shall see Quakerism as a logical outcome of the Puritan impulse, Quakerism as the legatee of Continental spiritual religion, and finally Quakerism in its connections with political radicalism in the aftermath of the English Civil War.

The meaning of the word 'Puritan' is a matter of lively debate among scholars. Below a certain level of precision, however, some generalisations are reasonably safe. The root of the word is 'pure', and Puritans were people who were not satisfied that the state church was either sufficiently free of Catholic practices or sufficiently faithful in its doctrine to what they supposed the Bible to teach. Puritans of various shades of opinion united in the view that scripture was the final authority in matters of faith and practice, and was entirely sufficient to decide all questions of religion. Their criticisms of the organisation, worship and doctrines of the established church were based on the conviction that, as they stood, these things were offensive to what the Bible taught.

First, they objected to the idea that there should be any government of the Church except through Christ, its head. They therefore rejected episcopacy, the system of church government by which authority extended downwards from (in England) the monarch, through the archbishops and bishops to the parish clergy. This system fitted neatly into the authoritarian structure of the state, and any alteration of it would have entailed considerable social and religious change. The main Puritan alternative was Presbyterianism. This was an hierarchy of assemblies and synods with both clerical and lay membership. There was a place for ministers and elders, for teaching, preaching and the ordinances of baptism and the supper, but not for an authority that by its actions supplanted Christ.

In the same way, the Puritans sought to base their worship firmly on the Word of God and the apostolic precedents. They rejected all practices that could not be justified from these sources, and came into conflict with those who argued that what the scriptures did not forbid was permissible. Among Puritans, the whole congregation sang praise in psalms and hymns, not just the choir. The main feature of the service was a sermon which expounded the Word directly to the worshippers, not the reading of a printed homily. A similar defence against second-hand sentiment lay in the rejection of responses to recited or chanted prayers and litanies. Puritans preferred to pray standing. At the communion service the minister faced his flock, who often communicated seated. The bishops' courts engaged in a constant battle throughout this period with Puritan vicars and congregations who would not bow to episcopal instructions as to how worship should be conducted.

One such engagement was fought at Fenny Drayton in Leicestershire, the birthplace of George Fox, the first Quaker. One Anthony Nutter became rector there in 1582. In 1590 he was imprisoned as one of the leaders of the Elizabethan Presbyterian Movement and in 1605 he was deprived of his living for failure to conform to the Book of Common Prayer. The Bishop's Transcripts of the Drayton parish registers reveal that a number of parishioners were also disciplined or punished in various ways for Puritan leanings, and some were even excommunicated. It was a strong Puritan parish, enjoying such protection as the Puritan Lord of the Manor could provide, and, significantly, the father of George Fox was twice a churchwarden there and would have been closely involved in these events.

The third target of the Puritan movement is less clear. Perhaps particular statements about Christian doctrine should really be seen as expressions of a particular kind of spirituality. If they are, we can treat formal doctrines with a degree of sympathetic freedom that we might otherwise withhold if they are not really to our liking. If we do this, we shall see in Puritanism a beauty and an idealism that we might overlook. Many people have puzzled over the fact that they find much to admire in Puritanism but not much that they like.

If we balance its doctrines with its spirituality, then we shall understand it better and perhaps be able to understand why some Quaker historians seek the origins of their denomination there, rather than in the traditionally acceptable quarters. We should also be clear that we are dealing with a movement rather than a school of thought with consistently thought-out positions: some Puritans followed John Calvin; others did not; Puritans differed over doctrine, strategy and tactics; the word had a strong political connotation over and above its religious use; some people came to essentially Puritan positions independently of the influences operating within the movement, and so on.

What we can say is that it was a loose body of doctrine and attitudes which sought to change the nature of the established church in England in a consistent fashion towards the main positions of the continental reformers. That meant a more thoroughgoing Protestantism than the Anglican compromise would allow, or, it seems, will still allow, to judge from the continued existence of the Free Churches and the successive collapses of ecumenical initiatives designed to heal this four-hundred-year-old breach in the unity of English church life.

The Puritan Experience

At the centre of Puritanism was a profound experience of divine grace, an awareness of the reality of God, a confidence in his providence, and a reliance on his illimitable love. This experience came painfully, through crisis, through the acknowledgement of one's status as sinful and lost, and through the realisation that personal acceptance of Christ's sacrifice on the cross meant forgiveness and freedom from the dire penalties that were the destiny of the unrepentant. The first notes of the Puritan's reformation symphony were glory, triumph and joy.

The development section worked out the consequences of this. If God were all powerful, all wise, all loving and all good, mankind was in comparison wicked, depraved and lost. Since the story of God's love in Christ was only to be found in the inspired word of scripture, it was there that the key to salvation was to be found. The Puritans thought that they had found this key. They were the elect, the saints, those predestined for salvation from the beginning of the world, and to them, through their experience, a true understanding had been given. They looked for moral regeneration in all things – in the heart, the family, the job and the nation. Aware that a church that admitted reason and tradi-tion as elements in its theology was substituting intellect for experience, many of them antedated the Quakers in taking a critical attitude to the historic creeds. If they were chosen to see and hear, those who were deaf and blind to God's message were doomed to eternal damnation.

But these considerations led to a restatement of the theme. They did not provide ease and comfort, for God had also withheld certainty that one was really of the elect. One could never be sure. So the salt of insecurity was also present in Puritanism in some measure. As the Puritans strove to attain personal perfection they also strove to make the nation into a godly community.

At this point the political aspects of Puritanism emerge. For some, the solution was to constitute themselves into an autocracy, able to govern people properly for their own good. The Quakers were to experi-ence their first sufferings at the hands of this brand of Puritanism in the period of the Interregnum between 1649 and 1660. The other solution was to emphasise the equality and freedom that is inseparable from life within the redeemed community. Quakerism left its Puritan home very early in life and it was perhaps through this door that it departed.

The Puritans came to be seen as cold, joyless people, hardy and unforgiving, censorious, withdrawn, fearful of contamination by the ordinary pleasures of life, obsessed with sin, strangers to culture, nar-row-minded and self-righteous. Shakespeare poked fun at them in the character of Malvolio in *Twelfth Night*. Jonson lampooned them through the ludicrous Zeal-of-the-land Busy, who overturns a display of toys in Bartholomew Fair because he sees 'the peeping popery of the stalls'. Everybody knows the gaiety of the Cavaliers. Equally, they know the gloom of the Roundheads, the Puritans-in-arms who secured un-dying opprobrium by daring to abolish Christmas.

But caricatures are intentionally false. They are designed to achieve their effect by distortion, and while many Puritans undoubtedly were austere and lifeless, it is significant that the great historian J. R. Green takes the character of John Milton, graceful, cultivated, heroic and profoundly religious as '. . . not only the highest, but the completest type of Puritanism'. Possibly the finest short summary of the Puritan philosophy of life is expressed by Lucy Hutchinson, wife of Col. John Hutchinson, regicide and defender of Nottingham during the Civil War, 'By Christianity I intend that universal habit of grace which is wrought in the soul by the regenerating Spirit of God, whereby the whole creature is resigned up into the Divine will and love and all its actions designed to the obedience and glory of its Maker'.

So there were Puritans and Puritans, and some were purer than others. One way of testing people's purity was to question their relationship to the establishment. Many, probably most, aimed at a reform of the church from within, a gradual gaining of influence so that it could be changed by weight of conviction. Wealthy Puritans purchased 'advowsons', the right to present clergymen to parishes, and then appointed men of Puritan persuasion. There was even an attempt to set up a trust to raise funds for this purpose on a larger and more organised scale, but it was scotched. Preachers had to be licensed by bishops. Since preaching was the main medium for the communication of Puritan ideas, licenses were withdrawn from the outspoken – so 'lectures' were given on weekdays and stipends arranged for lecturers, often by the mayor and corporation of the larger towns who were thus able to sidestep episcopal authority. The Book of Common Prayer was ignored, reinterpreted or used selectively. Clergy, sometimes with laity, met for 'prophesyings', or groups at which common interpretations of scripture, and thereby policy, were arrived at. Such Puritans as these 'conformed' and agitated from within. They were the reformers. The revolutionaries, however, were impatient. They would not wait for disobedient loyalty to change the face of the national church.

As the seventeenth century dawned, a movement began to gather momentum. It wanted 'reformation without tarrying for any'. This, the title of an epoch-making book by Robert Browne (1550–1633), was the watchword of the Separatists, groups of Christians who gave up the establishment to go it alone, to set up their own churches under their own discipline, free from government control. As George Fox and the other early Quakers were growing into maturity, this movement was gaining strength, though Brownism itself was a spent force. Any attempt to classify the Separatists runs the risk of reading back into their lives the distinctions of doctrine and organisation which have meaning for us, but which they might not have considered of comparable importance.

Perhaps they were distinguished from one another largely by emphasis. Perhaps our hindsight picks out those movements that were to survive rather than those that were important at the time. However that may be, the period sees the emergence of three recognisably historic communions. The Presbyterians, who conformed, lent theological colour to other groups who did not accept the policy of one all-inclusive state church on their pattern. The churches of the Congregational principle, Independency, believed authority to lie with each gathered local church based on a covenant entered into by each member with the other members of the congregation and with God. They themselves did not accept the label 'separatist', for many, if not most, looked for the 'comprehension' of different tendencies within the one state church. The Baptists, whose roots, we shall see, were only partly Puritan, took the issue of believers' baptism as their point of departure with all the rest.

The archetypal Separatists were the little congregation predominantly from around Gainsborough and Scrooby in Lincolnshire which sought refuge in Amsterdam and later Leyden in the Netherlands, some members of which sailed for America in 1620. They completed their journey in the immortal *Mayflower* and are known to history as the Pilgrim Fathers. Separation meant persecution, and whatever else one may say about the Puritans, they had the courage of their convictions in fullest measure. The Quakers, who possibly suffered more at the hands of the national church than other groups, were not breaking new ground in this respect. In 1652, George Fox encountered a large group of Christians in Westmorland and North Lancashire. They have been variously described and variously characterised. It is significant that Fox himself calls them separatists. (It is worth noting in this connection that some years afterwards, the early Friend James Parnell, 1636–1656, appears to have been connected with the small worshipping community who remained in England after the Pilgrims had departed.)

Thoroughgoing Reformation

For some centuries, while there was a bitter vitality in the controversies and animosities that it engendered, the Reformation was seen as a process whereby new ideas were able to survive by the protection of enlightened princes and rulers. In England, Scotland, Switzerland, the Netherlands and much of Germany, Protestant churches were established by law. However, while freedom to dissent from Rome was permissible, it was only allowed on terms. It seems that outside the Netherlands and some of the free cities of Europe, the particular brand of reform favoured by the state became a new orthodoxy and for many, Protestant authoritarianism was substituted for the Catholic variety. It has gradually become clear that in the shadow of this 'Magisterial Reformation' there was also a 'Radical Reformation', the growth of a widespread grass-roots movement which was based on different conceptions of Christianity and was regarded as subversive. Intertwined with the story of the Puritans there is the English end of this radical movement, and this is where the other main tap-root of Quakerism is to be found.

For many years before the rise of the Quakers, there had existed in England small communities of people and many isolated individuals whose religious experience conformed to other patterns than the self-conscious biblical rectitude for which the Puritans strove. For the most part they are hidden from the eye of history. Most were humble, most were discreet. Occasionally they appear in the records of the time as heretics to be punished in the bishops' courts, or as subversives whose views were dangerous to the state. But they represented an essential strand in the Christian tradition: they looked not to a written record for the way to salvation but to a direct encounter with the Saviour himself. Recognising the truth of Paul's dictum that the letter kills and the spirit gives life, they sought the life of the spirit. When the first Quaker preachers roved the length and breadth of England, these people found a coherence that they had not known before. From diverse standpoints, from obscure places in separatist congregations, from silent dissent from the established church, they came into the Society of Friends to find there, as many ex-Puritans did, a different kind of fulfilment.

It is certainly possible, for example, that the beginnings of Quakerism overlay the last dying embers of Lollardy, the great medieval movement for the reform of the Church which began in the halls of Oxford, spread over much of the country, was driven underground and surfaced finally some two hundred years later in the Tudor period, when it seems to have merged with newer and more vigorous expressions of dissent. The name 'Lollard' was originally given to the preaching priests associated with John Wycliffe (d. 1384), a trenchant critic of the establishment of his day. If Chaucer and Langland were cutting, Wycliffe's criticisms were potentially lethal.

He struck at the Church in three directions. He advocated free access to scripture and translated the Bible into English to make it possible. He attacked the functions and privileges of the priestly caste, notably the abuses of confession and elaborate theological sophistry. He called for 'evangelical poverty' and faced a worldly, political Church with the challenge of separation from the world. He was opposed to war, luxury and waste. He was, therefore, a dangerous man. Protected by his patron in his rectory at Lutterworth in Leicestershire (not twenty miles from the birthplace of George Fox), he sent out his 'hedge-priests' to preach his message.

Their success was not inconsiderable. Despite later persecution they were numerous and widespread enough to be the objects of official policy formulated at the highest level. Unlike many sects that were merely a nuisance, the Lollards were a serious threat. Their name lent itself as a term of abuse for dissenters generally in official propaganda. The direct influence of Lollardy on the English Reformation is hard to portray, though it doubtless provided a focus for the loyalty of radical Christians in England over a period of at least two centuries, down to Tudor times. In many ways, it prepared the ground for new growths. One of these was Anabaptism, which, a cursory reading of the Thirty-Nine Articles of the Church of England will reveal, was a heresy the Establishment loved to hate.

There are many swirls and eddies in the Anabaptist tradition. The word itself simply designates that group of Reformation Christians who believed in the necessity of adult baptism and hence required the re-baptism of all those who had received the sacrament as children. The horror the word aroused depended largely on the events at Münster in Westphalia between 1534 and 1535 when a group of enthusiasts set up an independent theocratic state which practised adult baptism, naturally, but also polygamy, an enforced communism and fanatically violent resistance to the besieging forces of their dispossessed bishop, which finally retook the city and killed them all.

Needless to say, Anabaptism was in fact a far less lurid phenomenon than this. Its central tenet was that the Church was a fellowship constituted through the Holy Spirit of those who had come into membership of it by their own free choice. It was also a 'gathered' church of those fully committed to obedience to Christ's teachings, notably the Sermon on the Mount. Thus, the rite of Christian initiation, baptism, could only be conferred on the adult believer. Since the essential feature of baptism was that it was voluntary, there could be no coercion by the state in spiritual matters. The Anabaptist tradition, therefore, stood for non-violence and for freedom of conscience.

It had other features less familiar to modern mainstream Christianity. It saw the contemporary Church outside itself as 'apostate' from the true faith and irredeemably corrupt. It believed in the imminent end of both the world and the apostasy, and that it was therefore the duty of each Christian to take part in a world-wide mission that would prepare the way for the imminent judgement.

When the wraps were taken off English Protestantism on the demise of Henry VIII in 1547, Anabaptism was already seen as a serious threat. There was certainly a native English Baptist tradition, but we also know that in 1567, when the Duke of Alva assumed power in the Netherlands, large numbers of Anabaptist and other refugees sought asylum in London and the towns of south-east England, notably Norwich, where by 1587 a majority of the population was reputed to have been immigrant. By this time, however, Anabaptism was itself being overtaken by the development of Separatism within Puritanism, which gave scope to many of its ideas in an indigenous key, and the flow of refugees was moving once more from England to the Continent.

The flow and counter-flow of religious refugees at this time promoted considerable intellectual and spiritual intercourse among Christians of a radical disposition in England and Continental Europe. On one view this connection is crucial for the understanding of Quaker origins, for when we focus on earlier European Anabaptism we find within it several emphases or tendencies, one of them being what we might cautiously call the 'spiritualising' tendency, and its adherents 'spirituals'. What is remarkable about them is the close similarity between some of the ideas they put forward and the message later preached by the Quakers. In Hans Denck (c.1500–1527) and Sebastian Franck (c.1499–c.1542), for example, to name two among the half dozen or so usually cited, we can observe a preoccupation with certain themes which certainly antedated, may well have influenced, and arguably even caused, Quakerism to take the course it actually did among the possible lines of development open to it when the radical log-jam broke in England in the early 1640s.

Anabaptism and Apostasy

The first published work of Hans Denck provides an excellent point of departure for a consideration of these themes. In 1525 he was sacked from his position as principal of St Sebald's school in Nuremberg when his views as outlined in his *Confession* were deemed unacceptable to the kind of Lutheran reform the city council was seeking to promote. Denck begins by asserting his own weakness and describing himself as a 'pitiable' man. Nevertheless, he says that he has experience of 'something' which is strongly opposed to his 'natural obstinate nature'. This points him towards a life of blessedness which appears 'as impossible for my soul to attain as it seems impossible for my body to climb up into the visible sky'.

Faith is obviously that which would provide the way, and Denck is at pains to point out that such faith cannot be the product of his own natural understanding operating on the words of scripture, by definition, as it were. Accordingly, scripture is a lantern shining in darkness, unable by itself to disperse the darkness completely. 'But when the day breaks in our hearts, the eternal light, the morning star, faith, like a mustard seed which presently points to the sun of righteousness, Christ . . . the darkness of unbelief is overcome instantly.' In all honesty he adds, 'This has not yet taken place within me.'

Later on Denck is more specific. In his *Recantation*, as he moves back from his Anabaptist phase, he says, 'I hold the scriptures dear above all of men's treasures, but not as high as the Word of God which is living, strong, eternal and free of all the elements of this world; for inasmuch as it is God Himself, it is spirit and not letter, written without pen or paper so that it can never be erased. Consequently, salvation is not bound to Scripture, even though Scripture may be conducive to salvation. The reason is this: Scripture cannot possibly change an evil heart even though it may make men more learned.'

This view has profound consequences for all departments of Christian doctrine. If only Christ in the heart can unlock the meaning of scripture, the weight of importance will shift from externals to internals, from theology to spirituality. Salvation will come to be seen less as the once-and-for-all reconciliation achieved by the historical Jesus on the cross, perceived intellectually, and more as a process maturing within the soul as the Christian is led to become more Christ-like. This in turn could give rise to renewed interest in the sacraments as symbols of grace and the development of an inward understanding of their significance.

The Anabaptists felt the inner grace of regeneration so strongly that they set great store by baptism and the sort of personal commitment it signified. 'Do you not know that all of us who have been baptized into Christ Jesus were baptized into his death? We were buried therefore with him by baptism into death, so that as Christ was raised from the dead by the glory of the Father, we too might walk in newness of life' (Romans 6:3). They emphasised the spiritual truth of these words, and this made them distinctive.

Conceived in this way, baptism was release from death, and the believer strove to realise Christ's life in his or her own. The pattern of spiritual discipleship was therefore Christ, who lived a life of obedience, love, non-resistance and martyrdom. This last was seen as the inevitable outcome of the Christ-like life, and willingness to undergo the sufferings imposed on them was central to the Anabaptists' witness. Believers' baptism was not to be undertaken lightly, for it involved very demanding ethical and spiritual standards.

The theme was repeated in the Anabaptist understanding of the Lord's Supper. They attached no importance to the elements themselves, and shifted the focus of the ceremony from the table to the participants. Bread symbolised the Gospel, which drew them to Christ and sustained them. The wine was Christ's sufferings, which had redeemed them, and in which they were as a consequence granted a share. Again there was the emphasis on the links between discipleship and suffering. Christ was present at his supper, but not in some metaphysical transformation. He lived in the lives of his followers.

If high standards of discipleship were expected, a strong corporate witness was also required. The Church was seen as a visible community of the redeemed in a sinful world, and nothing could be tolerated that would stain its purity. So both individuals and the community as a whole had to be worthy of the Lord, and a strict discipline was maintained to ensure that they were. This was the origin of the Anabaptists' 'ban', a form of excommunication more stringent than that of the historic Church. Theoretically, a Catholic could be excommunicated and remain in a state of grace. For all its worldly pretensions, Rome did not presume the right to anticipate the Last Judgement. To the Anabaptists, this was a part of its apostasy, a departure from the visible rule of Christ which they sought to restore. To ban someone from the community was to ban them from Christ.

Underlying Anabaptism was the central problem of the Reformation. Across the whole spectrum of dissent there was general agreement that the Church (the late medieval Roman Catholic system) had fallen seriously away from New Testament standards, and was therefore corrupt and in need of remedial action. Against the economic, political and theological power of this Church it was therefore necessary to provide some kind of rationale for this judgement, some account of the forces which produced the corruption, some diagnosis as to how deeply it had bitten, and what was going to be done about it.

We can distinguish three main kinds of approach to this problem. The first was taken by main-line churches of the Lutheran or Calvinist pattern. They sought straight reform on lines they believed to be dictated by the correct application of scripture to the traditional formulations of Christianity. The Puritans in England belonged mainly to this type. The second was the line taken by a number of Anabaptist groups, whether scripturally or spiritually oriented. They looked for a restitution of the Church of the Apostles, and, as we have seen, looked to discipleship for their models, and were in this sense revolutionary rather than reformist. So why was a revolution necessary? The answer lies in a conception they shared with the third group, the Spirituals, who were really looking for an entirely new Church. This conception of a 'fall' or 'Apostasy' of the Church was later developed at great length by George Fox in his celebrated sermon at Firbank Fell at the outset of his mission to Westmorland and Lancashire at (significantly) Pentecost 1652.

One clear statement of the idea comes from Sebastian Franck, ex-priest, theologian, historian, mystic, typesetter and soap-boiler extraordinary, a spiritual reformer whose vision and self-confidence kept him outside the Anabaptist groups with whom he nevertheless had considerable common ground. The Anabaptists generally pointed to the reign of Constantine the Great (306–337 AD) as the time when the Church fell from its true vocation as a voluntary religious organisation into the corrupt status of an agent of social control. Belief in infant baptism and in the sacrificial nature of the Eucharist became enforceable by law. Greater doctrinal precision drew the Church even further from its true path of humble discipleship and there thus began an era which made the persecution and killing of heretics an integral part of the practice of official Christianity.

It was this dispensation that the Lutherans sought to reform but the Anabaptists sought to sweep on one side. Franck is even more radical. In his celebrated *Letter to John Campanus* (1531) he traces the corruption of the Church back to processes referred to in the text of the New Testament itself, and states his opinion that for fourteen hundred years before his time there had been no truly gathered Church nor any valid sacrament anywhere in the Christian world. The outward Church had retreated to Heaven, though the inner truths of the sacraments and church order were revealed by the Spirit to the truly faithful wherever and whenever they had lived.

The true Church was therefore not the visible company that the Anabaptists proclaimed, but an invisible fellowship of all those who had received this inner revelation. In an earlier work he had looked forward to the emergence of a purely spiritual Church that would gather these souls and would neither have nor need vocal prayer, preaching, sacramental observance or formal structure. There was to be a continuity of this pure Church with the Apostolic Church, but it would consist in the revelations of the Spirit and not in sacrament, tradition or scripture.

The Netherlands Connection

Two religious movements in the Netherlands exemplify the options available to sensitive souls as the sixteenth century gave way to the seventeenth. There was considerable intercourse between England and the Low Countries at this time, and while it cannot be shown that these movements directly influenced the precursors of Quakerism, there are strong similarities between them at a number of points.

The Waterlander Mennonites are perhaps the first body to notice in this connection. These were an Anabaptist group originally numbered among the followers of Menno Simons (1496–1561). They stressed the authority of their local congregations and allowed considerable doctrinal latitude. Their tolerance was such that they accepted as members folk who had been excluded by the 'ban' from stricter assemblies. They baptised. They celebrated the Lord's Supper seated at tables. Like the modern Mennonites, many observed the ceremony of foot-washing, following to the letter Christ's command in John 13:14. Many felt uneasy with ceremonies altogether and preferred to sit in silent contemplation.

There were further similarities with the Quakers. Congregations had not one pastor but several ministers each – the pattern that later developed among Friends – and many of their meeting houses were on the familiar intimate pattern with a raised facing bench. Bartholomew Legate, burned at Smithfield in 1617, reputedly the last person to be martyred in this way in England, was a London merchant who was also a minister in a congregation that was said to be an offshoot of the Waterlander Mennonites.

The second group with similarities to the Quakers were the Collegiants. These were a minority group which resulted from the strictness of Dutch Calvinism following the Synod of Dort in 1619. They had much in common with the Waterlanders, though stemming from different roots. They found inspiration in the teaching of a number of figures including the multi-talented Dirck Coornhert (1522–1590), who was thoroughly familiar with the ideas of Sebastian Franck. They, too, espoused the idea of the invisible Church and, though baptising, ceased to observe the Supper as an ordinance until such time as God would send new teachers or prophets or apostles to purify and reunite the Church in a way that the reformers down to their time had, they thought, signally failed to do.

We now face the question of how these groups are related to the rise of the English Baptist churches with which many early Quakers, including Fox himself, had intimate contacts. As we have seen, there had been Continental Anabaptists in England at least since Henry VIII's reign. Under Elizabeth I there was a campaign explicitly designed to root out Anabaptist doctrinal heresies and to enforce conformity with the state church. The foreigners were deported, or forced to flee, or, as in one sordid case in 1575, were executed by burning, in spite of the efforts of John Foxe, the martyrologist.

In his *Acts and Monuments* (now known as Foxe's *Book of Martyrs*), published in 1570, Foxe produced a peculiarly English version of the apostasy theory which had great influence among subsequent generations of dissenters and was certainly available to his near namesake, George Fox. An ancient copy of the work is displayed in the church at Mancetter, the next village to Fenny Drayton. So it ought to be clear that, particularly in London and south-east England, religious radicals were not innocent of the many varied practices and shades of doctrine on the Continent. Moreover it is inconceivable that news of controversies there did not receive wide circulation in England.

We have, therefore, to imagine a situation in which, through trade and personal travel, there is considerable intercourse between England and the Netherlands and the considerable currency of Anabaptist and Spiritualist ideas. By about 1600, or at any rate, as James Stuart comes to the English throne, or as Shakespeare dies, or as Raleigh fails to find Eldorado, the streams of separatist Puritanism and Continental-style Anabaptism move together, as several of the main Anabaptist positions were taken by two of the great English separatist leaders, who nevertheless did not accept their teaching *in toto*.

Robert Browne, who led the Separatists at Norwich and later at Middelburg, had much in common with Anabaptism, though he is now seen largely as one of the precursors of Independency or

Congregationalism, for that is how he influenced subsequent events. This is a good example of our tendency to read things backwards. John Smyth the Se-baptist, or self baptiser, led his congregation into exile at Amsterdam, and in 1615, three years after his death, they joined the Waterlanders.

One Richard Blunt, in similar straits, doubtful that he had been properly baptised, went to a Collegiant congregation at Rijnsburg in 1641 in order to be baptised by immersion, and returned to institute this practice in his own nation. So connections were intimate, and boundaries difficult to draw. As the seventeenth century progressed, so did the English Baptists. The older Anabaptist ideas seem to have survived best among the General Baptists, among whom George Fox moved during his formative period. There were also the Particular Baptists, who accepted that Calvinist theology which was encountered on all wings of the Puritan movement.

The Puritan Dilemma

The events of the 1640s, however, were to reveal the shortcomings and contradictions within Puritanism. The state church that was the outcome of Elizabeth's middle way was unstable. It needed the support of the political system to survive. While its doctrine and structure were taken care of by the secular arm it was secure, but when Cromwell's Ironsides shot away its support, it rapidly collapsed. Such was the consummation the Puritans desired, but when they actually obtained the political leverage to reform the state church along their own lines, they found there were a number of replacement models available and they could not agree which should be chosen. They were the prisoners of history. Repression placed a very high penalty on Separatism which only a few heroic souls were prepared to pay.

When the High Commission and the Court of Star Chamber were abolished in 1641, the means to enforce conformity were gone and it rapidly became clear that there was no consensus among the Puritans as to what actual pattern of church government should replace episcopacy. Some wanted one united national church to which everybody would have to conform, but not on the episcopal pattern. Some wanted 'comprehension' as we have seen, a degree of latitude or toleration, but within this national institution. Others were prepared to accept such arrangements so long as toleration was granted to them outside the national institution.

As we shall see, controversy on this point was one of the inherent weaknesses of politics in the Interregnum period and partly explains the arbitrary and inconsistent policy pursued towards the Quakers at the time. The Cavalier Parliament in 1660 finally settled the point by driving the successors of the Puritans, including Friends, wholly outside the establishment and giving them the status of a permanent minority of dissent, rather than of an integral part of national religious arrangements.

If the Puritan movement was fragmenting politically, it was also showing signs of theological stress. The conservative 'presbyterian' grouping was still expounding a faith little different from that of its Elizabethan predecessors. Among the more advanced, however, two of the main themes of the Calvinist system were developing into something radically different, although hardly, in European terms, new. Calvinism insisted that, because of human sin, the gap between human and divine was so vast that the human being was, of his or her own volition, entirely unable to cross over it and enter into relationship with God. This view was accepted by many of the leading 'spiritual Puritans' and, indeed, was shared by George Fox.

On the other hand, so great was God's love towards the creation, and so lavish the grace waiting for the repentant that conversion came to be seen as perhaps the most important human experience, hence the Puritan's high-mindedness and seriousness of purpose. But many perceived an inconsistency at this point, for the received view stated that God elected, or chose, some of his human creatures for bliss at the expense of the damnation of the rest, who were denied involvement in any kind of real spiritual encounter with him. If maintained uncompromisingly, this doctrine seemed to many to neutralise the claim that this self-same God is the origin of that glorious liberation the Puritans believed themselves to have experienced.

Hence, various devices were employed to tone down this stark aspect of their thinking about God, and a number came to place increasing emphasis on the ways the Spirit works before conversion to engage the interest and then the commitment of the soul. They gave attention to the development of faith in the converted. They campaigned against 'notional' theoretical or formal religion untouched by inner fire. They called their flocks to a ceaseless battle with sin through prayer, self-discipline and Bible study.

Not content to withdraw from the world into enclaves of the Kingdom of Heaven, they sought to transform the world into a holy community. In America this was easier than in the Old World, where it meant an engagement with society and the state. It therefore involved politics as well as religion, and in the frenetic 1640s two tendencies came to the fore, which left an indelible stamp on the nascent Quaker movement. The Seekers and their kind sought the spiritual kingdom within. The Fifth Monarchy Men and their kind sought it without. The Quakers would come to hold a unique balance between the two.

It is clear that in the early 1640s there was a considerable number of individuals and a few groups who were known to their contemporaries as 'Seekers'. They were often tender souls who had frequently sought their spiritual rest among a number of the persuasions of their day – Anglican, Presbyterian, Independent or Baptist – without finding satisfaction. They had an intense sense that reality had gone out of the practice of the reformed religion and that, by looking for renewal in the preaching and practices of the churches, they had mistaken the proper direction of their search. Like others not of their company, they said that the New Testament Church was obviously characterised by the presence of the Holy Spirit. Equally obviously, they claimed, the Church of their own day was not. Not surprisingly, few, if any, actual communities of Seekers have been identified.

In view of what they saw as at least a century's failed attempts to reform the Church by human activity and initiative, they concluded that true reformation would only come by the direct action of God himself. They felt themselves to be in a period of dereliction so that the only constructive religious posture was to wait for the expected divine initiative and to prepare for the same. They accepted the disciplines of prayer, works of charity and searching the scriptures. They rejected all outward show of religion including sacraments, a ministry and church order. Some were solitary, some continued to attend public worship, but some came together in silent waiting in the spiritual conviction that very soon new prophets or Apostles, enjoying the miraculous powers that were the gift of the Holy Spirit, would appear, to do away with the apostasy, still the clamour of the divided churches of the Reformation, and re-establish the true Church in visible glory and unity.

It would appear, therefore, that the Seekers were occupying a transitional position, and of this they were fully aware; indeed it was the essence of their teaching. So it is a mistake to regard them as unsettled people or representatives of a mere rebellion against formality. Their ideas lie deep in the Radical Reformation, as we have seen, and their similarity to people like the Netherlands Collegiants is far too close to have been coincidental. Equally, concern with spiritual religion within the frame of reference of mainstream Protestantism produced development in this direction from the Puritan tradition. But what was to be the fulfilment of this search for a new dispensation of the Spirit?

By the late 1640s the Seekers were at a crossroads. One turning led in the direction of an outward millennial hope that some earthly figure would arise to institute the rule of the saints, perhaps even that there would be the second coming of Christ. The other turning led away towards conceptions of a new universal mission to be effected by the Holy Spirit working purely within. Both scenarios were on offer. Influential groups appeared, proclaiming that the last times were imminent and calling for political, or even military, preparations for them.

One group arose which proclaimed that the Day of the Lord was indeed here, but that it was a spiritual and not a temporal reality. Outward preparations were futile, for Christ had come to teach his people himself. With this key conception George Fox, in the years following 1652, brought many 'Seeking' people into the Quaker fold with a teaching that gave reality to their hopes and substance to their dreams. In return, they gave the experiences, the practices and the spirituality that did so much to make his original vision an enduring religious movement.

We are now beginning to pick up the threads of destiny which led to the appearance of the Quakers. Certainly the major factor was the rise of spiritual religion out of the disappointment with the perceived results of the Reformation. But political factors are also important. As we have seen, politics and religion were two aspects of one social reality in those days, and men and women with other than Seeker sensibilities felt drawn towards Quakerism. Indeed, most newly convinced Friends had not been Seekers in the strict sense. Many came from the more political end of the spectrum of religious understanding, and it is to them that we must now turn, passing to review the events that led up to the great constitutional crisis that brought about the Civil War and the period of republican government between 1649 and 1660. It is in this period that the Quakers emerge into the glare of public debate.

The Environment of the Earliest Friends

I N 1629, FOUR YEARS AFTER HIS ACCESSION, KING CHARLES I dispensed with Parliamentary assistance and began a period of personal rule. The price of what freedom of manoeuvre he gained was the necessity to resort to all manner of subterfuges to maintain the income of the state. People were forced to buy knighthoods; the ancient forest laws were revived and fines exacted for technical breaches that had become commonplace and unremarkable; monopolies were granted in a number of trades at attractive prices. The exactions of customs duties were stepped up and John Hampden achieved renown through his unsuccessful attempt to prevent the imposition of ship money for coastal protection on inland counties.

The landed and mercantile classes were both antagonised, and, where possible, they passed on the cost of the King to those lower in the economic and social scale. The glories of Whitehall Palace blinded the establishment to the disaffection of the nation which became focused on two symbolically hateful personalities – Archbishop Laud and Thomas Wentworth, the Earl of Strafford. In 1638 war broke out between England and Scotland, and as it drew to a drab defeat for royal policy, a fiscal crisis arose which obliged Charles at last to call a Parliament to ask it to vote him money.

Parliament put a very high price on co-operation. Its mood has been variously estimated. Some see the Civil War as the natural outcome of an irreconcilable constitutional conflict. Others discern nothing but a slow drift to catastrophe as politicians lost their grip on events. Whatever the truth of the matter, in 1642 Charles withdrew to Nottingham to raise his standard, and the Civil War began. After four years of near stalemate, Parliament secured an important victory at Marston Moor, near York, in 1644. In 1645, at Naseby, thirty miles from Fenny Drayton, the King was defeated by Cromwell and the New Model Army. You cannot hide thousands of fighting men, guns, baggage trains, fodder and horses in the Leicestershire countryside. George Fox was twenty-one and must have seen it all. He makes few references to these great events, but it was they that carried him to his destiny.

The Levellers and the New Model Army

Almost by mistake, certainly with heart searching, clearly with a sense of unease, Parliament had effected a revolution. It had not accomplished it on its own and it now had to reach a reckoning with the various political interests whose support it had been essential to enlist. Chief among these were the Scots, whose army, strongly represented at Marston Moor, actually took the King into custody following Naseby. The price of Scottish arms was the establishment of Presbyterianism in England, and in preparation, in 1643, Parliament had ratified the Solemn League and Covenant of the Scottish Presbyterians and called together the Westminster Assembly of Divines to consider what changes would be appropriate in the doctrine and discipline of the Church of England.

In due course, this body produced the Directory of Public Worship in the Three Kingdoms (which was intended to replace the Book of Common Prayer), the Confession of Faith and the celebrated Shorter Catechism which begins with the splendid assertion 'Man's chief and highest end is to glorify God and fully to enjoy him forever.' In 1645 and 1646 the machinery was set in motion for establishing Presbyterianism, and the process was begun of imposing a new order on the church. The scheme adopted was conservative and authoritarian, and was well suited to the members of that party in Parliament that wished to halt the revolution where it stood, without allowing further development in the direction of religious freedom. This would, such people rightly saw, lead to an even greater demand for political and economic liberty – if not equality. So the victors began to quarrel over the spoils, Parliament and the Army disputing the question of who spoke best for the people.

The New Model Army enjoyed good command, sound discipline and the cachet of victory. Its social composition was far more representative than Parliament and it rapidly became a fortress of the Independent, or Congregational, form of Puritanism. It took religion seriously. It was served by devoted and distinguished chaplains and many units constituted themselves as gathered churches. It knew its Bible and why it was in arms. It is hardly surprising, therefore, that in its camps and billets and barracks there developed the first serious English political movement in favour of liberty, democracy, freedom of conscience and the redistribution of wealth.

Cromwell wrote: 'I had rather have a plain russet-coated Captain that knows what he fights for and loves what he knows, than that which you call "a Gentleman" and is nothing else.' These words are capable of a democratic gloss, but in Cromwell's army there were people whose ideas about representative government were rather different from his. These men, political, religious, democratic and egalitarian were known as 'Levellers'. The full Leveller programme would have transformed the country. They wanted the House of Commons rather than Parliament to be the centre of power, an almost universal manhood suffrage, a re-distribution of seats to centres of population, and elections every one or two years. They stood for devolution, complete equality before the law, the abolition of trading monopolies, the opening up of enclosed land, security of tenure for copyholders, the abolition of billeting and the press-gang, the abolition of tithes and freedom of religious worship and organisation.

Politically they were under pressure from the conservatives, who held the levers of power, and from the radicals who wanted to go further. So they had to engage in manoeuvre and in 1647 at Putney church they presented to the Army Council the *Agreement of the People for a Firm Peace*, a form of declaration or social contract by which they intended to secure legitimacy and popular approval for the post-war regime. They were unsuccessful. Cromwell was in process of outflanking them when the King escaped from captivity and the army was recalled from politics to its proper business. The brief Second Civil War flared up and died away. A Leveller mutiny at Burford was put down and in 1649 the King was executed. Cromwell assumed complete control and the popular threat to his rule was at an end. Leveller sentiments, however, lived on.

Within ten years of these events the Quaker movement had come into being and attracted widespread support. Though we have presented it as a spiritual movement, its political connections contributed in a large measure to the suspicion with which the authorities viewed it and the persecution which it suffered at their hands. There is a fair amount of evidence that the Levelling spirit lived on among Friends. In the first place, a number of eminent personalities in the early Quaker movement are known to have fought in the war, mostly on the Parliament side, and would have been involved in the intense religious and political debates which took place there, without necessarily having had a formal connection with the movement. These include William Ames, Gervase Benson, John Crook, William Dewsbury, William Edmondson, Richard Hubberthorne, William Meade, James Nayler, Edward Pyott, Amor Stoddard and John Stubbs.

Over a period the Quaker officers in the army were cashiered, ostensibly for insubordination, but presumably for 'democratic' sentiments. The great publicist John Lilburne, after supporting the Levellers, became a Quaker, and so, possibly, did the radical 'Digger' leader Gerrard Winstanley. The reasons for these connections are complex and not entirely clear. However, it seems that the Leveller movement reached a crisis of failure in the early 1650s, some looking to the fanatical millenarian sects for a completion of the revolution, others opting for less radical groups which set their sights on toleration rather than the creation of a brave new world.

It is important to notice also, that, though the Levellers used reason rather than theology to advance their cause, it grew out of the religious world-view that we have here associated with Anabaptism – toleration, equality and the end of state interference in religious matters. Spirituals and Seekers joined the Quakers, to be sure, but equally, we must not ignore the strong evidence that it was to the Baptist congregations that the Quakers primarily made their conscious appeal. Many leading Levellers came from that branch of radical dissent, and Quakerism must have seemed to many a logical destination on the disappointment of their political hopes. The crucial point is the nature of the Quaker critique of the inequality the Levellers sought to abolish. If you believe that the solution to social problems lies in collective action to alter structures, you will enter the political arena. On the other hand if you see the basic cause of ambition, greed and the desire for power in the spiritual condition of pride, you will seek spiritual regeneration as the only lasting route to true justice, and that is the route the Quakers ultimately took.

Ranters and Fifth Monarchy Men

One of the difficulties with the literature of this period is the venom of public debate, the exhilarating delight in insult, the liberal use of smear tactics. So, if somebody is described as a 'Quaker' or a 'Leveller', this may not be an accurate description at all but a handy gibe to hurl when some correspondence, possibly trivial, is noticed between what one's adversary is saying and what some other, entirely different group is saying, particularly when the other group are the baddies. The times were harsh. One gets the feeling of an inchoate fear deep inside many of the controversialists. One group which cast a long shadow over the period were the much-abused Ranters, people who took liberty seriously by exercising it rather than just talking about it, or struggling for it. The fevered official mind called them 'Ranters'. There was no Ranter organisation as such, nor any agreed body of beliefs, nor even a sense of corporate identity so it is best to ask what kind of attitude or behaviour attracted this description, and how the Quakers might be connected with them in the popular mind. How many 'Ranters' there actually *were*, is a nice question.

It is an easy step from the Spirituals' experience of the Holy Spirit to a sense of the divinity in all things, and thence to pantheism. Many Christians are willing to make some such affirmation about the nearness of God, but the so-called Ranters went further and freed their conception of God from dependence on the Christian scriptures and doctrinal formulations, admitting other models of the relationship between human and divine. If the Quakers did not reject their Christian vocabulary and conceptual framework it was not because no alternatives were available; the Ranters got their name from the flamboyant and intemperate manner in which many of them proclaimed that there were.

The most favoured alternative was a mystical pantheism involving conceptions of God as being resident in all things, or as being life itself, as being one with reality and nothing more, or indeed as having such a nature that he could fully reveal himself in the human personality which was therefore either actually or potentially divine. But this personality was transient, and Ranter conceptions of soul differed sharply from Christianity, which taught some kind of heavenly reward as against the Ranters' mystical union or re-absorption of the soul at death by the greater reality of which it is a part.

The second step forward from spiritual religion is antinomianism, the doctrine that by faith and the dispensation of grace the Christian is released from the obligation of adhering to any moral law. This view is a permanent part of Christian thinking, for it is the illogical development of certain clear New Testament principles. Some Spirituals taught it and so did the Ranters. It fits easily into the Christian doctrine of grace, in the sense that the inwardly pure cannot sin. The Spirit will supply the moral discrimination the law cannot, for mere obedience is no guarantee of salvation in the absence of grace. It also fits neatly into any doctrine of divine immanence in all things. It is easy to see that these principles can lead to pure and holy lives. Equally, they could be used to justify licentiousness and immorality, and doubtless many Ranters, not clearly appreciating this aspect of their beliefs, provided a good reason for the horror with which the rest of society viewed their outrageous activities and violent and intemperate preaching.

So quickly did the Ranter bubble swell that in 1650 the authorities moved equally swiftly to burst it, and a bill was introduced into Parliament to suppress 'obscene, licentious and impious practices used by persons under the pretence of liberty, religion or otherwise.' The Blasphemy Act of that year was aimed at these two main Ranter doctrines and provided that an offence was committed where any person (a) affirmed himself or any other creature to be God, or infinite, or almighty, or equal with God, or that God dwelt in the creation and nowhere else (*contra* pantheism), or (b) affirmed that acts of gross immorality were either neutral or positively religious (*contra* antinomianism). The first offence brought a fine, the second banishment for life under pain of death. The statute had the desired effect, and Ranterism retreated to the footnotes and margins of history.

Quakers, however, proved vulnerable to the Act, for through both ignorance and design, prosecutions were brought against them, most notably in the person of George Fox. Actually, it is perfectly understandable that persons of little religious sophistication should notice only the outward similarities between Quakers and Ranters, who did not take the scriptures as their final authority, who judged all things by what light was in them, who preached that perfection was an attainable ideal, and who had a clear sense of the indwelling spirit of God. It is no wonder that one of the Friends' most difficult tasks was to show that in spite of these similarities, Ranterism and Quakerism were not the same thing.

Visions of the future are always built on perceptions of the past. Our ideals are always conditioned by our experience. Our conceptions of the possibilities of social or political action depend on what we take the motive power of history to be. This was as true of the seventeenth century as it was of the twentieth. The horrors of the religious wars that racked Europe in the later phases of the Reformation – including the English Civil War – produced a renewed interest in millenarian doctrine, an aspect of the Christian faith that tends to come to the fore in times of stress.

The New Testament clearly envisages the return of Christ and a period of temporal rule by the saints. Indeed, that he will come again is one of Christ's own promises. But Christians differ over how and when. Some see the millennium as a thousand-year period preparing the way for the end during which the saints will rule as a spiritual aristocracy. Others envisage the millennium as a period following the second coming in which Christ rules with the elect and gathers the world into a holy confederation with him.

Numbers of Spirituals and Seekers had variants of these beliefs, and the explicit doctrine was strong among the Independents. John Owen (1616–1683) taught a spiritual doctrine of the millennium and saw the gathered churches after the congregational pattern as harbingers of Christ's return. Others were more specifically political, and thought that the second coming would inaugurate, rather than fulfil, the thousand-year rule of the saints. These were the Fifth Monarchy Men.

Their name is derived from the way they interpreted the seventh chapter of Daniel. The beasts described there were understood to represent the four great world empires of classical and modern times, of which the last was Rome. By implication, the Roman Empire lived on in the Roman Catholic Church (another subtle twist of the Apostasy theory) and by interpretation the conquest of the fourth beast was taken to indicate the completion of the Reformation. As this process was thought to be well advanced, the second coming was therefore imminent. By weird mathematics the date of Christ's return was calculated to occur at some time in the 1660s. So the political task was to prepare for this advent by putting down worldly governments by force, if persuasion failed to convert them to policies designed to establish the rule of the saints.

The Fifth Monarchy was, therefore, the political rule of the saints which the Fifth Monarchy party sought to inaugurate. An emphasis on their revolutionary political intentions may play down their spiritual quality, and that would be a shame. In our own times we can find plenty of counterparts to both the Ranter and Fifth Monarchy impulses among contemporary secular concerns and we should not be as dismissive of their apocalyptic reasoning as we should of those who say exactly the same things today – they were using the limited intellectual materials of their age for an audacious purpose. Who would have thought that Lenin-in-exile seated in an obscure émigré café in 1916 had the key to the twentieth century in his pocket?

In 1660, what was one to say about the Fifth Monarchy Men? We know now the true extent of their weakness. In 1661, shortly after the restoration of Charles II, they rose in revolt in London and controlled the City for three days, anticipating the second coming which many others were expecting to occur in 1666. As they were put down, there took place the precautionary arrest and detention of anybody who might have been thought to have been implicated in their plot. Astonishingly, the largest group so considered was Friends, and it is estimated that some 4,230 Quakers were rounded up and imprisoned as a direct result of the Fifth Monarchy uprising.

Once more, we encounter the hidden assumptions we have when we read back into history distinctions that are clear to us, but were not so clear to those we are reading about. Most modern Friends would find precious few similarities between their own spiritual forebears and these apocalyptic revolutionaries – Jehovah's Witnesses with guns, perhaps. But there are clues beneath the beautiful and inspiring words of the Declaration of the Quaker Peace Testimony, which begins, 'All bloody principles and practices we . . . do utterly deny, with all outward wars and strife and fightings with outward weapons, the spirit of Christ which leads us into all Truth will never move us to fight and war against any man with outward weapons neither for the kingdom of Christ nor for the kingdoms of this world.'

This Declaration was addressed to the King to dissociate the Quaker movement from the Fifth Monarchists and all who were prepared to take arms to oppose the restoration of the Stuart line and the return of the episcopal form of church government which so many had suffered so much to destroy. Its vocabulary repays close study. The distinctions drawn in the Declaration are not between resistance and acquiescence, struggle and surrender, but between outward weapons and inward ones. There is no denial of the millennial hope, but a direct reference to the kingdoms of the world becoming the kingdom of the Lord and of his Christ.

The question is one of means, not of ends, for many Friends felt themselves part of a spiritual struggle given classical form in the pamphlet by James Nayler entitled *The Lamb's War*, published three years earlier. Certainly, Nayler says unequivocally, ' . . . these are the last times.' Equally clearly, his apocalyptic vision is a spiritual one taken as a whole. He says, 'But his kingdom in this world, in which he chiefly delights to walk and make himself known, is in the hearts of such as have believed in him, and owned his call out of the world, whose hearts he has purified, and whose bodies he has washed in obedience and made them fit for the Father to be worshipped in. And in such he rejoices and takes delight; and his kingdom in such is righteousness and peace, in love, in power and purity. He leads them by the gentle movings of his Spirit out of all their own ways and wills in which they would defile themselves, and guides them into the will of the father by which they become more clean and holy. . . . As any come into his kingdom they are known, and their change is to be seen of all men. He keeps them low in mind, and a meek spirit does he generate in them; and with his power he leads them forth against all the enmity of the evil one, and makes all conditions comfortable to them who abide in his kingdom.'

Thus we come to the authentic Quaker voice as it was heard by so many in the middle of the troubled seventeenth century. Quakerism can be seen in many ways, it can be treated historically, sociologically, psychologically. It can be described, classified, assessed, proclaimed, justified, criticised. It can be seen as an ideal, a technique, a refuge, an expression of deeper things in another guise. But to those who first came to it, it provided an experience of the Christian faith like no other they had known. All the first Quakers came into the Society from elsewhere. The sects and churches from which they came had failed to meet their needs. Nowhere did they find rest for their souls until they heard and responded to the first Quaker preachers, or 'publishers of truth' as they came to be known.

So as a matter of simple fact Quakerism came to be for many thousands of people the completion of their search, the fulfilment of their hopes and the destiny towards which they had travelled. To look for the 'origins', or worse the 'causes', of Quakerism is to ask far too wide a question. It had as many causes and origins as it had members. What it did was to appeal to ex-Baptists, ex-Levellers, ex-Seekers, ex-Independents, and ex-Ranters and ex-Fifth Monarchy Men and to proclaim to them that it could show them the reality which they sought. Rather than being able to trace one line of development from Puritanism or Anabaptism or Continental Spiritual religion, we can see that it had elements of all these things. In the religious alembic of the seventeenth century it was distilled as pure spirit, and to its main features we must now turn.

A Quaker Convincement

There can be no doubt that the generality of Christians were clear that they were living at a time of grave crisis. Most were content to let others worry for them, but for those who felt a personal responsibility there was a heavy burden as they contemplated a Church that fell far short of what they felt it should be. They saw disunity and a persecuting spirit, a clergy which often displayed worldly ambition rather than religious achievement, and a prevailing theology that confirmed and worsened the sense of sin and inadequacy from which they desperately sought relief. They suffered from a deep spiritual disturbance. They had mostly been through an experience of conversion, sometimes sudden, sometimes slow, but the joyous freedom of which the Bible spoke was denied them. They felt chained to the letter, but they also knew that somewhere there was the life. The Christ they were offered was too small. He was in the Book and not in the world, and too many clergy wished to keep him there. So, at a deep level many thousands of people were in despair, and this is probably the psychological fact that underlay the various beliefs we have looked at which sought a salvation from these feelings at some time in the future. But in their heart of hearts, many people knew that the Reformation, indeed religion, had reached a dead end. Restoration, true redemption would come, but not yet.

So how could such a condition be reached? Catholic confessors might have diagnosed the condition of accidie, or spiritual sloth. They might have prescribed a spiritual shock to jerk people back from their path of resignation to a renewed involvement with present realities, to face again the possibilities within themselves that over-concentration on the future permitted them to ignore. A sense of *personal* crisis was required, and it is this that the Quaker preachers provided, contrary to what we might have expected in view of the Friends' present reputation as healers and reconcilers. In the earlier parts of George Fox's *Journal*, for instance, in the crucial months of 1652 when he gathered the Westmorland separatists, he records that his preaching dealt with two main themes – a Pentecostal proclamation that a new beginning was taking place, that the Day of the Lord had come; and also the message that it was idle to seek for a new dispensation. For those who repented, he proclaimed, Christ was already here and was to be found within. To find him, one condition was necessary. It was not to search the scriptures. It was not to discover the reality of the passion in Jerusalem all those years ago. It was not to realise that one's sins were remitted at the price of a debt too great ever to be discharged. It was simpler than that – it was to exercise true repentance, to turn to the living Christ within, by whom alone the reality of these other discoveries would be revealed.

In seeking to express this inward reality, Fox chose to use the figure of 'light', one of the most universal symbols for the divine among mankind, and one of the key expressions of the Gospel of John, which also carried themes of crisis that resonated on the sounding board of the times. He was very free in his use of the word, never forgetting that its power comes from the fact that its meaning can never be finally pinned down. The light is that of God within you, and is not your conscience or intellect, though it may work through them. It is active and loving. It will show you your sins. It carries power and will enable you to overcome them. It is in all people, and if listened to will lead its hearers into unity with one another. It guides, warns, encourages, speaks, chastens, cares. It is that to which the scriptures witness. It is something on which you may place total reliance. It is the Christ you seek. It is what saves you and what gathers the true Church. We should note here the use of words. In those days to be convinced meant to be convinced of your sin in the sense of 'convicted'. It meant your first opening to the light. Convincement led to true repentance.

One of those convinced in 1652 was Francis Howgill. He describes his experiences: 'And then I told them there was guilt in me; and they said, "sin was taken away by Christ, but the guilt should remain while I lived," and so brought me the saints' conditions, who were in the warfare, to confirm it. I said to myself, this was a miserable salvation . . .' Then he heard George Fox, and writes, '. . . as soon as I heard him declare that the Light of Christ in man was the way to Christ, I believed the eternal word of truth, and that of God in my conscience sealed to it. And so not only I, but many hundred more who thirsted after the Lord, but were betrayed by the wisdom of the serpent; we were all seen to be off the foundation, and all mouths were stopped in the dust. We all stood as condemned in ourselves, and all saw our nakedness, and were all ashamed, though our glory was great in the world's eye, but all was vanity.' Many of the other early Quaker writings tell the same story, that convincement, the turning to the light within, was not a pleasant experience. The element of shock was present.

We should not be surprised at this, of course, for the newly convinced Friend was at a beginning not an end, and was facing the truth possibly for the first time – the truth about him – or herself, how far there was a falling short, and how terrible were the judgements of God. We begin to see a pattern that appears in later periods of Quakerism in other forms; the waiting, the stillness, the self-examination, the period of preparation. Francis Howgill continues: 'I became a perfect fool, and knew nothing, as a man distracted; all was overturned, and I suffered loss of all. In all that I ever did, I saw it was in the accursed nature. And then something in me cried: "Just and true is his judgement!" My mouth was stopped, I dared not make mention of his name, I knew not God. And as I bore the indignation of the Lord, something rejoiced, the serpent's head began to be bruised and as I did give up all to the judgement, the captive came forth out of prison and rejoiced, and my heart was filled with joy. . . . Then I saw the cross of Christ and stood in it. . . . And the new man was made.'

In this way the Quaker came to the light. He or she accepted its discipline and was remade, as Francis Howgill had been remade. The discipline was a necessary stage, and the tribulation that went with it enhanced the joyous feeling of release when it came. So deeply was this experience of salvation felt that it had to be shared, and this is the genesis of two further stages in the development of the Quaker message – the proclamation that Christ's injunction to be perfect was not to be taken figuratively, but was to be a serious purpose in the Christian life, and what we have already encountered as the 'Lamb's War', the proclamation to the whole of the world of the message that Christ was come and that in the Quaker movement the night of apostasy was over and the true Church was being restored. The themes of the Spirituals, Anabaptists and Seekers, Mennonites, Collegiants, Levellers, Ranters and Fifth Monarchy Men were taken up with immense enthusiasm and dedication. The age of outward and formal religion was over. The age of scriptural bondage and sacramental symbolism was done. Worldly pride and ostentation were doomed. Power was draining away from the kingdoms of the world and into the restored kingdom of God, for Christ was here to teach his people himself.

Appropriately, it is possible to find an extended account of such a conversion in the *Journal* of George Fox, the most widely circulated and read of all Quaker books. It was published in 1694, according to Fox's wish, and edited by one of the most influential of early Friends, Thomas Ellwood. It draws on a number of sources, including two accounts of his life, dictated by Fox in 1664 and 1675, accounts of his travels in Ireland

and America and copies of letters, pamphlets and documents appropriate to points he wants to make. It is not a systematic book, and strictly speaking it is neither a journal nor an autobiography. It is, however, colourful and fast moving, and perhaps unconsciously it shows us Fox, warts and all.

The *Journal* can be read in various ways. John Wesley heard it for pious entertainment at his mother's knee, but that is not likely to be the experience of many people today. It is a basic source for any account of the growth of Quakerism, for it takes us chronologically through the main events in Fox's life. He was an evangelist, and an evangelist's primary concern is people. So, as we would expect, they come tumbling through the narrative in profusion and variety. They run the whole gamut of response to Fox from violent hostility to adulation, and not many are indifferent. Evangelists also have a gospel to preach and we can find a substantial amount of Fox's doctrine in his account of his doings. Finally, successful evangelists preach from what they know, and here is an open and painstaking account of Fox's own spiritual experiences.

So what sort of a man was this George Fox? What sort of life was it that began to crystallise so many influences into an enduring religious community? It would be dangerous to take him at his own estimate because he was pugnacious and tended to take himself too seriously, but on the other hand he was capable of generating a remarkable devotion in people. We will not go far wrong if we let him speak for himself as far as possible, and supplement what he says with a little judicious interpretation.

The Young George Fox

There are no fully authenticated portraits of George Fox painted or drawn from life, so we do not have any of those revealing quirks of character that painters often capture. In 1858, in London, a painting attributed to Sir Peter Lely was found to have on the back the words, 'Geo. Fox by Sir Peter Lely'. The writing is not contemporary with the picture. Whether it is a likeness we have no way of knowing, but the face certainly shows those qualities of fearless repose, compassion, dignity and strength which William Penn records in his preface to the original edition of the *Journal*.

The head of the Lely portrait sits well on broad shoulders, and though we do not know the sort of measurements George Fox's tailor might have had, we know from William Penn that he was 'bulky', in spite of the fact that he ate little and slept less. Whether this choice of words conceals a plumpish, or even fat, Fox we shall never know. What we can say for certain is that he displayed on occasion an immense physical strength, particularly when the victim of violence. He also enjoyed extraordinary stamina and powers of recovery. He survived eight separate imprisonments in the foulest of conditions, spent two years travelling in the West Indies and the backwoods of America, and rode in a bumpy wagon through the Low Countries and northern Germany when he was over fifty.

Fox was probably comfortably off. The picture of a humble country weaver's son turning out to be a religious genius is unlikely. He records in the *Journal* that he was apprenticed to a shoemaker who was apparently also a sheep and cattle factor, buying and grazing beasts in anticipation of the market. This was not a career opportunity open to a son of the labouring class, and this fact probably places Fox in the ranks of the rural petite bourgeoisie. At any rate, he tells us that, while he was with his master, he did a great deal of business, but after he left the man went bankrupt. The message is clear. George Fox was a prudent businessman and knew how to take care of his affairs.

The conclusion is borne out by other things he says. When he was on his travels as a very young man, he carried on his trade wherever he was, but also says that he had enough to prevent himself from being a burden to people, and also had something to spare for the necessities of others. His will is instructive. His assets were valued at £700. He had property near Swarthmoor Hall that he used to endow the meeting there. He had shares in ships and over a thousand acres of land in Pennsylvania granted to him by William Penn. His own estate was always kept scrupulously separate from that of his wife, who can only be described as rich.

Nothing is known of Fox's education. There was a grammar school at Atherstone near his birthplace, and since there was a proposal at one point to make a priest of him it is conceivable that he went there. On the other hand, he was remarkably innocent of the classical curriculum and entirely lacked that wider perspective, even in religious matters, that informs the prose of a man like William Penn. He was accustomed to dictating to others, and while his own handwriting was just legible, his spelling was eccentric enough to be misleading even in those relaxed times. The likelihood is that he suffered from agraphia.

These are matters of formal education, however. Implicit in many of the incidents of the *Journal* there is a self-possession and savoir-faire which suggests that Fox was quite unworried by his lack of clerkly skills, indeed that they were just not relevant to the way he wanted to lead his life. On one occasion he was moved to exhort the Justices of Mansfield to be fair to workpeople when fixing the current rate of wages, which was their responsibility. So he went and told them, and there is never any suggestion that he might be refused an audience. He either had a sufficient reputation, or else he knew the ropes.

Fox's main reading was the Bible, which he probably knew as well as anyone ever has. The earliest historian of Quakerism, Gerard Croese, reported in 1696 that a number of Friends competent to judge had agreed that 'though the Bible were lost, it might be found in the mouth of George Fox.' There is more than one Friend who has attributed the words of St Paul to the apostle George. Of the ninety-nine books known to have formed part of Fox's library, two thirds are by other Friends. There are works by mystical writers antedating the rise of Quakerism, a book on natural religion, some works of current controversy on tithes and the establishment of a state church, Culpeper's *English Physician Enlarged* and a law book that has obvious uses to one as prone to court appearances as Fox. Two writers thought to have influenced Fox whose books do not appear in the list are John Foxe, the martyrologist, and the German mystic Jacob Boehme, whose thought has certain parallels with Fox's. He had other books, but it is not known what they were.

There is no thorough modern study of Fox's personality and psychology, though there is plenty of material in the *Journal*. He was certainly subject to bouts of depression, some occurring at crucial points in his career. The uncertainty connected with the imminent Restoration in 1660 weighed heavily on his mind, as, apparently, did the challenges to his personal authority that emerged in the decade thereafter. In 1670, shortly before his voyage to America, the *Journal* records a breakdown, in which Fox lost his hearing, sight and sense of time. He says that he lay under 'great sufferings and groans and travails, and sorrows and oppressions' for several weeks. Towards the end of this time, he says that he had come into the deep, that man-eaters were all around him, and he warred with their spirits.

Fox was both a born-again Christian and a mystic. His conversion does not appear to have arisen out of a sense of personal sin. Instead, he appears to have experienced a sense of release from temptation and despair. So he had a conversion with a difference. Equally, he records what can only be described as ecstatic experiences in graphic, highly symbolic terms. But the quest for such experiences was not his main purpose. He was a mystic with a difference, who did not follow what is usually understood as the mystic way.

The sense of living in, and assisting the work of divine power was so deep in George Fox that nothing could overcome it, and he takes his place in a long line of preachers and martyrs who were similarly inspired. Fox continually uses the phrase 'and the Lord's power was over all', and his experience of this power is an important factor in his temperament. He has a penchant for the dramatic and unusual. He has great capacity to accept persecution and violence. There are startling healings and a hint of hidden powers. His narrative heightens the response of people to his message. If they are positive, his unconscious exaggeration emphasises God's goodness. If they are not, God's judgement is underlined. Fox did not live on milk and water.

Tantalisingly, there is another side to his character that shows more plainly in what others said about him and what the record shows of his achievements. Fox not only preached the gospel but built a church that has endured out of many disparate elements. His constancy and willingness to stand by his principles are matched by diplomatic skill and organising ability, but it was above all as a loving pastor and spiritual guide that he was remembered.

George Fox began life in the small village of Fenny Drayton in Leicestershire in 1624. He was born at a time when kings claimed to rule by divine right. He died in 1691, three years after the revolution which finally substituted parliamentary control for what royalty thought was the will of God. He lived through a civil war and was imprisoned by both King and Parliament. A contemporary of Cromwell, Milton, Bunyan, Wren and Newton, he belonged to an heroic age. Nor was the village he came from a backwater. It was part of a cluster of settlements, including Mancetter and Atherstone, that lie across what was once Watling Street, the Roman road from London to Chester. In Fox's day the route had been extended to Holyhead, and it was the main line of communication between Whitehall and Dublin Castle, strategically important in the pacification and colonisation of Ireland that was proceeding at the time.

The district round about was well farmed and prosperous, and had a history of religious independence. In the fourteenth century, John

Wycliffe had been the rector of Lutterworth, less than twenty miles away. Joyce Lewis of Mancetter, and Robert Glover of the seigniorial family there – who actually figure in Foxe's *Book of Martyrs* – were both burned for their Protestantism between 1555 and 1557. Fenny Drayton itself was a Puritan stronghold as we have seen. This was the radical environment in which George Fox grew up. His father was a church-warden, and he tells us that his mother was 'of the stock of the martyrs'. We do not know why. Perhaps one of her relatives suffered with the Glovers in the Marian persecution, which would make him from the stock of the martyrs too. Fox received a tradition of religious serious-ness that did not compromise with worldly power.

He left the village in 1643, when he was nineteen, and never really returned, except on visits or in periods of melancholy. He was already deeply religious but he was neither master of himself nor conscious of his vocation. Though his *Journal* ignores the fact, the country was racked by civil war and immense upheaval, but the only turmoil he knew was what was going on in his soul. He spent about four years wandering the country between the Midlands and London, sometimes seeking out ministers to consult and at other times seeing them as a threat to what spiritual balance he had achieved. He also sought out individuals and groups of people who might be of help to him, and was preoccupied with reading the scriptures. He was deep in spiritual travail and underneath the somewhat incoherent descriptions of his condition there is the feeling of a slow but momentous change which he could not, as yet, understand.

He was, we might surmise, lonely, stand-offish and troubled in mind – reasons enough to run away from home.

The Years of Searching

The two years 1647 and 1648 were crucial in the development of the young George Fox. By this time he was moving around the east Midlands on the borders of Leicestershire, Nottinghamshire and Derbyshire. Things were happening and he was coming out of his prolonged despair. His account of these years is full of passages that most Quakers know by heart and it is interesting to see how they all form part of a whole. In 1646 Fox was still young and relatively inexperienced in spiritual mat-ters but sensible enough to know that he would not undertake other people's religious commitments second-hand. By 1648, when he was twenty-four, he knew where he was going.

In these years, George Fox went through a period during which he experienced total dereliction. He says that he sought help from ministers of the established church, but they could not help him. Then he tried the dissenting congregations but got nothing there either. He says bitterly that being bred at Oxford or Cambridge is not sufficient to fit a man to be a minister of Christ. One can feel the disillusion in his words, and it was at this point that he came to the moment of conversion. He says that when all his hopes in all men were gone, '. . . then Oh then, I heard a voice which said, "There is one, even Christ Jesus, that can speak to thy condition", and when I heard it my heart did leap for joy.'

The tempo of self-discovery increases from then on. In 1647 he preached for the first time at a Baptist conventicle at Broughton, Leicestershire, about ten miles from home. Concealed beneath the words of his *Journal* lies the conception of his ministry that he had come to much later, when he recorded these incidents from early in his life. One can debate the relative influence of the Gospel and Letters of John and the Letters and recorded speeches of Paul on Fox's preaching about the 'light', but in his account of his first words of public ministry at Broughton, Fox alludes to Acts 26:18 in unmistakable terms. Paul has described for Agrippa the blinding light that surrounded him on the Damascus road, and how Jesus had spoken to him in it. In this verse he describes the commission Christ gave him – to turn the gentiles from darkness to light, and from the power of Satan to God. That is exactly what Fox says was the purpose of his own preaching.

There is a difference, however, between taking part in a religious meeting and devoting your life to religion. Fox was not yet clear about the future, but he now knew he was not lost. God had preserved him from sin but put him through agonies of doubt, temptation and despair so he could understand the heart and mind of wickedness without being tainted by it. This was the only way for him to obtain the sense of all conditions that (by implication) he was going to need. He still had a way to go but he now saw the infinite love of God in what he had experienced. 'I saw also that there was an ocean of darkness and death, but an infinite ocean of light and love, which flowed over the ocean of darkness. And in that also I saw the infinite love of God . . .' By the end of 1647 Fox reports that his sorrows and troubles were beginning to wear off, and that he had been brought through the ocean of darkness and 'through the power and over the power of Satan by the eternal glorious power of Christ'.

By 1648, George Fox was nearing maturity and people were beginning to gather around him. He says that he continued to have 'great
openings' (insights into the meaning of life and the scriptures) and was
obviously gaining a reputation, for many people, including clergymen,
sought him out to talk. There are increasing references in the *Journal*
to 'the Lord's power' and to individuals and groups who were convinced. Fox continued to move about the towns of the Trent valley and
it appears that numbers of people from the Baptist congregations there
accepted his message. By this time his teaching and the theological system on which it was based were probably reasonably complete, and he
became a man who knew his own mind. His own account of these years
runs, 'The Truth sprang up first, to us so as to be a people to the Lord,
in Leicestershire in 1644, in Warwickshire in 1645, in Nottinghamshire
in 1646, in Derbyshire in 1647 and in the adjacent counties in 1648, 1649
and 1650.'

The exhilaration of these months must have been enormous. With
the dark years suddenly behind him, and with a mind and a spirit
sharpened to a needle's point, George Fox was ready for the work he
sensed that God had been preparing for him. He put it thus: 'Now was
I come up in spirit through the flaming sword into the paradise of God.
All things were new and all the creation gave another smell unto me
than before, beyond what words can utter. I knew nothing but pureness
and innocency and righteousness, being renewed up into the image of
God by Christ Jesus, so that I say I was come up into the state of Adam
which he was in before he fell . . . And the Lord showed me that such
as were faithful to him in the power and light of Christ, should come
up into that state . . . Great things did the Lord lead me into, and wonderful depths were opening unto me, beyond what can by words be
declared; but as people come into subjection to the spirit of God, and
grow up in the image and power of the Almighty, they may receive the
Word of Wisdom that opens all things, and come to know the hidden
unity in the Eternal Being.'

These words of George Fox can be interpreted away as an exaggeration or some other form of literary device, a memory of a dream,
trance or some other form of abnormal psychological state, a conceited
posture, wish fulfilment, a genuine experience of something else which
the words only approximately convey. Taken at face value, however,
they assert that Fox himself attained the ultimate experience of which
Christianity offers the possibility – total sanctification. What marks Fox

off from nearly every other reformer in Christian history is that he not only claimed to have had this experience, but taught that everybody else could have it too. If it was an impossibility, why did Christ die? What was the gospel for?

Immediately following this description of his feelings (during the high summer of 1648, one might speculate), Fox records a clear call to become an evangelist – to go out into the 'briary, thorny wilderness' of the world to proclaim the day of the Lord, to preach repentance, 'to turn people from darkness to the light that they might receive Christ Jesus . . .' It is clear by now that he has moved a long way from the Calvinism in which he was brought up, and, indeed, from the principles of the Baptists among whom he mainly moved. His message could easily have been a thing of shreds and patches, stitched up from a variety of other people's religious garments. But it was not. Out of loneliness and prayer, a deep acquaintance with the Bible and what looks like depression, Fox had built a personal faith of great strength and flexibility. He did not call it 'Quakerism' – it was simply the Truth.

George Fox's collected works were published in three parts and these remain the main sources of his thought. These are more or less an official selection, and for a balanced view it is nowadays necessary to refer to many other letters and tracts that have not been collected and reprinted, notably those from the Interregnum period. Apart from the *Journal* (1694), there is a volume of *Epistles* (1698) of a pastoral nature, written on various occasions to Friends and meetings, and *Gospel Truth Demonstrated* (1706) usually known as the *Doctrinals*, a collection of letters, tracts, and polemical works, many with curious titles. His first major work was *The Great Mistery* (1659), a detailed reply to over a hundred anti-Quaker pamphlets that had appeared in the years before 1659.

Similar difficulties attend the study of George Fox as with the study of Paul. The subject in each case is an energetic, fast-moving figure, labouring in the gospel and more concerned to build up the Church than to leave permanently important written records or an intellectually coherent account of his doctrine. Any attempt to draw a system of thought out of George Fox's writings is therefore to be made with caution. It can be done with reasonable accuracy, but there will be important loose ends.

As we have seen, the England of the time was in deep political and economic crisis. There was a marked contrast between wealth and poverty. Government was frequently arbitrary and unjust. Dissent was often severely punished. Puritans such as Prynne or Bastwick had their noses slit or their ears cut off. Before the 1640s taxes were levied without Parliament's consent and even afterwards, dissenters still had to pay tithes, one tenth of the annual produce of their land to the upkeep of the state church. Institutional religion supported the status quo and served the interests of power and wealth.

At its baldest and simplest, George Fox and those who thought like him, not all of whom became Quakers, by any means, were revolted by all this. The streams of Puritanism ran at a deep emotional level and provided a response to contemporary social life that was both religious and revolutionary. In order to return to the purity of New Testament times, the Christian community – and this meant the English nation – had to purge itself of its abuses. Though this purification would have to take institutional forms, it had to begin with individuals. Thus, the message George Fox preached was neither narrowly spiritual nor even peculiarly religious. It attacked contemporary attitudes on a wide front and involved a perspective on history, a theory of the Church and a doctrine of salvation. To understand his appeal we have to give due weight to all these elements in his thought.

From his acquaintance with the works of Foxe and the time he spent in discussion and debate about the country with the General Baptists and others, Fox would have been familiar with the radicals' diagnosis of the disease of the Church. Since the conversion of Constantine the Great (so the argument ran) what appeared to be the Church had been an arm of the state in disguise, not the outpost of the Kingdom of Heaven which was a community of true believers. The true Church continued 'in the wilderness' from that time, or, as we would say, underground. It was a common conviction on the religious left where Fox moved, that the restoration of the true Church was under way, and that their little communities had been chosen by God for a special role in bringing it about.

'Truth'

Like a frame round a picture or a jug round a pint of milk, this estimate of Christian history and his own place in it gives form and relationship to all the other elements in George Fox's thought. He was not a reformer nor a preacher of a new doctrine, nor one just to gather a small community round himself. He felt he was called to preach a message to the whole world, and he was confident that it would be heard. 'But with and by this divine power and spirit of God, and the light of Jesus, I was to bring people off from all their own ways to Christ, the new and living way, and from their churches, which men had made and gathered, to the Church in God, the general assembly written in heaven, which Christ is the head of, and from off the world's teachers made by men to learn of Christ . . . and from off all the world's worships, to know the spirit of Truth in the inward parts . . . And I was to bring people off from all the world's religions, which are vain. . . . And I was to bring them off from all the world's fellowships, and prayings, and singings, which stood in forms without power. . . . And I was to bring people off from Jewish ceremonies and from heathenish fables and from men's inventions and windy doctrines . . . and all their vain traditions, which they had gotten up since the apostles' days.'

Fox believed that all the errors and deceit that he discerned in the church of his times stemmed from this apostasy or betrayal of the principles of primitive Christianity. His four years of wandering, culminating in his conversion, had taught him that it is useless to rely on external, worldly things in matters of religion. In spite of their good intentions, friends, relatives, priests, ministers, sacraments, outward observances, doctrinal formulations, even the scriptures themselves could not guarantee the truth, nor verify his discoveries to his own satisfaction. The only pathway to salvation was inward submission to God, the inward reception of grace, an inward hearkening to the voice of Christ.

This led him to distinguish sharply between the world of the Spirit in which God's will and presence are known to those who repent and are redeemed, relying on nothing but the inward revelation of Christ, and 'the creature' – the world of ordinary unredeemed human society. The two exist side by side, but in the latter, instead of total reliance on God, people place confidence in their own traditions or natural abilities, in reason or conscience, for guidance in matters of faith. This is where humanity is vulnerable to corruption, and this is precisely where the Church fell victim to the tempter, when she lost sight of the distinction Fox had been raised up to reassert.

Here we can see the origin of some of the distinctive Quaker testimonies. George Fox had a clear understanding of preaching and pastoral ministry. As a student of the New Testament, he knew what the gifts of the Spirit were, and that their presence was one of the marks of the true Church. He vigorously denied that educational qualifications were a necessary precondition for ministerial gifts. He asserted that their divine origin clearly precluded any payment whatever for their exercise, and that therefore the whole structure of hierarchies and synods, ordination and benefices, tithes and taxes existed not to carry out God's will, but to facilitate human greed. Hence, no church which displayed these features could be genuine – it was part of the apostasy from Truth and would be swept away.

One of the ways such churches maintained their control over men and women was to preach false doctrine, particularly about the sacraments (or, as they were called, ordinances) of baptism and the Lord's Supper. Fox was not so foolish as to say that baptism and communion were unnecessary to Christians. He knew the New Testament texts to the contrary. What he did assert was that outward signs belonged to the old dispensation of Temple worship, law and ritual that Christ had come to fulfil, and to terminate, with the spirit and freedom of the gospel. As Christ said to the woman of Samaria, worship must be offered in spirit and in truth. Fox saw the symbols of water, bread and wine as pale, spiritually barren outward shadows of the inward reality of true baptism and communion. They were a standing invitation to people to miss the substance for the form, and the corrupt system of the apostasy ensured that this took place, drawing a veil of Christian appearance over an anti-Christian reality.

This attitude showed up even more clearly in the sorry tale of inhumanity, torture, rackings and burnings which Fox thought had been the concomitants of doctrinal development within the Church. Like many reformation radicals, he rejected the historic creeds out of hand, not so much because he disagreed with them, for on many points he can be shown to be in agreement, but because he objected strongly to the way they had been composed and the use to which they had been put. In the first place, they had been created by Church Councils to meet political and diplomatic needs rather than spiritual requirements, and they utilised a non-biblical and therefore non-authoritative vocabulary. In the second place, they were used as tests of orthodoxy, and history showed that the punishments for dissent were so far from the spirit of Christ as to be devilish. One would expect no less a judgement from one of the stock of the martyrs, and this attitude to creeds was by no means confined to the Quakers.

Fox's clearest challenge to what he saw as an apostate Church came in his attitude to scripture. He had a clear understanding of the

Catholics' objection to the reformation doctrine of scripture as the ultimate authority for Christians – it is easy to state but not so easy to apply. The Bible is so ambiguous that any number of equally attractive and authoritative doctrines can be spelled out of it. How do you know which is right? Without some countervailing source of authority, you have no way of telling. If you have a state church you are likely to find that interpretation prevailing that is politically convenient. Where there is a multi-national organisation like the Roman Catholic Church, you will expect an interpretation that serves its particular interests best. Fox would have none of that. It was all outward, worldly, of the creature not of the *life*. He did not believe that the scriptures were the standard by which to judge doctrines, religions and opinions, he told a congregation at Nottingham in 1649, 'But I told them what it was, namely the Holy Spirit, by which the holy men of God gave forth the Scriptures, whereby opinions, religions, and judgements were to be tried; for it led into all Truth, and so gave the knowledge of all Truth.'

Perhaps most of these ideas would have found an echo among many different kinds of people in the 1640s. They were trenchant, but they were negative, not really enough to found a new movement of the spirit. If the Society of Friends still relied on them for its theological justification, it would soon wither away, for they are things of the past. But they were not all that George Fox had to say. They were the preliminary to his distinctive and characteristic teaching about what happened when the individual followed the path he had taken and surrendered everything to the leadings of God. He called this 'turning to the light', and we must now examine this most characteristic of Quaker expressions.

The Universal Light

Though there were other translations available, George Fox usually used the Authorised Version commissioned by King James I in 1611. In the Prologue to John's Gospel, at verse 9 we read of Christ 'that was the true light which lighteth every man, that cometh into the world.' This is a mistranslation, and should read, 'The true light, that enlightens every man was coming into the world.' Happily, this correction enhances rather than detracts from Fox's understanding for it makes even clearer the central Quaker doctrine that the 'light' of Christ is in everyone, regardless of their religion, culture, nationality, race or anything else. The early Quakers rejected any idea of predestination or that God would fail to save those who were of pure heart but not in a position to give outward consent to the doctrines of Christianity. What mattered was the way you responded to the light.

George Fox took a dualist view of human nature. He was neither liberal nor optimistic. He was quite clear that human nature cannot regenerate or save itself, and that redemption from the sin and evil of the world is only possible through the supernatural grace of God. It was no part of his understanding of the light that people had a portion of the divinity within them. Nor did he take the fundamentally mystical view sometimes attributed to him that at one point of our nature we share the divine essence. We are creatures, we sin, and unless God comes to save us, we are doomed to destruction. He took an intensely practical view of the light, never defining what it is, but always saying what it does. It is the active principle of God within us, working for our salvation. When he talked about the light, George Fox was not referring to anything human – he was talking about one of the attributes of God.

Its main principles can be stated briefly. We have seen how Fox used the experience of Paul on the road to Damascus when Christ spoke to him amid a light from heaven. Fox uses the word in a number of ways. Sometimes the light is *from* Christ, as in this case, or else it *is* Christ, as in the Prologue to John. It does not matter as long as we understand him to be describing an essentially Christian experience. Light illuminates. Where there is light there is revelation. At the end of his own spiritual quest Fox received just such a revelation when the light told him that Jesus Christ could speak to his condition when all his hopes in worldly things had gone.

So the light was there in everyone, just as it was in him, and it was the source of salvation. He knew it, because he had experienced it personally. Thus, his preaching was intended to turn other people to this light or power within them. He did not primarily direct them to the Bible or the sacrifice of the cross, though he used both – his main thrust was to get people to bring their lives to the light. We have already seen the effect this had in his life, and in that of another early Friend, Francis Howgill.

The first result of turning to the light was conflict, for the light was antagonistic to human nature. It showed up one's sins. As the shadow gives a true profile of the body, so the light shows up all the nooks and crannies in the sinful soul that most people prefer to keep hidden. This was the point at which one quaked with fear at the power of God. It was the religious experience that gave the Friends their name.

It would have been morbid to remain like that, however. Hard and inevitable though it was, Fox taught that it was a stage of transition, for the light also gave the power to overcome the sins and inadequacies of the unredeemed human nature. It was a release, for at last there was a way to throw off the burden of guilt. The challenge of the Quakers was that sin itself was conquerable, and the life of perfect love was no longer an impossible ideal.

So the light operates at a personal level to redeem those who turn to it; but it would be a mistake to regard it as a part of human nature, a personal possession, a fragment of divinity, our bit of God. The light is in all, but it is the same light that is in all, not sparks from the eternal flame. There are not many lights, but only one. We all have a different measure of it, thought Fox, depending on the stage of our spiritual journey, but our own lives are only a part of the matter. Because it is common to all of us, the light calls us into unity with one another, into the community, into what we have seen George Fox call 'the Church in God, the general assembly written in heaven'. This is the fellowship that was to replace the Church of the Apostasy.

This is why it is probably a mistake to see Quakerism as a spiritual movement untrammelled by doctrines and structures which lost its momentum as it became better organised in its first fifty years of life. It offered people a new conception of themselves, a new conception of fellowship and a new conception of their place in the order of things. The doctrine of the light was a doctrine of the real presence of Christ as fundamental to the Friends as transubstantiation to the post-Tridentine Roman Catholics, and capable of generating the same power and conviction.

So you could not practise the sort of religion George Fox preached in isolation. Your personal experience was of turning to the light, but the light now brought you into the true Church which alone understood the inwardness of true religion and which, in the contemporary understanding, was then emerging from the wilderness to accomplish the true Reformation. Hence, the group experience is as important a part of George Fox's message as his challenge to individuals, and it is clear to see why he and his companions first took the name Children of Light.

The early Friends lived in an atmosphere charged with symbolism and figurative speech, and on occasion it is hard to know whether they are using metaphorical or literal ideas. One such difficulty surrounds the proclamation by George Fox of what he called 'the Day of the Lord', a concept deriving from the crisis passages in Joel and the great sermon at Pentecost delivered by Peter in the second chapter of Acts. It seems that the early Friends did not speculate as others did about the time to come when Christ would come back to rule the world. They preferred to preach that Christ had already come, and this was their challenge to their times.

To those who were apostate from the truth, there was judgement, the Day of the Lord. This was the process of reckoning and the inevitable punishment that followed failure to turn to the light and receive the everlasting gospel. Fox and his friends could be savage in their denunciations of the wickedness of others who refused to submit to the chastening of the light within. The times were ones of heightened crisis and many felt that history was moving to a climax in a way totally foreign to modern secular understanding.

To those who accepted Truth, on the other hand, there was salvation and life within divine providence. Life in the restored Church was different from what people had experienced previously, for those who had come into the light received 'the same power and spirit that the Apostles were in'. This was another claim made by George Fox for himself and the community that gathered round him. What it meant was that the restored Church was identical to that which had received the Holy Spirit and written the New Testament all those years before. It was under the immediate and continuing guidance of its Lord, whose revelation of himself continuously added to the understanding of the community. Fox therefore called people to a new and fuller relationship with Christ. He said he called people to sit down under Christ their teacher to teach them, Christ their king to rule them, and Christ their bishop to take care of them.

The last feature of George Fox's thought will need further discussion, but it is the element that gave a coherence and an esprit de corps to the first Quakers. Fox's central proclamation that Christ had come to teach his people himself meant that the mid-seventeenth century was God's appointed time to restore the Church. The restoration had begun in England but it was a mission to the whole world. Membership in the Church meant involvement in this spiritual warfare against economic, social and religious evils. You needed to have a convincement that endured, but also a willingness to be enlisted in what they called 'The Lamb's War'.

So this was the mental world of George Fox as he set out on his commission to change the real world at the beginning of 1649. In the next two years he was imprisoned twice, at Nottingham for interrupting a sermon, a crime of which he was guilty, and at Derby under the Blasphemy Act 1650, a crime of which he was certainly innocent. Fox recorded of his encounter with the law at Derby, 'This was Justice Bennet of Derby that first called us Quakers because we bid them tremble at the word of God, and this was in the year 1650.'

Fox's apprenticeship was now almost at an end. He was approaching thirty years of age and was at the height of his powers. He was confident of his message and his vocation. He had a considerable reputation and there were already Friends' meetings in existence. But he had not yet reached national prominence. By the winter of 1651 he was travelling in the North, ranging across Yorkshire. His progress was probably being noted by the authorities, but he was no real threat to the established order. Nevertheless he had now gathered about himself some pretty formidable people. For some time he had known Elizabeth Hooton, and in various places he had made important contacts with magistrates and military people who had influence with the regime. From this time we date his association with Thomas Aldam, Richard Farnworth, James Nayler and William Dewsbury. He must have known in his bones that great things were about to happen to him, and it is as if he were being carried along on the bow wave of religious history.

The Establishment of a Religious Society

A T LANCASTER CASTLE IN 1613, EIGHT WOMEN AND TWO MEN were hanged as witches, following a macabre series of incidents in the Forest of Pendle. The Lancashire witches, once the victims of horrific brutality, are now celebrated in literature and folklore. In the villages of Pendle, the tourist souvenirs feature black cats and broomsticks. The cattle plague, the madness, the accidents the witches were alleged to have caused are forgotten, for we cannot take seriously the people who took witchcraft seriously. The coven is supposed to have met near Pendle Hill, a long, steep gritstone eminence which stands out in grandeur from the neighbouring Pennines, looking like an immense sleeping lion. In modern times it is the haunt of curlews, sheep, hikers, self-conscious Quaker pilgrims and rowdy motorcyclists shattering the peace of everybody else. In the seventeenth century it was thought to be the haunt of demonic powers.

In the late spring of 1652, George Fox arrived in the district from his recent travels in the West Riding of Yorkshire. He felt drawn to go up the Hill, and he did so with great difficulty, leaving his travelling companion, Richard Farnworth, below. He did not climb to see the view, or enjoy the effort, as a tourist might – such activities were not the thing at that time. What took him to the top was a distinct sense of obligation, and even of expectation. What occurred there was an incident that is often regarded as the turning-point in his life.

Fox's narrative reveals that at that time much of his preaching had been devoted to proclaiming the Day of the Lord. By this he meant pointing people to the crisis of decision with which the indwelling

Christ faced them. His New Testament model is clear, for the phrase he chooses to describe his message is the link between the prophecy of Joel and its fulfilment as proclaimed by Peter in his sermon at Pentecost. Packed into Fox's formulation was a message of prophecy, judgement and salvation. Its individual dimension was that people were called to repent and believe the gospel. Its collective dimension was that these were the last days, when extraordinary things would be seen. They were beginning in England, in 1652.

He tells us that he ascended Pendle Hill in obedience, and when he got on top, he was moved to 'sound' the Day of the Lord. This could refer to some action or proclamation regardless of the absence of an audience, for Joel records God's instruction to blow a trumpet on Mount Zion as a warning of the day of judgement. On the other hand, the usage may be that of sounding the depths – as at sea – as if Fox was working out the implications, or estimating the significance of his calling. The word he uses is ambiguous and could mean either course. But the context may favour the second alternative, for he is thereupon granted a vision: '. . . and the Lord let me see a top of the hill in what places he had a great people to be gathered.'

The Quaker Pentecost

It is presumably with a heightened sense of expectation that George Fox travelled on northwards. His route lay through the Dales of the West Riding and finally he arrived at Brigflatts, at the headwaters of the westward-flowing Lune. Once a thriving centre of the flax trade, Brigflatts is now a quiet hamlet. Apart from a few dwellings it has a Quaker meeting house and burial ground, and an old house called Borrats at the end of a lane. It was there, on Whit Sunday 1652, that George Fox attended worship at a separatist conventicle. Though he rejected observance of the liturgical year, he must have felt the significance of the day, for he wrote, '. . . this was the place that I had seen a people coming forth in white raiment.' His imagery was, as always, scriptural. Moreover in this case it was also apocalyptic. In Revelation it is the remnant of faithful souls at Sardis who shall walk with Christ in white raiment. Augmented, they become the multitude which stands before the throne of the Lamb. 'These are they who have come out of the great tribulation; they have washed their robes and made them white in the blood of the Lamb' (Revelation 7:14). This was the beginning of the Society of Friends.

The group that met at Borrats, the home of Gervase Benson, a local Justice of the Peace, appears to have been part of a widespread separatist network that had connections across Durham, the North Riding of Yorkshire, Westmorland and the Furness district of North Lancashire. This was one of the poorest and remotest districts of England. It was visited by the plague in 1649, but never by its king. Its parishes were too large and grossly understaffed. It had few schools. By and large, the tenant farmers and independent 'statesman' farmers had neither Royalist nor Parliamentarian sympathies, and the religious radicalism of the district stems probably from an independence fostered by official neglect, rather than a reaction against the impositions of authority.

In those days, contracts of employment ran for a year and many towns had an annual 'hiring fair' at which workers released from service were able to seek new employers. A vivid description of such a fair in later times is given in Thomas Hardy's *Far from the Madding Crowd*. It was frequently the occasion for the Justices of the Peace to attempt to fix the official wage rates, though the market frequently frustrated their intentions. On the Wednesday of the week of Fox's appearance in the ministry at Borrats, a hiring fair was held at the nearest town, Sedbergh, just up the road. It was a big day. The town was packed with people. To the statesmen farmers, the town was full of shepherds and labourers. To the merchants' wives, there were cooks and maids to be had. For Fox, there was a great people waiting to be gathered, and he went to preach to them.

According to his own account, he perched in a tree in the churchyard and preached for several hours. As luck, or fate, or providence would have it, one of the separatist preachers, Francis Howgill, was present and so were Thomas Blaykling and his son John. Fox had stayed with one of their kinsmen up in the hills. Hospitality ran in the family. Fox had refused money from the kinsman, but he went home with Thomas and John.

Fox scored a considerable measure of success, and his preaching in the open air emphasised what he was saying about a new and living way to Christ unencumbered by the traditional understanding of what made the Church. He refused to go into the parish church of the establishment, and the following Sunday made the same testimony by refusing to enter the separatists' place of worship either. The Church, he insisted, was people, not buildings, and his conduct left his hearers in no doubt about his meaning.

The next Sunday, John Blaykling took Fox up another of the great hills that figure in Quaker history. Near Sedbergh was Firbank Fell, a long hog's-back with dramatic views to the north. Nestling under the summit was a chapel to which the separated people of the district used to resort and where Francis Howgill and John Audland preached. Fox declined to take part in the meeting and stayed outside, and when it broke up he gave notice of his own meeting to be held up on the hill after dinner.

Refreshing himself with nothing but a drink from a brook he went and sat on a rock, and gradually the people and some of their ministers gathered round. Fox says there were upwards of a thousand people present. Again, he took a long time, three hours to present his message, for it is likely that he had a comprehensive exposition of his teaching which he put before people in some detail. The development of an enduring religious movement out of this man's ministry was based on more than passing religious enthusiasm. He was beginning to find that it appealed to minds as well as hearts, and very large numbers of people were becoming involved.

A few miles to the south was Preston Patrick, an ancient settlement that was once an outpost of the abbey at Shap. At the chapel there, the Westmorland separatists held a general meeting on a Thursday once a month, and it was due three days after Fox's visit to Firbank Fell. By now, John and Ann Audland had befriended him, and, after staying briefly at their house, he accompanied them down to the general meeting, where again Francis Howgill was present, as were John and Thomas Camm and Richard Hubberthorne. This time, perhaps because he was invited, Fox worshipped with the congregation. After an uneasy period during which Francis Howgill more than once rose to preach, and found that he could not, Fox began to speak. In their different ways, Howgill and Thomas Camm, who was twelve at the time, have left accounts that show that for many of those present Fox's message was a turning-point in their lives.

With astonishing speed, George Fox had won the hearts of this 'seeking and religiously inclined people', and, as can be imagined, the wiser ones were concerned. Even if what Fox said was the fulfilment of their secret hopes, the corporate aspect of their fellowship was affected. The attitude of similar groups elsewhere in the north could not be presumed. Fox's doctrine needed to be tested, and reservations discussed. The position of those who did not go along with Fox needed to be considered. At that time Fox adopted some extreme positions, which we shall see he may have got from the Baptists. He tells us that on Firbank Fell the elderly watched him from chapel windows and thought it strange to see a man preach on a hill and not 'in their church (as they called it)'. The shock to such tender people can be gauged by the concluding remark of his account of his visit to Preston Patrick when he told them that their bodies were the temples of God and that Christ was their teacher, 'and after they met in houses'.

After visiting Kendal, the main town of the district, Fox travelled on to Underbarrow, accompanied by a number of people including Edward Burrough, with whom he engaged in deep controversy. A gathering of concerned people assembled at Miles Bateman's house, and Fox asked them to arrange a meeting for him the next day. There was considerable opposition to his request, and the debate on it continued the following morning. Finally they agreed, and though there were convincements at the meeting, the records show that Fox encountered opposition. Quaker tradition is correct in its assessment that the Westmorland congregations provided the numbers and the leadership without which the nascent Quaker movement could scarcely have survived. However it tends to underestimate the misgivings people felt in the charismatic presence of the man from Fenny Drayton.

Swarthmoor Hall, the spiritual home of Quakerism, is an old house standing on the windswept coastal plain near Ulverston in the Furness district of Lancashire. It belonged to Thomas Fell, landowner, Judge of Assize, member of the Long Parliament and Vice-Chancellor of the County Palatine of Lancaster. Fell was a parliamentary nominee in a royalist area and he had a tricky political position to maintain in addition to his administrative responsibilities. Long after Fell's death, his wife Margaret married George Fox. She was mistress, i.e. manager, of the property and was engaged in bringing up eight children, of whom the seven eldest were daughters. Both played a part in giving the new movement the vital breathing space it needed.

Margaret Fell quickly became a Quaker but though her husband opened the Hall to Friends for meetings, and appears to have supported his wife, he was never formally associated with the Society. Thomas Fell was a man of affairs and could not have survived without a clear grasp of what was going on. We can safely say that Swarthmoor Hall became the headquarters of the Quaker movement with his consent not his complaisance. Fox arrived here in late June 1652, and for much of the remainder of his life this was his base of operations.

He stayed in the district for about a year, plainly with considerable success. James Nayler visited him, and a number of the separatist preachers now committed themselves firmly to 'Truth' as the Quakers' gospel was coming to be called by those who espoused it. What people would later call 'revival' was sweeping Lonsdale, Furness and hill country thereabouts, and this disturbance was troublesome to the authorities. George Fox became the victim of a slowly rising level of personal violence and what appear to be concerted steps taken to shut his mouth by judicial means.

He was arraigned for offences under the Blasphemy Act 1650 at Lancaster Quarter Sessions, and everybody knew a second conviction meant banishment on pain of death. Fox had friends with influence and the charge was dismissed on technical grounds, whereupon attempts were made to bring him back to the Assizes, and even to bring his case to the attention of Parliament. Both moves were ultimately unsuccessful. Fox left for Carlisle and the other side of the Pennines in the summer of 1653, about the time that his less fortunate companion, James Nayler, was released from Appleby gaol, where he had been put at about the same time that Fox escaped the same fate in Lancaster.

It was now clear that quite a widespread religious movement was springing up in the northern counties. In terms of doctrine, it took itself outside the usual frame of reference within which the Puritans conducted their own arguments and therefore upset everybody. Socially, it offered a serious challenge to the class distinctions practised by the laity and the economic privileges of many of the clergy. This meant that it could not be ignored. Something had to be done. But what?

Standards of justice and administration were anything but consistently applied in these post-war years, when feelings still ran high and the republican government was under pressure from royalist sympathisers on one side and its own radical wing on the other. The Justices of the Peace carried wider responsibility than they do today, and as a body had connections in the army, trade, law and Parliament. They therefore had their own intelligence network, and, presumably, factions and parties that reflected the situation in the New Model Army and at Westminster. Fox records in the *Journal* his first interview with Thomas Fell, from which it is quite clear that the judge already knew a great deal about him. Fell had influential contacts in Yorkshire and Durham, and while within their spheres of influence Fox and the increasing number of itinerant Quaker preachers would have been reasonably safe. Otherwise they tended to run foul of factional prejudice as well as the antagonism they attracted on their own account.

Early Quaker Preaching

By 1653 the Quakers were established on a firmer basis than the scattered Baptist communities of the East Midlands. Fox had recruited Richard Fainworth, Thomas Aldam, James Nayler and William Dewsbury in Yorkshire two years earlier, and Elizabeth Hooton in Nottinghamshire well before that. The leadership was now augmented with the likes of Edward Burrough, Francis Howgill, John Audland, Richard Hubberthorne and John Camm. In 1653 at least thirteen of the major Quaker preachers passed through County Durham (or Bishoprick as it was known), and south into Yorkshire. At the same time, partly by invitation, Friends began to move through South Lancashire and Cheshire towards North Wales. Quakerism was still a regional phenomenon, but its successes were about to turn it into something else.

The first itinerant preachers were engaged in what they called 'publishing Truth', which, as we have seen, was another name for preaching the gospel as Quakers understood it. These travelling Friends included women, and most of them came from the more comfortable sections of society. In religion, many had tried a number of persuasions before finding fulfilment in the Quaker message. They therefore combined a personal spiritual search which gave them a sense of other people's conditions, and the discovery of such a strong commitment that many of them came to sing hymns of joy in the foul dungeons into which they were not infrequently cast. Like most English people of their day they were rooted in the Bible, and its images, its phraseology, its teachings were second nature to them. In Quakerism they also found what they believed was its true meaning.

From what has been said so far it should be clear that the first Quaker evangelists did not enter unprepared or unheralded into the briary thorny wilderness of the world. When they came into a district, it was often already known who they were and why they had come. Their message was preached at market crosses, at inn-yards, on commons, and anywhere that people would assemble, often in the open air, and often by invitation in the church, though also in people's houses. There was a patchy network they could key into and they often carried letters of introduction to possible sympathisers along their route. The period was not really denominationally conscious, so it is possibly inaccurate to see them in the same terms as the door to door evangelists of unfamiliar sects today. They represented a radical and challenging emphasis within a generally accepted religious culture.

Hostility did not stop them, and in parts of the country where they were unwelcome, they suffered considerable inconvenience and harm. Duckings, beatings, insults and imprisonments came their way, and such was the extravagance of some of their utterances that one is not really surprised. Where they did preach in churches, they either did so by invitation or because they claimed the right to do so under the Directory after the minister had finished his sermon. Whatever right they had was reduced almost to nothing by the extension of the offence of disturbance under the Lord's Day Act 1656. This area of law is as murky as contemporary English law on the question of picketing in industrial disputes. Similar issues are involved. The reputation they enjoyed as deliberately ill-mannered interrupters of other people's devotions was largely undeserved. Only on two or three occasions did George Fox speak out when he was not entitled to, and he is careful to make clear that these were exceptional circumstances.

Fox advised Friends in the ministry to 'thresh out the corn, that the wind may scatter the chaff that the corn may be gathered into the barn'. The early preaching was divisive, as Christ's gospel had been divisive, and the first publishers of Truth were well aware that there would be less than universal acceptance of what they had to say. What seems to have happened was that their first action in a new place was to hold a meeting like the ones George Fox held in Sedbergh churchyard or on Firbank Fell. These were not occasions for schooling but for an act of commitment and may have involved elements of debate.

Fox's *Journal* frequently records that people in varying numbers were 'convinced' at these gatherings and the other preachers found the same. Later the same day, or in the week, there were more intimate gatherings of those whose interest was serious, and out of these more private gatherings the Quaker meetings began. A 'threshing' meeting seems to have been one at which various viewpoints were represented, and there was usually some sort of agreement over the agenda and rules of procedure.

It seems that they often developed on the basis of a church fellowship that was already there, so the Quaker experience was not entirely novel – indeed, the fellowship of the meeting was a necessary part of Fox's scheme of things. Christ had come to teach his people himself, and it was as they gathered for worship that he carried out his office. Clearly such an understanding of worship involved a personal convincement by Christ's light as a necessary preliminary, but in spite of the individualistic appearance of his doctrine, Fox's call to people was in the community of the church. There is reason to believe that 'Gospel Order' was one of his concerns from the beginning. Vocabulary can be illuminating – the Quaker meetings were 'settled', like flocks of sheep in the fold.

Their thinking did not proceed very far beyond this point, however. In the disorder of the times, a clear definition of the new movement vis-à-vis the rest of the Church was not possible. Quakers settled down in the future as one of the dissenting denominations, regardless of their own wishes or self-image. This was far from their intention at the beginning. The scope of their vision was so wide that unfamiliarity blinds us to it.

Fox and his fellows were quite clear that they were proclaimers and witnesses of the final redemption of the whole world, and no account of Quaker origins is adequate that fails to give fullest weight to this aspect of their thought. Their preaching was not intended to reform the church, still less to set up another sect, movement or fellowship. Gospel Order was not another sort of ecclesiastical set-up. It was the life blood of the true Church. That is why they sought to protect it from the influence of those whose understanding of Truth underplayed its historical and collective aspects in favour of its spontaneous and individualistic ones. But they did not envisage an organisation to integrate the true Church as it emerged from the wilderness. That was the work of the inward Christ. He would call individuals to go into the world on the final mission. He did not need a committee to help him.

So the travelling ministers set up meetings, where possible leaving them in the charge of one or two 'most grown in the Power and life, in the pure discerning in the Truth', as William Dewsbury said. Such Friends were supposed to be responsible for discipline, and to make sure that a three- or four-hour silent meeting was held once or twice a week, and that every month or so there was a general meeting with other nearby Friends – an occasion for worship, business and social intercourse. The early fellowship was a network rather than a pyramid.

Friends grew haphazardly, and were quite content. They had no clergy or church buildings to maintain and they were strongly opposed to the payment of tithes for the upkeep of a 'hireling' clergy. While rejecting priesthood and ordination, they nevertheless recognised ministerial gifts. In other places, worshippers usually expected a service with psalms, sermon and scriptural readings which were either in the form prescribed by the Book of Common Prayer or the Directory, or else one devised by the minister or the congregation itself.

Among Friends, worship was based on a period of silent waiting that usually lasted several hours. Other meetings were punctuated by personal testimony and lengthy extempore sermons known as 'ministry', as such speeches are still known to this day. It is possible that these forms of meeting were separate at the beginning and were assimilated to one another soon after. The Quakers rejected all sacramental observance as a corruption of the new covenant, which they understood in purely inward and spiritual terms. To others, they appeared to devalue the Bible by emphasising the continuing revelation of truth by the Holy Spirit as a present reality. In fact, this was far less radical than it appeared, for the doctrine merely provided a way of correcting the false interpretations that the false church was bound to produce. In no sense was it understood as providing a corrective for the 'errors' of scripture.

Contemporary records show a significant drift of membership from the Baptists to the Quakers. A large number of practices which are nowadays associated with the Friends can be shown to be paralleled or antedated among the Baptists. In turn they were probably employed by other groups as well, so what became integral to organised Quakerism represented a pattern of thought and feeling that was quite widespread among the many experimental separatist congregations of the time. Nevertheless, when all is said and done, these things have an unmistakable Anabaptist ring about them.

In the first place, at a time of political as well as religious trouble, members of these congregations regarded one another as equals in the gospel, not persons graded and divided by the irreligious conventions of secular society. A church like this could clearly not accept the authority of the state over its religious life. Its members would not swear oaths in law courts, nor take life at the state's behest in armies, nor pay money for a state-controlled church it believed to be depraved.

Then, at the confluence of spiritual and radical Puritan faith, there was the conviction that revelation continued through the Spirit and was not confined to the word of scripture, but that, paradoxically, religious discourse should be very wary of employing a non-scriptural terminology. The Quakers were by no means alone in their belief that academic learning was not essential to a minister, nor in the conviction that if the Holy Spirit suffused a gathered church, there would be free and spontaneous ministry.

This sense of the sufficiency of the Holy Spirit in the church provided a basis to challenge the extravagance of the world. By adopting certain standards of attitude, speech and dress, the radical separatists could constantly and obviously remind the worldly that they were forsaking a saving reality for a destructive appearance. So radicals used the familiar form of 'thou' and 'thee' instead of the polite form 'you'. The Quakers irrationally stuck to the old usage even when the distinction had disappeared, and its spiritual truculence had become merely quaint. They dressed plainly, without superfluous lace and decoration. They knew that Wednesday was Woden's day and August was named after one of the Caesars. So, as Christians, they refused to use these pagan names, and insisted on the use of numbers for the days and months of the year. They knew the church was a community not a building, so they had 'meeting houses' to emphasise the fact. That remains the correct noun for the Quakers' place of worship. Until the nineteenth century, it was in common use in the other dissenting denominations too.

In common with Baptists and others, Friends considered the church to be a social unit as well as a purely spiritual society. It was customary to have a number of elders, a practice continued by Friends, although, lacking the sacraments, they did not need to ordain ministers. Women were allowed to take part in service and nobody derived an income from church work. Monthly and quarterly meetings for worship and business are another old separatist practice Friends have continued. There are precedents elsewhere for such customs now seen as characteristic of Friends, like using written queries to obtain information about the health of the church, using a form of oversight as well as eldership, and protecting the group by disowning any of the members who fell short of its standards, particularly by contriving to marry a non-member.

There is a complex reciprocal relationship between the position women occupy in society and the possibilities open to them as church members. It is in this period of considerable social dislocation that women appear in numbers as preachers, pamphleteers, controversialists and evangelists, and begin to enter spheres of influence previously reserved for men. The women we read about come from a wide range of social backgrounds, and they, and the religious communities to which they belong, attract a great deal of hostility. Aspersions are cast on their morals and they are dismissed from consideration because they have no formal training. Conventional views about the relations between the sexes remain, but within the religious sphere irreversible long-term changes are occurring. The separatist churches in general, but the Baptists and Quakers in particular, are the seed bed of these changes. Perhaps among Friends what was significant was the kind of utterance people understood was being made. Preaching might be criticised by the normal (male-devised) canons of understanding. Prophetic utterances were not. The sanction behind them was *divine* and came directly to women regardless of humanly constituted authority, fulfilling Acts 2:17.

The Quaker form of separatism was attractive, and its appeal had a number of features. Through its proclamation of the Day of the Lord and the inward presence of Christ, it communicated a sense of great urgency – it was a matter of life and death. It was not limited in appeal – whatever the class basis of its first generation of members, the message was intended for high- and low-born alike. Though it had radically new features it was sufficiently similar to what had gone before that it could ring bells and strike chords in the consciousness of its hearers – it had a world-view that was understood.

'Truth' – the message the Quakers proclaimed – was a coherent system, an ideology. It had the great merit of providing self-consistent answers to a wide range of religious difficulties, and could be mastered by the unsubtle. It proved capable of convincing people from a whole range of social and economic classes and dramatically changed many lives. There was an element of high risk in joining Friends, and Truth proved capable of inspiring acts of great heroism in Christian patience and love. Above all, Quakerism was a spiritual and only secondarily an intellectual movement. It spoke to the needs of its time and only later had to face the test of rational scrutiny. The most important features of early Quakerism were its missionary endeavour and the persecution it attracted, not its theological novelty.

We can see these features in miniature in the period 1652–5, during which Friends emerge on to the national stage. Clausewitz says that the first rule of successful strategy is to secure your base, and Margaret Fell achieved this as efficiently as any Prussian general. She began to maintain contact with the itinerant Quaker preachers by letter and by personal contact, keeping open house for them at Swarthmoor Hall, and much of her correspondence survives. At the same time she took a leading part in building up the 'Kendal Fund' which was intended to meet the costs of the ministry and to support Friends in prison. At first the Quaker mission was concentrated on the northern counties but in 1654 the Friends emerged determinedly into the other parts of the nation.

It is impossible to underestimate the importance of Margaret Fell to the survival of the Quaker movement, though previous generations had a good try. Certainly she had wealth and social position, organising ability, contacts and influence. But her personality was also one which fitted the needs of the hour. While pious and devoted, she was used to getting her own way, and possessed, perhaps, an even stronger character than Fox. The military metaphor is exact. She held the fort securely at a time when any breach in the unity and resolve of the early Quaker mission may well have resulted in its becoming just a footnote to seventeenth-century history.

Politics and Persecution

In that year a large company of Quaker evangelists, not quite seventy in number, spread out through the kingdom in pairs like the seventy sent forth in Luke 10. Known as the 'Valiant Sixty' by modern Friends they began to take their message into all parts of the country. In the few years that followed many became leaders of the Society, and some were to die in prison. Already the Quaker movement was known, and Edward Burrough and Francis Howgill made their way to London, where their coming had been prepared for. Camm and Audland were successful in Bristol, but at Norwich, the third town of England, in strongly Puritan East Anglia, Richard Hubberthorne and George Whitehead ploughed a barren furrow for Friends. Scarcely more receptive were the universities. For some reason the first Quaker preachers at both Oxford and Cambridge seem to have been women. Each group was roughly handled. The seats of learning dealt out beatings for those who dared to disturb their fragile tranquillity.

The persecution Friends suffered was neither as systematic nor as horrendous as the treatment meted out to the continental Anabaptists or the Protestant martyrs in England. It was arbitrary and callous, cruel even, but the Quakers' sufferings were caused far more by local prejudices than a deliberate policy of vindictiveness on the part of the state. In the period 1652–60 there are plenty of examples of appeals to central government putting right illegal or badly judged actions by provincial magistrates. In some places, like their strongholds in the northern counties, Bristol and London, the Quakers suffered few disturbances. Elsewhere, and at certain times, the authorities set out to harass them with some severity. Friends were objectionable not so much for what they were, as for what they represented. Their success in gaining converts added a dimension to the current political struggle that the authorities could have done without.

Above the Puritan republic of England, which lasted from 1649 to 1660, there floated the spectre of the restoration of the monarchy, the reimposition of the episcopal system of church government, and the curtailment of the considerable political and religious freedom that had been won. From a confused sense in 1641 that royal power had somehow overstepped the mark, opinion crystallised throughout the rest of the forties round the view that on the basis of a Parliamentary victory in the Civil War, England could be remade. As the new republic had to face the realities of power, this vision began to dim. The radicals found that they had been betrayed by the moderates. The moderates suffered losses to the conservatives. Through these shifting currents, Oliver Cromwell had to sail his course, and policy-making gave way to the need to maintain the regime.

The political and religious centre, loosely called 'Independency', was the group that really counted. Any alliance of loyalties that could be forged to support the republic would have to be made round them. Some of its members were inclined towards a complete separation of church and state. Others were prepared to settle for a measure of independence within a state church. Perhaps the final disintegration of England's only republican experiment can be attributed to Cromwell's failure to satisfy the expectations of either group.

For example, the conservative Independent John Owen (1616–1683), later Vice-Chancellor of Oxford University, stated his principles before the House of Commons in 1647. He, and those who thought like him (who were numerous), considered it to be the duty of the state to ensure that the truth of the gospel was preached to all people; to protect the worship of orthodox Protestants; to prevent the spread of Catholic practices and Unitarian ideas; and to oppose the Leveller and sectarian demand for complete religious freedom. People of this mind were numerous in the Rump Parliament between 1649 and 1653 but they overplayed their hand and Cromwell was forced to look leftwards to maintain the political balance.

The Barebones Parliament (named after 'Praise God' Barebone, MP for the City of London), which contained several Quaker sympathisers, was nominated by gathered churches and army units, and sat for less than a year. It attempted a wide range of reforms, including the introduction of civil marriage, special protection for infants and the insane, and relief for debtors and poor prisoners. It also turned its attention to the problem of tithes, as intractable a problem for legislators in the mid-seventeenth century as the exact form of local taxation remains for their counterparts in the twenty-first.

Tithes were originally a feudal payment due to the rector, or incumbent of a living for his support, and comprised one tenth of the produce of the parishioners' land. By the 1640s this apparently simple way of supporting the church had grown immensely complicated. There was a mass of law defining what counted as tithable produce, which varied from district to district. The right to tithes became negotiable, and, partly because of the sale of monastic land and its rights, 'impropriations' became widespread. These were arrangements whereby a landowner could purchase the right to receive tithes, substitute a vicar on a stipend as the incumbent in place of a rector, and thus make a profit.

The offence that this gave to religious sensibilities is obvious. As the *Communist Manifesto* remarked of capitalism in general, 'It has drowned the most heavenly ecstasies of religious fervour, of chivalrous enthusiasm, in the icy water of egotistical calculation.' Some estimates say as much as one third of the nation's tithes were impropriated by 1640, and the Long Parliament was deluged with petitions for abolition, the agitation getting within ten votes of success. The system bore hardest on small farmers and caused considerable unrest in the country. It also meant poverty for many clergymen and was a real obstacle to the provision of proper pastoral care.

Political radicals and separatists of all colours favoured outright abolition as part of the dismantling of the state church, and the Friends were part of this body of opinion. But the Independents, who could see merit in some system of state support for religious institutions, doubted the value of tithes on the practical grounds that there might be better methods of finance available. When the Barebones Parliament was about to grasp this nettle, the conservative members carried a motion which effectively dissolved it. Cromwell accepted the fait accompli. Having alienated the conservatives in 1652, he now alienated the radicals.

The institution of the Protectorate in 1653 brought about England's only written constitution, the *Instrument of Government*. This ensured considerable religious freedom, making the 'public profession of the Christian Religion' an object of state policy, but maintaining the system of tithes until some other arrangement 'less subject to scruple and contention' was found. 'Faith in God by Jesus Christ' was the test by which to decide whether the separatist sects were to be allowed to meet, for there was no intention to force people to adopt the 'public profession', though it must be said that Roman Catholics were not granted toleration thereby.

Within the established church some persisted in using the Book of Common Prayer but since the Presbyterian reform had been given statutory backing, the Directory was the official service book. In an attempt to raise clerical standards, the Triers and Ejectors were appointed by Ordinance in 1654 to examine ordinands as to their suitability, and to ensure the removal of unsatisfactory ministers. The effect of these reforms was that a wide variety of opinion was now officially envisaged within the state church, but complaints began to be heard about the strictness of the ministry. Debate continued, and the scandal of tithes remained. One permanently important event of the period was the readmission of the Jews, who had been barred from settlement in England since 1290.

The Quaker tradition looks back on this period as a time of persecution, and we must examine why. How could it come about that so many Friends were imprisoned when it looked as if an age of uneasy toleration was dawning? To answer this, we have to look at the laws they were alleged to have broken, to see why it should have occurred to the authorities in many parts of the country that they were a subversive force which had to be put down by one means or another.

We should be clear that the Quakers came well within the prescribed test for tolerating sects. Their theology may well have been distasteful to the majority, but they clearly preached faith in God by Jesus Christ and were as strongly opposed to Unitarianism and Ranterism as they were to the establishment. As Fox says, 'And many other disputes we had with such like and with all the other sects, as Presbyterians, Independents, Seekers, Baptists, Episcopal men, Socinians [Unitarians], Brownists, Lutherans, Calvinists, Arians, Fifth Monarchy Men, Familists, Muggletonians, Ranters. But none of them would confess to the same power and spirit that the Apostles had and were in.'

On the other hand, they differed (with others) from the mainstream Calvinism of the time. There, the grace of God operates on the sinner by convincing him of his sin and showing him through the medium of scripture how he can be forgiven through the merits of Christ's sacrifice on the cross. Though he remains a sinner, Christ's righteousness is imputed to him, and he is saved. For the Quakers, this saving grace operated independently of the scriptures in the light of Christ within. The sinner can then see the meaning of scripture by direct inward revelation, for he can say, with Paul, '... yet not I, but Christ liveth in me' (Galatians 2:20). To the uninterested, the unsophisticated, the underhand, such statements looked very much like a breach of the Blasphemy Act 1650. With the possibility of banishment on second conviction this might appear a forbidding weapon in the hands of magistrates. As it turned out, they only used it against one or two leading Friends, and then without success, for they were clearly not guilty under it.

More common were two statutory offences to which Friends often succumbed. We have seen how itinerant ministry was an important part of the Quaker mission and many travelling Friends were convicted on spurious charges under the Vagrancy Acts, notably a statute of Queen Elizabeth dating from 1597 – not very old – permitting rogues, vagabonds and sturdy beggars to be flogged. Many Friends, like the women evangelists at Oxford and Cambridge were deliberately proceeded against by this means, so that unjustified punishment could be inflicted.

Then again, we have seen that Friends claimed a legal and customary right to speak in churches after the minister had finished, and were even invited to do so. Though this was an integral part of their early mission practice, it was not very prudent. Word got round that Quakers were in the habit of interrupting services, and some of them ran into violent resistance from outraged congregations. On Friends generally, this is in all probability a calumny. Nevertheless, in February 1655 a proclamation was made, specifically naming the Friends, warning them not to disturb services. In April the same year another promulgation provided for the taking of an oath abjuring the authority of the Pope, so that, when Friends were brought to trial, their refusal to swear an oath meant a contempt, and they could be committed in prison for what was in effect an indeterminate period, before they ever got a chance to answer the charges against them. Once inside they were at the mercy

of whatever ill-treatment the gaolers chose to devise. Many of their testimonies to the world, like the use of plain speech and the refusal to
remove their hats were construed as contempts in the same way, with
much the same results. The classic example of this cat-and-mouse game
can be read in Fox's *Journal* in which he describes the events that led up
to his imprisonment at Launceston in 1656.

The last category of acts of witness which brought imprisonment to
Friends was the refusal to pay tithes. As was to happen in the future, the
Quakers found themselves called upon to make a stand against something which others opposed equally strongly but did not see as a matter
where personal testimony was required. The extent of the corporate
commitment to these principles can be gauged by the fact that Friends
claimed that down to 1660 over three thousand of their number had
suffered imprisonment, 'putting in the stocks, whippings, loss of goods
and other abuses for keeping a good conscience toward God and man'
and over thirty had died as a result of persecution. It is important to
note that none of these was for a capital offence.

The internal spiritual assurance that enabled the Quakers to make
these quite staggering (and it seems to the world, foolhardy) gestures,
was a reflection of their message. Their apparent lack of interest in the
historical Christ was the outcome of a faith in the resurrecting Christ
rather than the atoning Christ, and it provided an aggressive and uncompromising attitude to all the ways of the world, so that distinctions
between essentials and non-essentials were dissolved, and the demands
of Truth reached down to what others regarded as trivia. The doctrine
of perfection as an attainment open to all involved total consistency regardless of consequences, and only by accepting suffering could Friends
practise what they preached. They know that this was a necessary part
of the Lamb's War, and they took it as it came.

In some ways, however, the early Friends were not the best adver-
tisements for the faith they proclaimed. Perhaps it was the disturbed
times in which they lived, but we should not fail to notice the extravagance of some of their words and actions. They prophesied disasters,
went naked for a sign, fasted and, of course, quaked. There were alleged miracles. Their speech was exaggerated too. For example, some
played into the hands of their opponents by calling for the burning of
the Bible. They valued scripture very highly, but thought that this rhe-
torical device would make their point about the authority of the Holy
Spirit more effectively. It had the reverse effect.

Underlying the response of society to the Quakers' stiff-necked extravagances lay a fear that any success they might achieve would upset the precarious balance of the state. On the left there were people like the Fifth Monarchy Men who would grab at the chance of an armed uprising if one presented itself. Many people sought to silence the Quakers because they confused them with the Fifth Monarchists while others thought that the adoption of Quakerism on a large scale would break down the normal pattern of life to such a degree that the way would be open for further revolution.

In fact, the nation was then only four years away from the restoration of King Charles II, and the reviving hopes of the Royalists added a further ingredient of suspicion. Many influential people came to the conclusion that a continuation of the policy of toleration would create a confusion that would be resolved either by a descent into sectarian chaos or a coup that would restore the monarchy. So they set out to limit it in whatever ways they could.

The situation of the Quakers was not helped by the winding down of the Leveller movement. It began to be noticed that numbers of people formerly of this persuasion seemed to be opting for Quakerism as a fulfilment of their egalitarian ideals. Against this background it becomes clear why magistrates, landowners, army commanders and parish clergy should seek to turn whatever legal artillery they had on 'the innocent and harmless People of God called Quakers'. Beneath the arrest of Fox for sedition in 1656 and the savage treatment of James Nayler in the same year lay a wave of hysteria connected with the fear of an outbreak of revolutionary violence that would render worthless all the political struggles of the previous fifteen years.

Missions Abroad

The Friends, however, were unmoved by political considerations, for the kingdom to which they owed allegiance was not of this world, and they began to take their message beyond the confines of England. There was a large standing army and numbers of Protestant planters in Ireland, so Truth was proclaimed there. It was fairly successful among the settlers, but never made much headway among the vast Catholic majority. It was a similar story in Scotland, where the Reformation had taken quite a different course, and in any case social conditions were quite different. That nation was to produce the Quakers' greatest systematic theologian in Robert Barclay, but it never developed more than a few scattered Quaker communities, and to this day, like Wales, it forms a part of Britain Yearly Meeting.

In spite of commercial rivalry, there have always been close connections between England and the Netherlands, and from 1655 onwards there was a Quaker presence in that country. Meetings continued there for many years but perhaps the Quaker message did not take firmer root because it was so similar to that of some of the Collegiant and Mennonite Congregations already in existence. From Holland, two Friends travelled into Germany and as a result of their ministry a Quaker group came into existence at Griesheim in the Palatinate. Emigrating to America, this community settled at a place now called Germantown, Pennsylvania, and was involved in 1688 in the first corporate religious protest against the institution of slavery.

The most audacious early mission was carried out by two parties which left England for the Ottoman Empire in 1657. One Friend, Mary Fisher, who, as we shall see, had already given her witness in Massachusetts, managed to obtain an audience with the Sultan at Constantinople. He listened to her words but was not convinced by them, and with kindness she was sent on her return journey. Two members of the other group, John Perrot, an Irish Friend from Waterford, and his companion, John Luffe of Limerick, travelled round Greece, but were probably prevented from going further by the English consul at Smyrna. Eventually they found themselves back in Venice and had to think about a change of plan.

They set off for Rome intending to seek an interview with the Pope. Luffe succeeded, but not quite in the intended manner. He was examined by Pope Alexander VII who was even less impressed than the Sultan and his Council, the Sublime Porte, had been with Mary Fisher. He also behaved in a less Christian manner than the Muslims, for Luffe was hanged as a reward for his audacity. Perrot avoided this fate, and there is a hint that he betrayed his countryman. He was first placed in the madhouse and then removed to prison, whence he was released in 1661.

Though it scored some isolated successes, Quakerism did not make much impact on Christendom outside the Anglo-Saxon countries, and its pretence to be a world mission must be recognised as just that. For some time it retained its fervour and its witness to 'truth' against all the sects and religions of the world, but in numerical terms its achievement was slight. If the old world proved barren, a fruitful future awaited it in

America, which became the centre of Quakerism long before anybody recognised it as such.

The English settlement in America stretched from the plantations in the West Indies northward to the New England colonies, and two of the centres for Quaker settlement and mission there were Barbados, where Friends appeared in significant numbers after 1656, and Rhode Island, where the 1651 charter allowed for religious toleration. This was both the policy and conviction of its celebrated Governor, Roger Williams, who had earlier been a refugee from the intolerance of the Puritan regime in Massachusetts. New England provided an object lesson of the kind of religious exclusiveness that with all its troubles, Old England had avoided. In spite of the sufferings of the English Quakers, they cannot really show any example of suffering and injustice to match the witness made by the accurately named 'Boston Martyrs'.

In 1656 Mary Fisher and Ann Austin arrived in Boston, Massachusetts, to proclaim truth. They were promptly imprisoned and illegally deported to Barbados. The authorities then passed a series of draconian laws penalising any shipmaster bringing Quakers into the colony. Any Friends found there could be flogged, imprisoned with hard labour and deported. If they returned, they were to be flogged again, their right ears were to be cut off, and they were to be deported again. In 1658 a second return after banishment was made a capital offence.

This was a challenge that the Friends could not ignore, and the scene of the story switches to Bridlington, a sea-coast town in Yorkshire, Old England, where one Robert Fowler felt led to build a ship 'in the cause of truth' to sail to New England. It would be hard to imagine a smaller and less adequate vessel for his purpose than the one he produced, but he sailed her to London, where he found a number of Friends, three of whom were fated to end up in Boston, waiting for an Atlantic passage. Navigated by little more than faith, the tiny *Woodhouse* finally made her landfall off Long Island, and her passengers made their various ways to their ministries in America.

Of the first three friends to suffer the penalty of losing an ear, two were from the *Woodhouse*, Christopher Holder and John Copeland. Their travelling companion, William Robinson, went to Boston with Mary Dyer and Marmaduke Stephenson, and each of these three friends suffered the penalty of flogging and deportation. They went straight back, and this time were sentenced to death. The men were hanged, but Mary Dyer was once more expelled from the colony. Yet again she returned, and this time there was no reprieve. In the summer of 1660 she also went to the gallows. The persecution was ended by the newly restored King Charles II at the request of Edward Burrough. With nice disdain, his order that any Quaker accused of a capital offence should thereafter be sent to England for trial was carried to the persecutors by one Samuel Shattuck, himself a banished Quaker.

There had, of course, been Friends in the American colonies for some time. The controversies within English Puritanism were reflected across the Atlantic, though in due course they acquired a very different historical significance, helping to lay the intellectual foundations for the subsequent development of the United States. As in England, there was proto-Quakerism to be found in figures such as Anne Hutchinson, obliged to leave the Rhode Island colony in 1637 after an inquisition. It is a serious error to imagine that Quakerism is an English phenomenon and that therefore its English manifestation is somehow the norm. Rather we should see it in broad terms as one of the outcomes of the North Atlantic culture.

So while some Friends migrated for economic reasons, to avoid persecution at home, or with the encouragement of William Penn, the seeds of the Quaker movement had already germinated in American soil. The earliest communities are, of course, found on the eastern seaboard. Puritan Massachusetts was notoriously intolerant, and a place of early persecution for Quakers, as we have just seen. But Rhode Island turned out to be a beacon of toleration. New York was under Dutch suzerainty until 1664, so New Jersey became the first big Quaker settlement. It was overtaken when Pennsylvania was granted to William Penn and he encouraged a significant influx of settlers in the years following 1682. Civil disabilities did not prevent a Quaker community developing in Virginia, which came to an end in the War between the States, and there were Quakers in Maryland as early as 1656. Though the Carolinas had only few Friends, George Fox made a point of going there in the course of his visit in 1672, which was part pastoral, part evangelistic, and partly to consolidate organisational structures in the New World.

Strengths, Weaknesses and Challenges

We now turn to a consideration of the internal development of the Society of Friends. Though convenient, this is really a misnomer, for the first recorded use of the phrase in the modern sense seems only to date from 1793. Following the New Testament usage, the earliest title Friends gave themselves was 'Children of Light' (cf. John 12:36, Ephesians 5:8, 1 Thessalonians 5:5, AV). The name 'Quaker', as we have seen, was alleged by Fox to have originated with Gervase Bennet at Derby in 1650. According to this account, the Justice used the word as a riposte to Friends' injunctions to people to tremble at the word of God. Others, like Robert Barclay, were more willing to admit that it was the Quakers who quaked and the others who did not. On that account it was an accurate description of what actually happened in meeting. Whichever is right, the name quickly proved suitable and acceptable.

'Friends' seems to have been in use from the very beginning, often coupled with a reference to the message, as in 'Friends of Truth' or 'Friends *in the* Truth'. There was no reluctance to use the word 'church' but in the sense that implied a community rather than a building or an institution. Another favourite text was quoted by George Fox at Sedbergh, 'I said unto him I denied their church for the church was in God as in 1 Thess. 1:1.' Hence, the New Testament references were taken to describe the reality the Friends knew, to the exclusion of others' experiences. In fact, the usage 'Friends Church', which is now common on the evangelical wing of American Quakerism has a more respectable ancestry than is sometimes appreciated.

There is reason to believe that some form of church government was a part of Quakerism from the beginning though Friends would have insisted that only Christ governed them. Whether or not George Fox had foreseen the precise pattern that emerged was less important than that he appreciated Paul's dictum, 'for God is not the author of confusion but of peace, as in all churches of the saints' (1 Corinthians 14:33). In any case, unity was one of the outward marks of the guidance of the light. Many of the first Quakers had experience of Independent or separatist churches in which the sense of identity with the community was deep. A strong individual faith arrived at through personal experience was not regarded as inconsistent with submission to the authority of the group.

In early Quakerism, authority was sometimes confusingly dispersed. Its elements were the basic personal experience of convincement and submission to the light, and the continuous guidance of the light expressed corporately through the church, and measured against the testimony of the Holy Spirit in the scriptures. Other churches were able to trace their origins to a covenant between their founders, or else a historic and authoritative statement of doctrine to which they owed their distinctive witness. In cases of conflict, argument often centred on the meaning of these fundamental documents. The Quakers had no such thing. This was both their strength and their weakness.

The earlier meetings, for such was the name of the local churches, generally gathered in people's houses, and were often largely made up of members of some earlier congregation. They usually had members mature in the spiritual life who acted collectively as pastors on the familiar pattern. Each group appeared to be autonomous but not independent, and from the outset, several groups in one district would periodically meet. There was very considerable uniformity in faith and practice on the basis of similar previous experience, shared presuppositions, and an outside hostility which provoked a closing of ranks. The teaching and co-ordinating function was fulfilled by the essential institution of the travelling ministry.

The strength of these arrangements was that the nationwide Society rested firmly on a large number of small communities, each used to running its own affairs, so that there was a constant growth of leadership at the local level. Necessary for health, this was not sufficient for continued growth, and the corresponding weakness was that, if the travelling ministry was in some way impaired, the cohesiveness of the Quaker movement would be noticeably damaged. Quakerism began with a congregational form of church government in which primary responsibility lay with the local churches. As time went by, it developed a form of organisation which looked more like the Presbyterian model, in which the area synods have a regulatory function. Experience taught Friends that in a hostile world small groups could not survive. They would be isolated and destroyed by persecution, and they would be unable to provide the full range of necessary pastoral care. Moreover, when hard decisions had to be made in various sets of circumstances, different meetings might go different ways. Autonomy could be the enemy of unity.

In the first fifty years of Quakerism, therefore, we can discern four movements which led the Society away from its original form. There was a tendency to organise, and influence moved from the localities to bodies representing Friends over a wider area. There was a tendency to centralise. Political and other pressures made it necessary for national institutions to be created. These two trends were accompanied by opposition, and a tendency to divide made its appearance. Finally, as the Society became established as a permanent part of the religious landscape, there was a need for it to expound and defend its faith and a tendency to formalise faith and practice emerged. The eight years before the restoration of the monarchy in 1660 provided a foretaste of these things, but, thereafter, all four trends combined to weave a lifeline. The movement did not lose its momentum. It learned lessons necessary for survival.

The first Quaker schism occurred in one of its earliest centres, Nottingham. Rice Jones, a Baptist soldier, seems to have thrown in his lot with Friends for a while, and was certainly one of the leading local people. By 1651, however, he appears to have moved out of the Quaker orbit. He visited Fox in prison at Derby while on his way to take part in the Battle of Worcester, which ended the Civil Wars. It was during this imprisonment that Fox himself was offered a captaincy in the Parliamentary army and made his celebrated statement, 'I told them I lived in the virtue of that life and power that took away the occasion of all wars . . . ' Close though they might have seemed on the surface, there was nevertheless a spiritual chasm between the two men. If we had more information about Rice Jones than Fox supplies, we might find a classic illustration of the cross-currents of opinion on the frontiers of radical religion that we have already noted. What might also show up could be the real originality of the message George Fox preached.

Rice Jones appears twice more in Fox's *Journal*, over a period of nearly seven years. He is engaged in controversy with Fox, who speaks disparagingly of his followers, claiming oddly that many of them had become the greatest football players and wrestlers in the country. Some members of this congregation are reported as joining Friends over the period, but it is noteworthy that at the same time numbers remained loyal to Rice Jones. These Friends, known as the 'Proud Quakers', held their Meetings for some years at Castle Yard in Nottingham. It may be the strength of such quasi-Quakers in that part of the Trent Valley that caused Fox, Nayler and Elizabeth Hooton all to complain of a coldness towards Friends in what we now know to have been the cradle of Quakerism. It seems that yet another prophet found that he was without honour in his own country.

James Nayler

A prophet dishonoured was James Nayler, a yeoman farmer, born perhaps in 1617, near Wakefield in the West Riding of Yorkshire. He was a pious man and concluded over eight years' service in the army as a quartermaster in Major-General Lambert's regiment in the Scottish campaign of 1650. It seems that he had arrived at an essentially 'Quaker' position while still a soldier, and one member of the army records that his terror at the preaching of James Nayler was greater than his terror at the Battle of Dunbar. By all accounts, Nayler was an imposing personage and an eloquent speaker. In 1651 he encountered George Fox and hereafter devoted his life to religious work.

Because of subsequent events, some people have said, the Society of Friends tends to overlook the fact that at one point Nayler, rather than Fox, might have become the leading figure in the new movement. He was an early pamphleteer, a skilful debater in the public disputations that were a feature of the religious life of the Interregnum, and a compelling preacher. His remarkable defence to a charge of blasphemy at Appleby in 1652 was so powerful that it convinced Anthony Pearson while he was actually sitting on the bench in judgement. Nayler had fatal weaknesses, however. He was too much given to fasting and religious exercises that impaired his judgement. He was unable to withstand the adulation that he received in some quarters. The purity of his own soul prevented him from seeing the mixture of motives in other members of his own religious community.

These defects of character surfaced dramatically in 1656. In January of that year, George Fox was arrested in Cornwall on a holding charge of sedition and imprisoned at Launceston, where he spent part of the time in 'Doomsdale', the insanitary oubliette of the castle. The authorities were jumpy. The Barebones Parliament was outliving its usefulness. Cornwall was an area of strong Royalist sympathies and there were rumours of an uprising. The vagrancy laws were turned against a number of Friends who sought to visit Fox there, and Quakers were generally in a delicate situation. While Fox was out of circulation and Burrough and Howgill were away, James Nayler assumed the leadership of Friends in London.

At this critical point, the alternative leader of the Society of Friends took leave of his senses. A group of women in London began to disrupt meetings and act in a manner that the rest of Friends found scandalous, singing and chanting for hours on end, barracking and heckling preachers, and following their own leadings without considering their effect on Friends. They treated James Nayler with exaggerated respect, bowing and lying down before him, and singing in his presence, and one later claimed that he had raised her from the dead. So repellent was this conduct that some Friends even thought that Nayler had been bewitched. All the evidence, however, points to a deep and traumatic depression in which he allowed himself to be used by unbalanced people whom he originally did not have the courage to discipline.

On Friday 24 October 1656, James Nayler was brought into Bristol in circumstances that suggested that he was claiming to be Christ. He rode among the company of eight people, who sang and chanted 'Holy, holy, holy, Lord God of Israel', and spread garments before him. Crowds followed. The rain poured down on the bedraggled procession. Every member of the thousand strong Quaker community remained behind closed doors, and the demonstrators were taken into custody.

There was no case against Nayler under the Blasphemy Act 1650 for it was quite clear that his action was intended to be seen as a sign of Christ's coming not a personal claim to divinity. In any case, the penalty for a first offence was only six months' imprisonment, scarcely satisfactory to his opponents. Nevertheless, the form of his answers under cross-examination indicated theological views that were unacceptable to the authorities, and, it has been suggested, were only partly assimilated into what were then the received views among Friends. The magistrates in Bristol did not know what to do with Nayler, so they referred the matter to Parliament, which appointed a committee to look into the case.

After considerable debate, and almost certainly illegally, the House of Commons decided that it possessed the independent jurisdiction to punish Nayler. On 17 December 1656 he was pilloried for two hours in the Palace Yard at Westminster and then whipped through the streets to the Exchange in the City of London. Moves were then made to mitigate his punishment but they secured respite not reprieve. On 27 December he was pilloried again in the City, his tongue was bored through with a hot iron and his forehead branded with the letter B. He was returned to Bristol, exposed to ridicule and beaten again there, and imprisoned indefinitely in solitary confinement.

Friends were mortified by this whole episode. The adverse publicity was enormous. So many petitions were received that Parliament set up a committee to prepare a bill designed to suppress Quakerism entirely. The followers of James Nayler turned on those who had seen where his extravagances might lead, and the disturbance of meetings continued. Throughout the country there was a noticeable escalation in the hostility felt towards Friends, and sympathy for the execrable cruelty perpetrated on him had to be put in the balance against all the trouble he caused.

Indeed, one modern historian has remarked that on the rare occasion when anything deserving the name of torture was inflicted in England under the Commonwealth and Protectorate, it was by order of Parliament and not the judiciary or executive. In fact, Nayler was a victim of circumstances. What happened to him may simply have been the outcome of Parliamentary manoeuvring as Cromwell's critics sought to limit the Protector's freedom under the Instrument of Government. In such circumstances the episode may say more about the political antagonisms at the heart of the Protectorate than any specific offences committed by Nayler himself.

Three years later he was released, and was reconciled to Friends. His earlier consciousness of the possibilities of a life of perfect holiness and obedience remained with him. But his suffering had now given it quite a different basis. In October 1660 he was robbed near Huntingdon, and shortly after died at a friend's house. His last words describing the spirit in which he tried to live are among the classics of Quaker literature. Speaking of the Spirit which 'delights to do no evil nor to revenge any wrong' James Nayler concludes, 'I found it alone, being forsaken. I have found fellowship therein with them who lived in dens and desolate places in the earth, who through death obtained this resurrection and eternal holy life'. Not many people have come as close to their Saviour as James Nayler.

The whole episode raised fundamental questions about the effectiveness of the Quaker movement. In spite of persecution it had now touched nearly every part of England and was spreading overseas. The tension between individual leadings and the authority of the group, both parts of 'Truth', had to be faced. The weaknesses of the system of a loosely linked network of meetings co-ordinated by a travelling ministry were showing up, and in the period 1655-60 the first moves can be discerned towards a greater co-ordination of effort and activity. It was now more than an explosion of missionary endeavour. It had a continuing life of its own, and it needed steady nourishment.

The Beginnings of a Formal Discipline

By 1655 Quakerism had spread over most of the nation. It was no longer possible for Margaret Fell in her northern fastness to take the main burden of organising care for the poor and deal with problems of individual discipline. The need developed for national guidelines, and in due course was met. A meeting of elders from the north Midlands, held at Balby in the West Riding in 1656, produced a long 'advice' on church government, and its influence can still be seen in Quaker organisational handbooks the world over. It gives general advice about the times of meetings and gives directions as to how people who 'walk disorderly', or flout the commonly accepted standards of behaviour, are to be dealt with. The responsibility is placed firmly with the church and not the elders.

There then follows advice on ministry and instructions about dealing with inappropriate contributions to meetings for worship, and taking care not to say too much or too little in expressing the message which is given. There is mention of collections and expenditure on the relief of prisoners and the poor, the right holding of marriages and the proper maintenance of registers of births and deaths. Scriptural texts are recommended with advice for children, parents, husbands, wives, masters and servants. Traders are to be honest and punctual in paying debts, and proper service to the state is to be undertaken cheerfully.

The postscript is well known – 'Dearly beloved Friends, these things we do not lay upon you as a rule or form to walk by, but that all with the measure of light which is pure and holy may be guided, and so in the light walking and abiding these may be fulfilled in the Spirit – not from the letter, for the letter killeth, but the Spirit giveth life.' The use of this text, 2 Corinthians 3:6, summarises the whole approach to church order. The appeal is not made on the authority of the elders, as if issuing instructions. The appeal is from the light in them to the light in Friends. Their words are to be followed because they express Truth, not obeyed because they are written from the meeting. The question of disagreement will, therefore, not arise.

Thus, we can see the later organisational structure of the Society beginning to emerge. Friends gathered locally in their particular meetings, and several congregations came together at intervals, perhaps monthly or every few weeks, often at a common centre within a day's ride from each. It gradually became clear that this was the most convenient administrative unit, although there were also gatherings of Friends from a wider area still, like that at Balby, which produced the advice on church government.

The arrangements were haphazard and incomplete. There was no consistent practice in naming meetings, nor any clear definition of their respective responsibilities, so there is a degree of vagueness about what a 'General Meeting' was. Some were for elders, who tended to discuss business matters, some for Friends in the ministry. Large crowds often came, sometimes running into thousands, although the nucleus of the meeting consisted of nominated representatives.

The need to manage money is part of the reason for this widening of the horizon. Though local Friends remained responsible for the support of the travelling ministry, it came to be recognised that care for the poor and the relief of suffering needed to be co-ordinated over a wider area, and the cost of evangelists travelling to foreign parts should fall on Quakers as a whole. In 1657 this latter burden was shifted from the Northern Friends to the nation at large, and steps were taken to plan a national assembly. It seems that in preparation, the northern practice of church government, exemplified in the Balby advice, was widely introduced into the south. In 1660 a General Meeting at Skipton became the first representative gathering of the Quakers nationwide. It was not yet a Yearly Meeting, but at this point the centralising tendency began to manifest itself clearly.

Another reason for this development was the change, symbolised, and partly brought about, by James Nayler's extravagances. The new Society was running into some real opposition as people became accustomed to its methods and style. In debate, speech, pamphlet and book the Puritans began a counter-attack, and the Friends were forced on to the defensive. Organisational changes were carried out against a background of a much less colourful campaigning style, with much less speaking in churches and going naked (except for a loin cloth) as a sign to a wicked generation. Evangelists found the work tougher and the crowds smaller.

But even more far-reaching changes were coming. Those who only engage in discourse with those of like mind often fail to read the signs of the times. For many outside governing religious circles and the sectarian cliques, a silver lining was appearing in the dark clouds of republican rule. In 1658, Oliver Cromwell died, leaving no clear political settlement, and in two short years Friends needed to resolve the question of their relations with the state. They were now London-based and much better understood. But they were also ambivalent towards Parliament, still appearing hostile to the government and issuing apocalyptic warnings about what the future held.

As the constitutional crisis deepened, there were Friends with military experience willing to take up arms to resist the restoration of the monarchy. However, Fox and most of the other leaders were beginning to realise the pacific consequences of the Quaker message, and the peace testimony was about to make its appearance. Nevertheless, the question of the power of the state to preserve order and defend its sovereignty was not resolved and is debated to this day. In the midst of this crisis, George Fox entered a long depressive period. In August 1658, he sought refuge at Reading with one of his close friends, Thomas Curtis, who had been a soldier and was now to become a commissioner of the militia. The tide of events flowed on round him.

What course the Quaker movement would have taken if the relatively liberal religious policy of the Interregnum period had continued, one can only guess. Possibly it would have declined as animosities softened. As it turned out, a much more serious persecution was in store, and yet again, the blood of the martyrs proved to be the seed of the church. In 1660, amid general rejoicing, King Charles II was restored to his father's throne. The King himself favoured a conciliatory policy, but his Parliament took another view. The political and religious revolutionaries who had destroyed the old order would be put in their place. The national church would be Episcopalian again, and conformity to its worship would be enforced.

Persecution and Consolidation

T HE RESTORATION IS REMEMBERED AS THE TIME WHEN LIGHT AND laughter came flooding back into national life. The pageantry of the court returned and the playhouses were opened again. The King encouraged art, architecture, science and fashion, and was to be seen at Newmarket Heath. Symbolic of the age, the new St Paul's Cathedral rose out of the ashes of the Great Fire of London to dominate the skyline of the City.

But the regime was insecure. There was a general belief that conformity in religion would promote internal peace, and that the country should avoid further experiments in toleration. The exiles who returned with the King never really understood Puritanism or religious dissent, and too easily confused it with disloyalty, a confusion made worse by a number of serious plots against the state in the first few years of the reign. The Quakers, who were neither violent nor disloyal, suffered the guilt by association that had been their lot earlier, and they now found themselves joined by others. Presbyterians, Independents, Baptists and Friends were forced by history into a common identity. They stood against the national church and were collectively called 'Dissent'. They fought for, and won, both religious and political liberty in England, and their steadfastness in the 1660s and 1670s prevented their nation from undergoing the violent revolutions that later racked a number of other major European countries.

Soon after the King's return in May 1660, two great dissenters were arrested – George Fox, who was released after twenty weeks on a writ of Habeas Corpus, and the Baptist of sorts, John Bunyan, who spent the next twelve years in gaol, on and off. Many others were also given a foretaste of what would happen if they refused to conform to the usages of the Church of England. In January 1661, as we have seen previously, the Fifth Monarchy Men rose in rebellion in London, and for a period four thousand Friends were taken into preventive detention. The transfer of power to the monarchy did not go entirely smoothly.

To dissociate themselves from this violence, Friends addressed to the King their famous *Declaration from the Harmless and Innocent People of God called Quakers*, the effect of which has already been discussed. It contains a highly significant passage which says, 'The Spirit of Christ, by which we are guided, is not changeable, so as once to command us from a thing called evil and again to move unto it . . .' This marks the end of any tendency for Quakerism to become an individualistic faith, and shows us that, by 1660, the leading Friends had drawn the conclusion from the Nayler episode that Truth was Truth, and did not vary with individual conceptions of it.

Their resolve was tested in 1661 when John Perrot returned from his imprisonment in Rome and took up his place as a leading Friend. He started to criticise other public Friends including Fox and Howgill, neglected meetings of ministers and set up evening meetings of his own. In spite of his piety and humility, his abilities and his immense suffering, Friends came to the conclusion that he was breaking their unity and fellowship. This is what lay behind the preposterous and apparently trivial 'hat' controversy.

It was the custom to remove hats whenever a Friend offered prayer in meeting, and to shake hands at the close of meeting. John Perrot condemned these practices as remnants of the customary, traditional worship which belonged to the apostasy. He said he had been commanded by God to testify against them, thus raising the whole issue of whether previous guidance was in right ordering. If he was right, the collective wisdom had been in error. If wrong, his revelation was a delusion, and a dangerous one at that. It is easy to speak in generalities about continuing divine revelation, but when a hard case comes along, opinion is divided, and the Society of Friends has always had to live with this fact.

There is far more to the John Perrot controversy than arguments over hats. By the time he left England for Barbados in 1662 Perrot had attracted a considerable following and was to attract more in the New World. Though he was not the focus of an open schism, he represented a considerable number of Friends who were disaffected by the way the leadership of Friends was being carried on. His attitude and his influence touched nerves. He accused a body that preached against forms that in insisting that the hat be removed to pray, they were instituting a form. He thereby posed a direct threat to the body of leaders who had confirmed the practice, and his success raised the spectre of another episode like that of James Nayler. The Perrot affair was one of a series of controversies in the early period showing that deep in the heart of the Quaker community there was a strong counter-current to the moves towards a greater unity and cohesiveness.

The Clarendon Code

In the first five years of Charles II's reign, Lord Chancellor Clarendon put through Parliament a series of statutes designed to enforce conformity with the Church of England but which actually created dissent. The Corporation Act 1661 required all mayors, aldermen and councillors and holders of civic posts to communicate in the Church of England. The Act of Uniformity 1662 required compliance with the Book of Common Prayer and about two thousand Puritan ministers were ejected from their livings because they refused. The Five Mile Act 1665 forbade these 'nonconformists' to live or build chapels within five miles of any corporate town. This is the reason for the strength of the nonconformists, including Quakers, in some of the unincorporated towns like Birmingham which later became large cities. The full emancipation of dissenters from the provisions of these statutes was not accomplished till the mid-nineteenth century.

The two statutes at the heart of the Clarendon Code, as it has come to be known, were the Quaker Act 1662 and its successor, the Conventicle Act 1664. The Quaker Act provided penalties for maintaining that oath-taking is unlawful and contrary to the will of God, for any person wilfully refusing an oath or encouraging others to do so, and for printing any defence of these views. It rendered illegal any religious meeting of more than five people other than a household. The penalty for a first or second conviction was a fine. The penalty for a third conviction was transportation.

It was soon realised that there was a more effective way of attacking the Quakers and Baptists who (it was known) refused to swear oaths. Before the court got to the main issue to be tried, the Oath of Allegiance and denial of the Pope's authority was tendered and refusal to take it

97

was regarded as tantamount to treason. The penalty involved forfeiture of the accused's estate and imprisonment for life or during the King's pleasure. George Fox's most severe imprisonment was on this technicality, which was called 'praemunire' after the medieval writ on which it was based. He refused the oath at Holker Hall in January 1664, and, following a period in custody in Lancaster, was moved to Scarborough Castle, from which he emerged in a very poor physical condition in September 1666. Margaret Fell, arrested at the same time, was not released from Lancaster Castle until 1668.

The Conventicle Act 1664 was the Quaker Act stiffened to include all nonconformists, and was a response to a Puritan uprising in the north in 1663 called the Kaber Rigg Plot. It banned all religious meetings other than those of the established church, dispensed with a jury and increased the fines, facing all dissenters with the choice of meeting secretly or not at all. Many took the former option, but Friends met the challenge head on. Richard Baxter, a staunch opponent of Friends, nevertheless acknowledged their courage, describing how the meeting was kept at the Bull and Mouth at Aldersgate in the City of London. Every day Friends met, and were haled off to prison. The next day more came, till the prisons bulged. 'Yea, many turned Quakers, because the Quakers kept their meetings openly and went to prison for it cheerfully.'

The Middlesex county records show that in the year following the passage of the Act, 855 Quakers were convicted in the environs of the City, 94 per cent of the total, and we could expect the lost records for London and Surrey to show a similar pattern. The first sentences were light, for the authorities wished to press on to transportation to set a good example. There is evidence, however, that some grand juries were reluctant to convict in cases involving transportation. The Second Dutch War was in progress and it was hard to find a shipmaster willing to brave the narrow seas. One, the captain of the *Ann*, faced contrary winds in the Downs for nearly two months and finally put his seven prisoners ashore, saying that the hand of the Lord was clearly against him. The progress of persecution was then interrupted by the plague.

In May 1665 the Sheriffs of London found one Fudge, a sea captain, who boasted he would transport even his nearest relations. About forty Quaker men and women were bundled aboard his ship, the *Black Eagle* lying at Greenwich. Then Fudge was arrested for debt. Soldiers from the Tower came to guard the human cargo, and many of the crew deserted. Before the ship reached the North Foreland half the prisoners had died and were buried ashore. She made Plymouth after nine months, and shortly thereafter was taken by a Dutch privateer. At this point the two ships were parted in a storm, and the *Black Eagle* eventually sailed round Britain and arrived at Bergen in Norway. She went on to Amsterdam, where all the prisoners were reunited, finally getting back to England through the good offices of Dutch Friends.

Though Friends originally met in houses and barns, they now began to procure their own meeting houses, plain unadorned rooms with benches facing a raised bench or gallery where the leading members sat. There was as yet no formal recognition of elders or ministers, but strength of character and experience marked some Friends out for these responsibilities. Part of the campaign of intimidation was to damage or pull down places of worship. At Reading, Stourbridge and other places, the whole adult membership found itself in prison, and the children and younger women, often in the face of abuse and violence, managed heroically to keep the meeting going until such time as all Friends could meet again in peace.

Such treatment was obviously doing serious damage to the Society. Fox was in prison. So were Margaret Fell, Francis Howgill, William Dewsbury and George Whitehead. Edward Burrough, John Camm, John Audland, Richard Hubberthorne and James Nayler were already dead. In the countryside, Friends' meetings were threatened by all kinds of social pressures and in the larger towns the full force of the law was brought to bear on them. The travelling ministry, which had been the life blood, was stopped up. Unless there were some other way to nourish the body of Friends, it would die. Providentially, in the autumn of 1666, George Fox was released from gaol.

Settling the Society

Fox came south to London, and took some time to recuperate. In the next year or two, he showed what many consider to be his true greatness. Instead of taking steps to consolidate the Quaker movement at the centre, he chose to strengthen its limbs. In 1667 five monthly meetings were set up for London and an attempt was made to heal the divisions that had arisen in John Perrot's time. In 1667–8, Fox made an extended tour through the whole nation, touching Wales and Scotland also, reorganising the structure of meetings, giving attention to Quaker marriage procedures and encouraging the setting up of schools. At the same time, steps were taken to give greater disciplinary powers to meetings

99

and thus began the concentration of authority in the hands of leading Friends.

This was part of his response to long-term trends. In the mid-1660s, the Quaker movement had to decide how it was going to accommodate itself to a new reality. It was no longer moving in a world that observed the Puritan niceties and had the Puritan preoccupations. The new state knew its mind and was prepared to defend itself with none of the Puritan political ambivalence. The old targets were gone, the old methods bore no fruit, the old vocabulary no longer carried conviction. With hindsight one might say that the spiritual aspects of Quakerism were being salvaged from the shipwreck of its millenarian hopes.

This judgement is after the event, of course, but successful leaders move instinctively towards the accomplishment of their goals, and this was the task faced by Fox and the other leading Friends. It was not easy. Faced with a changed reality, the libertarian enthusiasm of the early period was out of place, though it continued to attract many. This created strong differences of opinion in circumstances in which only a united body could withstand persecution. If unity was a necessity, on what terms was it to be agreed? As the country edged slowly towards toleration, Friends found a way of surviving. At first, they accepted the consequences of isolation, and created in miniature a society of their own, with their own form of marriage, their own care for the poor, their own schools. Though they slowly found a place in the larger society, their private arrangements endured, and still lend colour to Quaker life today.

A significant and highly controversial part of these moves was the creation of a structure of women's meetings with considerable pastoral responsibility at each level of the organisation, for Fox took the view that women have an integral place in the Church and this was the best way to encourage them to take it. In old meeting houses there are still wooden screens, often worked by sash cords or pulleys, which can be hoisted up so the women's meeting room can be open to the main room.

This was not accomplished without opposition, as we shall see, and was probably never entirely completed. Women did not serve on the Morning Meeting or Meeting for Sufferings (soon to be the central business meetings of Friends) and did not take part in the business sessions of Yearly Meeting, though eventually, between 1784 and 1907, there was a Women's Yearly Meeting. Before this was formally laid down, Yearly Meeting was held with full membership of both sexes.

We have seen that, though Friends had a clear idea of what they called 'Gospel Order', the translation of its principles into a church structure was not accomplished without difficulty. What George Fox now did was to survey the country as a whole, and seek to bring order out of disorder by filling gaps in the existing arrangements, and defining more clearly the functions and boundaries of meetings. The basic unit remained the particular (local) meeting, but the main administrative unit was the area federation called the monthly meeting. On what might be called the provincial level there were quarterly meetings, but for the moment, there was nothing else.

The business side of the particular meeting became the preparative meeting because it 'prepared' any necessary returns, or replies to 'queries' from the monthly meeting. Statistical and other information has traditionally been sought from Friends' meetings by addressing short questions known as Queries to them. They usually emanated from the 'higher' representative meetings. The latter gatherings, the monthly, quarterly and yearly meetings were representative in character. There was no fixed membership but it was expected that meetings below would send 'weighty, seasoned and substantial' Friends.

Quaker business meetings were (and are) held on the basis of silent consideration of verbal contributions in an attempt not to achieve consensus, but to discern the will of God. At the table, as opposed to 'in the chair', the clerk, a servant of the meeting, listened to the discussion and 'weighed' what was said in an attempt to get the 'sense' of the meeting. It was not 'democratic'. A 'weighty' Friend was simply one whose judgement and experience in Friends' ways was more helpful to the meeting than one with less of those qualities. Though other Friends accompanied the representatives, and were gladly heard, the meeting need not hearken to them. The principle of delegation was no part of this system.

The modern Quaker marriage ceremony is anomalous and anachronistic. The Presbyterian *Directory* of 1644, which applied to the national church, abolished sacramental marriage and substituted a form of mutual declaration between the parties. In 1653 the Barebones Parliament enacted a compulsory additional civil marriage before a Justice of the Peace. Friends adopted their own procedure of a private consultation with older Friends, an announcement of intention, the consideration of objections at the next business meeting, followed by announcements of the forthcoming ceremony along the lines required by civil law, and the appointment of the meeting for the purpose.

Such marriages were publicly advertised and many reported to the civil authorities. The form of certificate, reciting the promises and witnessed by at least twelve, and often many more Friends, is in use to this day in Britain and is signed before the civil register. It is in itself a testimony that the validity of the marriage rests upon God's sanction, which is expressed directly and not through a medium, whether it be a minister of religion or a government registrar. The form of the declarations made on these occasions dates from the *Directory* of 1644–5.

Weddings like this were evidenced, but not strictly legal, until the Marriage Act 1656 withdrew the illegality attaching to unions not conforming to the Statute. We should therefore see the Quaker marriage as in part a religious testimony, in part a survival of the Interregnum, and at all events an institution with a slightly different emphasis from those of other churches. Civil marriage was abolished at the Restoration, causing some uncertainty. For example, if a brother who was a Quaker died, leaving property to his son, the son could be disinherited by the non-Quaker brother if he could establish that the marriage was invalid and the offspring therefore illegitimate. Quaker marriage was recognised as lawful at Nottingham Assizes in 1661. Though it was subsequently challenged, the precedent held and Friends were confirmed in their freedom to celebrate marriage in their own way.

One of the penalties of Dissent was to be denied access to the state endorsed education system – the two universities of Oxford and Cambridge, the great schools and the grammar schools. Hence, Friends and other nonconformists turned to the provision of tuition for their own children. The 'Dissenting Academies' were mainly for the training of ministers. Among the Quakers, the needs were more practical. Certainly Quaker teachers ran 'Latin schools', but by and large, Friends' schools were intended to meet the particular needs of the denomination. The testimony of plainness applied the same criterion of usefulness to secular learning as well as theology, and this predisposed Friends to a certain degree of innovation in curriculum, notably the importance many attached to the study of nature and what useful skills could be derived from the science of the time, such as the practical applications of mathematics.

Theoretically, the Five Mile Act 1665 should have closed many schools, for it applied to dissenting teachers as well as ministers. In spite of the Act, however, Friends do not appear to have been greatly hampered in their educational work. In 1668 George Fox set up a boys' school at Waltham Abbey in Essex, and a girls' school at Shacklewell near Hackney, a few miles down the River Lea on the eastern edge of London. Perhaps because of the contemporary apprenticeship system, Friends tended to favour boarding, and by 1671 it is estimated that there were at least fifteen boarding schools under the care of quarterly meetings quite apart from a large number of others opened by individual Friends, and often open to non-Quaker children. An interesting feature of the period was the attempt made by a number of Friends to improve methods of teaching Latin, and the disquiet many felt about the language and sentiments of some of the classical authors. Ovid deserved to be banished *in absentia*.

The persecution of dissenters eased towards the end of the 1660s. Clarendon fell from office and none of the members of the committee which succeeded him, known as the Cabal, was of similar convictions. So the number of dissenting conventicles increased and some members of the public seemed willing to entertain the thought of toleration. But as the price of obtaining finance from Parliament, Charles II had to consent to the passing of the Second Conventicle Act in 1670, which the Puritan poet Andrew Marvell described as 'the quintessence of arbitrary malice'.

Conviction was now in the power of a single justice – a far cry from the jury of the Quaker Act 1662. New offences of preaching at a conventicle or harbouring one were added, and there was a rapid distraint on the property of anyone fined for an offence. Transportation was dropped as a penalty and instead an attempt was made to ruin the nonconformists. There was power to search premises and use the militia. Meetings were broken up with violence and meeting houses pulled down. At Ratcliff, the meeting house was demolished but Friends continued to meet defiantly amid the ruins. Informers were used against suspected preachers, and many, including Friends, were convicted on perjured evidence.

Two Quakers who got the better of the authorities over the Conventicle Act 1670, and caused a fundamental freedom to be entrenched in English law, were William Meade, a draper of the City of London (who later married a daughter of Margaret Fell), and William Penn, gentleman. As the founder of Pennsylvania, a leading theologian of Quakerism's second period, a political thinker of vision and integrity, and by any standards a most romantic figure, it is to Penn that we must now turn.

William Penn (1644–1718) was born near the Tower of London, the son of an admiral who served the Commonwealth and was one of the military figures who paved the way for the Restoration. From the family home at Wanstead, Essex, William was sent to Chigwell School and matriculated at Christ Church, Oxford, in 1660, the year of the Restoration. After two years at the university, he was sent down for protesting against compulsory attendance at chapel, and was then packed off to Europe to broaden his experience. He stayed in Paris for a while and then went to study at the Protestant seminary at Saumur on the Loire under the liberal and eminent scholar Moise Amyraut.

In 1664, he came back to England and undertook legal studies at Lincoln's Inn. In 1665 the Second Dutch War was declared and Admiral Penn took a command with the King's brother, the Duke of York (who was later to reign briefly as King James II). William accompanied his father. By this time he was a well-travelled, well-educated, fashionable young man with excellent connections that might take him to the top in the service of the state.

Before the Restoration, Admiral Penn had been given an estate near Cork which had belonged to a Royalist, and on a previous visit there William had attended a Quaker meeting addressed by Thomas Loe, an Oxford shopkeeper. At this point the estate was returned to its previous owner and another allotted to the Admiral, so William, now ready to enter into the ways of the world, was sent to Ireland to manage some of his father's affairs. While there he heard Thomas Loe again, was convinced, and began to attend Friends' meetings, ending up in prison and needing political pull to get him out. The Admiral was not pleased, so William was summoned home. The Admiral was even less pleased at William's persistence in his faith, and the ripples were felt at the Admiralty itself. Pepys remarked to his diary that Penn's son had become a Quaker, 'or some very melancholy thing'. Though later reconciled with his relatives, Penn was thrown out of the family home.

In the next two years Penn appeared as a Quaker minister and a writer of pamphlets. His first major work, an attack on the doctrine of the Trinity, called *The Sandy Foundation Shaken*, was published without the Bishop of London's license, and as a consequence Penn was imprisoned in the Tower. While there he studied and wrote what is his most accomplished literary work, the spiritual treatise *No Cross, No Crown*. The earlier version of the book reveals in him a mature Christian sensibility which he would thenceforth put at the service of both society and the Quakers in his religious work at home and also in the colonies in North America.

Shortly after the Second Conventicle Act 1670 had been passed, Penn and William Meade found themselves addressing a meeting for worship held outside the Gracechurch Street meeting house in London, which had been locked up by the authorities to prevent people entering. There was a large crowd also, and in due course Penn and Meade were arrested. There then arose the problem of charging them. The assembly was plainly not secret, so the Conventicle Act was inappropriate. Neither preacher was ordained, so the Five Mile Act did not apply. Consequently the authorities chose to proceed on a charge of riot, which, unhappily for them, carried the right of jury trial. Penn and Meade were therefore indicted at the Old Bailey in the City of London for conspiracy to cause a riot.

The case has come down to us named after one of the more outspoken members of the jury called Bushell. The jury was directed to return a verdict of guilty on the charge, but they flatly refused to do so. The Recorder sent them to Newgate till they should change their minds, and Penn and Meade were detained for not paying their fines for wearing hats in court. Application was quickly made for Habeas Corpus, the jury was released, and the case reviewed by a higher court, which finally established the right of juries to bring in their own verdict, independent of judicial direction.

Though Bushell's case arose in the City, it was settled before the Court of King's Bench at Westminster Hall, an illustration that even then England had a centralised legal and administrative system. The relative spheres of influence of King and Parliament were not very clearly defined and the Royal Prerogative was much more important at that time than under the present British Constitution. The concerted effort to break Dissent brought Friends into collision with the state, and while many penalties were unjust but legal, some were neither. The question therefore arose as to whether Friends were justified in using legal remedies to obtain release from imprisonment, if that imprisonment were arbitrary and itself illegal. Opinion was divided, but it slowly became clear that Friends' religious witness had a political dimension and they had no organisation able to make representations to government at the highest level. There were individual Friends with influence at court such as Margaret Fell and William Penn, but that was not enough.

The Creation of Yearly Meeting

It took a decade, from 1668 to 1678, for Friends to round off their existing structure with a permanent, centrally organised representative body. They did this in a period of fierce persecution, and against considerable internal opposition. In spite of strains and arguments it was a logical step to take, and the outcome was the setting up of London Yearly Meeting.

In 1668, during the process of settling the local structure, there was a meeting of ministers from the whole country. It met twice in the next three years and in 1671 decided to set up a central body to advise on the management of Friends' public affairs. This assembly was to meet in London in Whitsun Week, and to comprise the body of ministers and representative Friends from the counties. It was envisaged that during the course of its deliberations, ministers would sometimes meet separately and nobody else would be eligible to attend without special leave. This plan probably reflected the actual constitution of the 1671 gathering, and a year later the prototype Yearly Meeting was actually held.

The whole idea was eminently sound. The general meetings of the previous decade had tended to be specialised gatherings with ministering Friends meeting at separate times and places from those whom we might call elders. Over time, this pattern could have resulted in some sort of senior ministerial synod, quite contrary to the original Quaker impulse. The precedent of a much more open gathering had been set, and although meetings lapsed after 1673, a workable scheme had been tried, and it only needed more favourable circumstances for it to be revived. While the full Yearly Meeting was in abeyance between 1673 and 1678, other necessary parts of the central apparatus came into being.

Within the general body of ministering Friends there was also the group known as 'Public Friends', whose specific vocation was to travel among Friends' meetings to strengthen and encourage them, more particularly in the London area. For years it had been the custom for all public Friends who were in London to gather on Sunday morning so that their activities could be co-ordinated and to ensure that the available ministerial assistance was spread properly through the city and its surrounding meetings. This meeting, which had developed more or less spontaneously, soon found itself at the national centre, under another name.

In 1673, at the initiative of George Fox, the Second Day Morning Meeting, thereafter simply called 'the Morning Meeting', took over official responsibility for the ministry in London and combined it with the task of collecting anti-Quaker books and publications to ensure that they were properly answered. This body was destined to become very influential. Its collections form the basis of the present Friends House library, and the printing function later delegated to it enabled it, in effect, to operate as a censorship committee. With its role in co-ordinating ministerial work, this gave it a crucial position in Friends' developing power structure. In all but name, it was the executive arm of the Yearly Meeting of Ministers, which continued to meet throughout this period while the full Yearly Meeting had lapsed.

By 1676 numbers of Friends were coming round to the view that the oppression which they suffered should not be endured passively, and that government should be faced with the consequences of its actions. For some time it had been laid on Friends to send details of sufferings in to London, and these had been carefully collected. Now the Yearly Meeting of Ministers sanctioned the use of acceptable methods of legal redress, and Friends began to resist injustices with publicity and with pressure. In those days Parliament met infrequently, and in civil cases the Assize Judges heard evidence in the country but gave their verdicts at Westminster Hall. From 1676 the new Meeting for Sufferings met at the commencement of the law terms three times a year and made what representations they could on behalf of Friends. There was a member in the Meeting to represent each of the counties, and in 1679 Yearly Meeting directed that the costs of legal action and political lobbying should be met by a collection from the counties at the discretion of the Meeting for Sufferings.

Though women ministers had been a part of Quakerism from the beginning, they were not always fully integrated into the administrative structure of the Society. Though in theory the sexes were on a footing of equality, in practice they were not. In the 1670s we find the development of women's meetings with responsibilities for the relief of the poor, the placing of Quaker maidservants, the supervision of marriages and other things of a pastoral nature. As time went by a shadow structure of women's meetings grew up alongside the existing system and in 1784, as we have seen, the Women's Yearly Meeting was set up to complete it.

Those favouring separate meetings took the view that there was a contribution to the corporate life of the Society which only women could make, and various matters in which men's attention would not be appropriate. Additionally, it was felt that in business meetings composed of members of both sexes, women would be overshadowed, and voices Friends needed to hear might be silent or muted. There was force in this argument, but this functional equality was not carried out in practice. Women took little or no part in the central meetings in London, and in some parts of the country monthly meetings did not separate. Women's meetings tended, ultimately, to be subordinate, and an early move to promote a regular yearly meeting of women ministers was headed off in 1701. London was probably behind the Quaker world at that point. Ireland introduced a Women's Yearly Meeting in 1679, and in spite of their limitations they were in general use in the American colonies.

So the 1670s see the completion of a central Quaker structure. Leadership was in the hands of the Yearly Meeting from 1678 onwards, but within this body the ministers kept their influence and identity. Though there was no direct constitutional link, the leading ministers co-ordinated policy formation and day-to-day administration through the strength of their presence on the Morning Meeting and the Meeting for Sufferings. The influence of other Friends was brought to bear by the hierarchy of representative monthly and quarterly meetings and the parallel system of women's meetings. Women's and men's meetings have now almost universally reunited, and the rest of the structure has served London Yearly Meeting (since 1995 called Britain Yearly Meeting) well for the past three hundred years, though it is now finding that modern communications and increasing diversity among Friends are seriously weakening the middle rung of monthly and general (formerly, quarterly) meetings.

This whole organisational structure, both national and local, was not set up without serious dissent, and many Friends took exception to the way in which it was done. Local autonomy was one of the principles of the new movement, but so, on the other hand, was a mission to the whole world, and the controversy over John Perrot and his ideas raised the question as to whether one could have co-ordination without leadership. Perrot's influence continued in his absence, and more worrying for Fox and those who thought like him, was the existence of a strong body of Perrotian thought in the Quaker settlements in the American colonies. The decision was taken for a group of Friends under Fox's leadership to cross the Atlantic and settle the meetings there on the pattern being established in England.

George Fox in America

In August 1671 George Fox took ship with a number of other Friends in a leaky sloop called the *Industry* to travel to North America. At that time many ships sailed south across the Atlantic, to pick up the trade winds that would carry them across to a landfall near Barbados, and thence to Jamaica and then north to various destinations on the mainland of North America. The journey was not a comfortable one, but then, in those days very few were. It was risky too. Unless one sailed in convoy there was the ever-present risk of being taken by Barbary corsairs as one skirted the coast of Africa, or by the buccaneers in the Caribbean.

Inevitably, the risk materialised, and off the Azores, the *Industry* fell in with a ship which gave chase. We have two accounts of this episode, one from Fox and the other from John Hull, the master of the ship. Both are given in Fox's *Journal*, and it is instructive to compare them. Hull outsails the pirate ship and manages to shake it off. Fox records that his advice was sought, and he gave it, but that the deliverance was an act of God.

The visit to Barbados is noteworthy for various reasons. There was already a significant Quaker population on the island, and though Friends were important to the economy, they were also thought to be unsound in belief, and too sympathetic to the slave population. One of the purposes of the visit was to reassure the authorities on these two heads.

In fact, Friends represented an awkward political dilemma. Barbados was important for its sugar, its strategic position, and the fact that it was assuming a significant role in the developing Atlantic mercantile system. London needed the Quakers' economic clout, but their faith might always become a focus of anti-government sentiment.

The document known as the *Letter to the Governor of Barbados* is very important in Quaker history. It provides an outline of Quaker belief designed to show its orthodoxy, which follows closely the order of the Apostles' Creed and is still reproduced in the Disciplines of almost all of the evangelical yearly meetings among Friends. It is hard to see how (unless one is liberal in theology) what it says is incompatible with Quaker belief. On the other hand, if Fox were preaching or writing to Friends, he would have utilised very few of these tenets and brought the Light Within to the centre of what he had to say. The *Letter* is therefore still alive and still controversial.

The second matter Fox dealt with is slavery. In due course Friends would follow their own logic and come out in active opposition to slavery, but here Fox is concerned to shore up the position of Friends in the colony by exculpating them from the charge that they were sympathetic to slave rebellion, not by calling for the abolition of slavery but by urging that slaves be well treated and be regarded as members of the families to which they belonged.

From the West Indies, the party sailed a long way up the coast to Maryland, a tolerant, Catholic-owned, largely white society. Their landfall was stormy and full of dangerous incident, as Fox records, but they came ashore safely. There is an air of optimism about the *Journal* account at this point, although it is not unqualified. A conference appears to have assessed the situation facing Fox's party and decided how it could best be used. The *Journal* reports that 'things were much out of order' in Virginia, and a party of four was despatched there while two other Friends set out for New England. Fox had received disturbing reports of Perrotian sympathies in New York, and he and some companions set out northwards in order to reach Long Island in time for the next half-yearly meeting in mid-May, which they did.

Having brought the meeting round to the Foxian persuasion, the party continued across Long Island Sound to Rhode Island, the colony founded and ruled by Roger Williams, one of the most interesting figures of the early colonial period. He believed in religious freedom and the separation of church and state, often acting as a mediator in disputes between the colonists and the Native Americans. Eventually his advanced opinions proved too much for the Massachusetts settlers and he was banished from the colony, going into the wilderness and setting up the Rhode Island colony, which became a haven or refuge for religious dissenters of all kinds. Having read Fox's first published work, *The Great Mystery*, Williams challenged Fox to a debate. Sadly for history, Fox left the colony before the challenge was received, though others took it up on his behalf. Fox records successful meetings in Connecticut but, interestingly, avoided going into the Puritan stronghold of Massachusetts.

They had a hard time of it in those days. Tidewater Virginia and the country round the heads of Chesapeake and Delaware bays was not the easiest terrain to traverse without roads – nor was what became New Jersey, for that matter. Boats and canoes were much easier. Even then, the rivers – and there are a number of major ones, the Potomac,

Susquehanna, Schuylkill and Delaware – hinder north–south communications because they run broadly west to east. Fox mentions 'tedious'
travel through bogs, rivers and creeks and adventures with canoes.
There is also the weather – fine when it is fine, dreadful when stormy.
To say nothing of the insects and snakes.

It is a tribute to the intrepidity of both these early Quaker travellers
and also the people who came to settle and farm and trade there, that
they were able to prevail against harsh conditions and flourish over the
many drawbacks of the country. On many occasions Fox mentions the
Native Americans, with whom he seems to have got on well. He stayed
with them several times, usually, it seems, with chiefs, or 'kings' as he
calls them.

Fox was on a mission to the world, so he was concerned to preach
to the Native Americans. He tried to do so on the basis of the Light
he was convinced was in them, and which he believed would lead
them to accept what he said, telling some that 'God is setting up his
tabernacle of witness in their wilderness countries and setting up his
glorious ensign and standard of righteousness'. No Indian meetings
seem to have been settled as a result, however. One cautious chief kept
his own counsel. He said that for those of his people who had adopted
it, the religion of the New England Puritans made them worse than
they were before. The Quakers sounded 'the best', but in case he got
on the wrong side of the Puritans, he was not going to take the risk of
joining them.

From New York, Fox and his party made their way south again,
visiting Virginia and Carolina (as yet undivided) probably with
pastoral rather than disciplinary motives. At any rate, the party
retraced its steps, setting out to visit isolated Friends in the South
before returning to Maryland to take ship for home in May 1673. The
party had seen and accomplished a great deal in trying circumstances
and had lost the great Quaker pioneer Elizabeth Hooton, whom they
buried in Jamaica. William Edmondson was to return twice for future
service.

So where is the Quaker heartland in America? Certainly Pennsylvania springs to mind, but one can make the case for other places
too. The great nineteenth-century expansion was set off from North
Carolina and, at the close of that century, reached its peak in Indiana,
where the largest organisation of Friends is still based. Then again, one
might look to Oregon, home of many of the missions which are now

supporting the continuing expansion of the Friends Church in the developing world. Not many people would choose Baltimore Yearly Meeting as the mother church of Friends in America. But, just perhaps, it is.

The Wilkinson-Story Separation

It was not to be expected that such changes could be carried through without doubts as to their wisdom and desirability. They represent a centralising, and therefore standardising, tendency which runs to some degree counter to the independence and personal responsibility by which Friends have always set great store. The breaches in fellowship caused by the ideas and activity of John Perrot had scarcely been healed, when two far more influential Friends went into separation with their followers. John Story and John Wilkinson were weighty indeed, coming from Westmorland and having been convinced at the very beginning. They expressed the views of many people who did not follow them out of the main stream of the Society.

The matter was opened up by the publication of a tract called *The Spirit of the Hat*, while George Fox was in America between 1671 and 1673. The title revealed immediately that it was from the Perrot faction, and it accused the leadership of 'Tyrannical and Persecuting Practises'. The anti-Fox party was emerging again, and in their Epistle for 1673 the Yearly Meeting of Ministers issued a strong rebuke to them. This was not well received in Bristol and its prosperous Wiltshire hinterland, where Story and Wilkinson had laboured in the gospel, nor in Westmorland itself.

Opposition surfaced at Preston Patrick in 1673. While London Friends had been meeting publicly and going to gaol in thousands under the Second Conventicle Act, Preston Patrick Friends had followed the practice of other dissenters and worshipped in secret. They had thus departed from the collective testimony, and it is easy to understand the feelings of Friends who had willingly accepted sufferings, particularly since those Friends who had met clandestinely also criticised the new structure of the Society on a wide front.

In certain matters of practice they were more lenient than Friends generally. They opposed the enforcement of discipline beyond what Friends were willing to submit to. Thus, they were prepared to accept compromises with the testimony against tithes, and objected to the practice of quarterly meetings in drawing up papers of condemnation against Friends who had infringed the discipline. In constitutional matters they were stricter. They opposed the setting up of separate women's meetings, and considered that the business meetings of the Society should be confined to representatives only. They did not like collections for the travelling ministry, and the last of their objectives we shall notice gives a fascinating sidelight on the worship of the period. Silence? They took strong exception to the 'groaning singing or sounding' which seems often to have accompanied ministry or vocal prayer in the meetings of the period.

Three conferences were held with the leaders of this faction, in 1675 at Worcester, where Fox was then imprisoned, in Sedbergh in 1676 and at Bristol in 1678. There was a separation in Westmorland which lasted some decades, but in the West Country the damage was limited. In 1680 John Rogers published *The Christian Quaker Distinguished from the Apostate and Innovator*, and set off a further round of controversy, but by that time Friends had more important problems on their plate.

The rise of an opposition party and the development of a central organisation are both aspects of the political situation of the time, which provided a breathing space in a period of persecution. King Charles II had secretly become a Roman Catholic and entered into an alliance and financial arrangement with Louis XIV of France in March 1672. Able to dispense with Parliament he exercised what he claimed was his dispensing power and by a Declaration of Indulgence suspended the penal laws against dissenters (including Friends) and the 'Popish recusants' as the Catholics were known. Thousands were thus released from incarceration.

For those imprisoned under the praemunire procedure, a pardon under the Great Seal was necessary to procure release. With great labour on the part of Friends' Secretary Ellis Hookes, and George Whitehead, who was to assume the mantle of George Fox, the necessary documents were prepared, and some had to be carried round the country on horseback to be shown to the sheriffs, though some were presented at Westminster at the opening of the law term. There was magnanimity all round. The King declined to accept his fee, the Friends included the names of some other dissenters, including their opponent John Bunyan, whom we last saw at his arrest twelve years before.

For the next three years there was a lull in persecution until policy changed again and the penal laws were reinstated by Order in Council in 1675. The situation now bore a strange resemblance to the 1650s. Certainly there was severe persecution of dissenters, but it was patchy and periodic, and connected as much with the vagaries of party politics as a consistent effort to crush nonconformity. There was a notable increase in activity in 1680–1, but in 1685 the Duke of York succeeded to the throne as James II. He was a Catholic, a friend of William Penn and a distant relative of Robert Barclay. His motives are still the subject of debate, but his actions are history. The pressure of persecution rapidly diminished, and in the year following the coup which removed him and permanently established the Protestant succession, the Toleration Act 1689 remitted all penalties on dissent.

We have now seen the effects of the tendencies toward organisation and centralisation, and how in the 1670s it begins to make sense to talk about the Society of Friends as an institution. Change is always disturbing, and as a counterpoint to these processes there are signs of a more or less continuous party of opposition, and though mild, there is certainly a tendency to divide. There are many parallels between the early history of Quakerism and that of the Church itself, and the fourth tendency affecting the Society at the time was the need for justification in the terms of the world. Quakerism needed its apologists, and they, inevitably, would lead to a trend of increasing formality.

The early message was simply known as Truth. In the heroic age of Quaker beginnings, it was the means of changing many thousands of lives. It held the community together in persecution and was a permanent inspiration to succeeding generations of Quakers. But the struggle for independence and the need to resist persecution brought their own demands. Friends were called upon to show greater clarity of expression, to draw finer distinctions. They were subjected to searching criticisms and needed to develop theory to answer unexpected and persistent lines of enquiry into the full implications of their message. Times had changed imperceptibly, and they were in a new rational and philosophical environment.

Penn's Defence of Quakerism

William Penn was one of the earliest and most formidable exponents of the Quakerism of the second period and his books and pamphlets combine rigour and vigour in equal proportions. As the title of one of his books shows, he thought the faith he had espoused was *Primitive Christianity Revived*. His writings raise the continuing problem of the orthodoxy of Quakerism and thereby its relationship to the Christian faith taken as a whole.

One possible view is that Quakerism is a spiritual and theological departure from the Christian dispensation, whatever its origins may have been. It is therefore fundamentally heretical. Another view sees the Quakers as a group clearly within Christian orthodoxy, but having reservations over details such as the nature of ministry and the non-observance of sacraments. There is much to be said for both views. What makes Penn interesting is his reversal of roles between the teachings of the rest of the Church (the 'orthodox' position) and what he takes as central to Quakerism. He seeks to show that Quakerism is perfectly orthodox and in keeping with the teaching of the New Testament, but that its peculiar testimonies are really the nucleus of Christianity, round which the elements of defective mainstream orthodoxy ought to revolve.

For example, Quakers always insisted that religion should be concerned with conduct and spiritual experience rather than with refinement of points of doctrine. So they refused to engage in theological speculation that went beyond the concepts and vocabulary of scripture. This is not wholly satisfactory, for it creates as many problems as it solves, particularly in the attempt to make sense of what the New Testament says about Jesus Christ. Friends discounted these difficulties. They did not approve of the attempt to clarify the doctrine, and they refused to accept the word 'Trinity' on principle.

They were therefore accused of denying the Trinity. In a formal sense they certainly did, and Penn caused a furore with his *The Sandy Foundation Shaken* (1668). It is important to be clear, though, for early Quakerism was certainly not Unitarian in the modern sense. What was being said in this rejection of Trinitarian doctrine was that you did not need to believe in an elaborate system of 'persons', essences' or 'natures' in order to have a saving faith in the Father, Son and Holy Spirit.

Friends also ran into trouble with their doctrine that the saving light of Christ is available to everyone, even those who have no knowledge of the historic Christ. Critics saw straightaway that this robs Jesus of Nazareth of any real role in the process of salvation. It was a spectacular own-goal in the Quakers' campaign to prove that only they were the real Christians. Much of *The Christian Quaker and his Testimony Stated and Vindicated* (1673) is devoted to a struggle with these matters. Penn faces the objections fairly and squarely, but uses the same frame of reference as those who differ from him. Though he asserts that the light, as Christ, is personal, he does use the pronoun 'it'. The critics claimed that the Quakers' failure to fix the reference of 'the light' securely enough to the Christ revealed in scripture, leads to imprecision, misunderstanding, and ultimately to some kind of Unitarianism.

Friends gave further offence by taking sin seriously in an age of immorality and growing religious indifference. The spiritual experience they talked about was the struggle for self-mastery, and the defeat of personal sin through the inward power of Christ the light. In *No Cross, No Crown* (1669), Penn set out what he understood the Christian life to be, and he was in unity with the rest of the Society in asserting that the path to heaven is a reformed life – we are justified to the extent that we mend our ways.

The critics castigated this view. It looked like saying that we could earn salvation by our own efforts rather than relying on divine grace. It also opened the way for the spiritually successful to close the door on the many who, try as they might, failed to measure up to Penn's exacting standards. It was, they said, the reappearance of the pre-Reformation doctrine of justification by works. And that was how it looked, regardless of the protestations of Penn and others to the contrary.

A fourth example of controversy was Friends' insistence that God's revelation of himself was not confined to the scriptures, but was a continuing process, and that without the illumination of the Holy Spirit, scripture was barren. The critics argued that just as Friends had effectively rejected the work of the historical Jesus, they now intended the overthrow of scripture as the ultimate criterion of Christian truth. Unlike many later Quakers, William Penn refused to make this inference. In *Quakerism a New Nickname for Old Christianity* (1673), he stated, 'We assert not a revelation of new things, but renewed revelation of those things God made former ages witnesses of; otherwise men are no more benefited by them, and to be benefited, they must be ours by the spirit which made them to the holy Ancients.' More briefly, he said, 'We earnestly contend not against the scriptures, but for that living experimental knowledge of them.' He was, perhaps, using spiritual language in a theological context; at all events, his subtlety was not appreciated.

There is no doubt that William Penn and Robert Barclay brought a new frame of reference to Quaker theology, and adapted George

Fox's views in a number of ways. But the Apostasy theory (which rapidly became an orthodoxy, if not a dogma) has the drawback that it sees theology as either pointless or harmful and thus precludes Quaker participation in the wider development of Christian doctrine. Consequently, William Penn's thought is in some ways a throwback to the period before the great ecumenical councils. His Trinitarian doctrine is vulnerable to criticism in a Unitarian direction, contrary to his stated convictions, and his understanding of the atonement falls into the so called 'dramatic' pattern, widely held among the pre-Nicene Fathers. The Apostasy theory resulted in Friends opting for the problems rather than the solutions and having to pay the price.

Most of William Penn's religious writings date from his first twelve years or so as a Quaker, when he was travelling widely in the ministry, suffering four periods of imprisonment, courting and getting married to Gulielma Springett, the stepdaughter of Isaac Penington, running the risk of losing his inheritance, and becoming involved on the fringes of Whig politics. This period of activity tempered his soul, and some of his devotional writings are classics in the genre. One of his earliest maxims was the theme of his later work in America, and has been an inspiration to Friends ever since: 'True godliness don't turn men out of the world but enables them to live better in it, and excites their endeavours to mend it.'

Pennsylvania – the Holy Experiment

Better known than these words – and a more practical memorial – is the Commonwealth and State of Pennsylvania and its capital, Philadelphia, the city of brotherly love. In 1675, Penn became involved in the colony of West Jersey, which lay on the eastern bank of the Delaware River, as trustee in bankruptcy for another Quaker, Edward Byllynge. The question of the relationship of colonies to the mother country was beginning to arise at this time, and Penn helped Byllynge to devise the 'Concessions and Agreements' of West New Jersey. Contrary to the policies pursued by constitution mongers elsewhere in America, Byllynge and Penn sought to promote liberty and democracy in the territory in their charge, and Penn soon got the chance to be more ambitious.

In 1681, when the prospects of religious toleration in England seemed bleak, Penn accepted an enormous tract of land on the west bank of the Delaware River in settlement of a debt owed to his father by King Charles II. It was all very amicable, and the King insisted that, in memory of the Admiral, the new province should be called *Penn*sylvania. The first Quaker settlers went out straightaway, and the following year Penn arrived to take charge of his colony.

Penn was already one of the leading advocates of political liberty and religious toleration, and he had been personally involved in one of the leading cases in English constitutional law. Even in matters of religion there was a rational side to him and it is not surprising that he took the chance to turn the American wilderness into a model state. In a letter in August 1681, he records his conviction that he had come into possession of Pennsylvania through divine providence, and that he was called upon to set up a model community there, '. . . that an example may be set up to the nations; there may be room there, though not here, for such an Holy Experiment.'

The land, of course, belonged to the Indians and was not the King's to give. Penn went out of his way to cultivate their friendship and earn their respect, purchasing land from them. Relations between the settlers and the Indians were regulated by a number of agreements including the Treaty of Shackamaxon, later depicted by the American painter, Benjamin West. It drew the ironic comment from Voltaire that it was the only such treaty that was never sworn to and never broken.

Settlers from Europe looked to the new colony for the air of freedom they did not breathe at home. Naturally, the largest single group were the Quakers, who stamped an indelible impression on the colony. Then there were many refugees from Germany, including members of a number of small sects very similar in outlook to Friends. Collectively, they became known as the 'Pennsylvania Dutch'. West of Philadelphia lay the Barony, the Welsh tract, where names from the Principality are common, such as those of two of the foremost colleges in the area, Haverford and Bryn Mawr. Later to play a part in the weakening of Quaker political power in Pennsylvania were the Scots-Irish settlers, many Presbyterian, who went to the back-country and did not take Friends' ideas of pacifism and tolerance with them.

The constitution, or Frame of Government of the colony, was based on Penn's Quaker ideals. Most important of all, it guaranteed freedom of conscience and the right to worship in accordance with one's own convictions. It sought to entrench this right at a time when it was very precarious on the other side of the Atlantic. The document itself contained provisions which allowed amendment when conditions were felt to require it. The laws enacted on the basis of this constitution touch a number of Quaker concerns. Considerable provision was made for the fair and expeditious transaction of legal business designed to sweep away all the bureaucracy and chicanery which oppressed Friends and others in England. The prisons were to be workhouses, where something constructive was done, not merely places of incarceration. All children up to the age of twelve were to be taught some useful trade or skill, and there were to be absolutely no tithes in Pennsylvania.

In the Preface to the Frame of Government occurs one of Penn's more famous maxims: '. . . governments, like clocks, go from the motion men give them; and as governments are made and moved by men, so by them they are ruined too. Wherefore, governments rather depend upon men, than men upon governments. Let men be good, and the government cannot be bad; if it be ill, they will cure it. But, if men be bad, let the government be never so good, they will endeavour to warp and spoil it to their turn.'

Actually, the colony was not as democratic as might be thought. Though libertarian between denominations, there was a strict religious test. Public office and the right to vote were restricted to 'such as profess faith in Jesus Christ'. Though an elected assembly was the legislative body, it was the Governor and the Upper House which retained the right of initiating legislation, thus ensuring proprietorial control. This was all right while William Penn was the proprietor, but the continuation of his benign concern could not be guaranteed. Moreover, the Crown naturally retained its powers. Slavery was not illegal, and though severely restricted in its application, the death penalty was retained, together with the power to raise and finance a militia and impose war taxes.

The Holy Experiment may not have developed exactly in the way William Penn had envisaged. In its formative years he was absent, and beset by political and financial troubles of his own. Despite his idealism and drafting skill, there was considerable scope for factional argument over the government of the colony. Nevertheless, it was an outstanding achievement and a very proper object of Quaker pride. The world was shown that religious toleration was a workable policy when very few legislators were willing to countenance the fact; Pennsylvania became a beacon of hope for all who shared the Quakers' belief in equality and human dignity; the relations of the Commonwealth with the Indians redeemed in some small measure the many atrocities otherwise visited on the Native Americans; the penal code was unparalleled in its humanity at the time. Out of the vision of one man and his religious Society sprang an application of those principles that would soon lead to the creation of American democracy, and an assurance for lovers of freedom everywhere that their hope was not in vain.

Quaker life in the colony was disturbed by the activities of George Keith (1639–1716), who became convinced during William Dewsbury's visit to Scotland in 1662, but who became the first serious Quaker heresiarch. Keith was a friend of, and an influence on, Robert Barclay. Also, he accompanied Barclay, Penn and Fox on their journey to Continental Europe in 1677. However, he found it hard to fit in with Friends. He raised eyebrows by his belief in reincarnation and became a nuisance when he started to deny the sufficiency of the light to effect salvation.

He emigrated to America and in 1689 he opened a school in Philadelphia. He began to quarrel with Friends, and set up a secessionist body, the 'Christian Quakers'. There were court cases. Following an uncomfortable Yearly Meeting in 1691 Keith's followers began to meet separately, though they did not consider themselves separated – indeed, their views on war and slavery, for example, were entirely in keeping with those of the Society. But there was to be no reconciliation. In 1695 London Yearly Meeting disowned Keith, significantly, for 'unbearable temper and carriage', not his doctrine. He later joined the established church and became an Anglican missionary in America. This was not to be the only crisis in the life of Philadelphia Friends.

Large numbers of Friends emigrated to America in those years. In 1682 alone, twenty-three ships carried over two thousand people to Pennsylvania. Life there would not be troubled by the insecurities of home. The burdens on dissenters were lifted slightly later by the Toleration Act 1689 which was part of the 'Glorious Revolution', the series of events which saw the flight of King James II, the Protestant succession in the persons of William and Mary, and the final constitutional victory of Parliament in its struggle with the institution of monarchy.

The Act provided for a permanent suspension of the penal acts, thus giving liberty of conscience to Dissent. However, it gave no relief from tithes, and excluded Catholics and Unitarians from its provisions. The disabilities of the Test and Corporation Acts remained in force, so higher education and the public service stayed closed to non-Anglicans. On the other hand, it now became an offence to disturb somebody else's worship. The Act worked by allowing dissenting ministers to subscribe to the Thirty-Nine Articles of the Church of England subject to reservations so they could benefit from the Act's policy. Baptists, for instance, were excepted from the article on infant baptism.

These matters were not really an issue for Friends, who were a special case. Quakers who scrupled to take the oath were allowed to make two declarations. One was against the doctrine of Transubstantiation. This would have been irrelevant to Friends, but it satisfied the state that they were not secret Catholics. The other was of faith in the Father, the Son and the Holy Spirit. The word 'Trinity' was delicately avoided and a form of words that would satisfy Friends negotiated. Quakerly exception was taken to the draft on two counts. The description of the Holy Spirit as 'co-equal with the Father and the Son' was objected to as unscriptural. The description of scripture itself as 'the revealed Will and Word of God' was just not what Quakers believed, but the government remained content with a commitment to the Holy Scriptures of the Old and New Testament as having been given 'by Divine Inspiration'.

It was now more than forty years since the rise of Quakerism, and the world was changing out of recognition. Many of the early leaders were dead and the younger generation was entering middle age. The need to preserve the memory of the life and works of the founders of the Society gave an added impulse to the process of formalising the faith. Collections of the works of notable Friends began to be published, and there was great interest in the journal, which later became a characteristic form of Quaker literary expression. The works of Robert Barclay and William Penn were double-edged swords – they defended Quakerism against its public detractors, and the Society of Friends against the tendencies within that would have compromised its unity. From being a people of the Word, Friends now became a people of their books. A long period of introspection was about to begin.

The Dawn of Quietism

George Fox died peacefully on 13 January 1691 and was buried close by Bunhill Fields, the dissenting burial ground outside the City of London. One of his letters, published posthumously, clearly shows that he hoped the Morning Meeting would together take over his individual role in counselling and guiding Friends. In fact, a joint leadership of George Whitehead and Stephen Crisp emerged. Crisp soon died, leaving Whitehead as the main guide of the Society, down to his death in 1723. Though George Whitehead had been one of the Valiant Sixty, times had changed him. He no longer believed in the convincement of the nation and the world, and, to be fair, not many others did either, in their heart of hearts. His sermons are a milestone on the journey into quietism. Friends were now a 'little seed', a 'Remnant', preserved from destruction by the special grace of God.

It is probably not to be wondered at that Dissent generally should have gone through a low period at the end of the seventeenth century. In a sense, its battle had been won. Though Quaker, Baptist, Congregational and Presbyterian ideas had not been adopted wholesale, the churches themselves had won the right to exist, and their struggle for an intellectually plural society was of profound importance in the relatively smooth transition to political democracy later on. Dissent was now an important feature of national life and would remain so.

This was not clear at the time, however. Numbers of dissenting ministers found their way back into the Church of England. All the denominations reported a loss of members and few recruits. The age was not receptive to strong and challenging messages, and Toleration considerably blunted the criticism Dissent was wont to make of the behaviour of the national church. In addition, there was the perennial problem of the second generation. Little evangelism was undertaken, and far more attention was given to the education and indoctrination of those already within the fold. Apart from the loss of ministers, Friends were affected by all these influences and, in addition, those which arose from their own particular circumstances.

The first Quakers had all come from outside the Society, and brought with them the influences of a variety of backgrounds as well as a depth of biblical and theological understanding. They were religiously educated in the proper sense of the word. Now, while other dissenters invested considerable care in the education and preparation of their ministers in the dissenting academies, Friends were cut off from outside influences through their lack of a trained ministry. This non-involvement with the religious concerns of others is part of the explanation for their increasing isolation and their failure to meet the need discerned by the Methodists, who were ready to take advantage of the spirit of revival when it came.

Some commentators feel that the Quakers lost their ardour as a result of the persecutions, and their retirement from the world was a recuperative process. There may be some truth in that, but it is not the whole explanation. It is also said that the growth of organisation began to hamper the spiritual freedom Quakerism had when it was a 'movement'. There may also be truth in that, but it seems that the rigid control which the elders of the Society came to exercise in the second century of its existence was a consequence of its weakness, not a cause. There is a case for saying that eighteenth-century quietism preserved the soul of Quakerism rather than losing it.

The halting of the forward movement of Quakerism cannot be attributed to one cause. It was a complex phenomenon, and did not spring mainly from weakness or defection in Friends themselves, as some are inclined to suggest. Underlying all apparently consistent theological positions, there is a world-view which their authors often do not fully appreciate. Such was the case with Quakerism. The whole system of ideas surrounding the apostasy and the millennium was beginning to creak. The issue of pluralism or uniformity had been settled. The contrast between spiritual and formal religion in Quaker terms was no longer the issue it had been. It was not yet clear what the issues of the future would be, but there was no doubt that Quakerism would need to be expressed in a different way, and a period of readjustment was undoubtedly necessary.

As the eighteenth century began, Friends were in a no more uncertain position as to their future than other dissenters. They had survived as a group and the strict codes of behaviour they had developed, coupled with what came to be a rather authoritarian method of church government, preserved them from dissolution. By 1715, Friends probably had the largest number of congregations of any dissenting community in England and Wales, 696 against the Presbyterians' 662. On the other hand, the average size of meetings was much smaller, for Presbyterian strength is estimated at about 179,000, as against 59,000 for the Independents, or Congregationalists, and 39,000 for the Friends. Dissent was considerably stronger in the towns, notably Bristol, where 20 per cent of the population were dissenters, and London and its environs, where perhaps 20 per cent of the total number of Quakers lived.

Friends now clearly stood for a distinct emphasis within Christianity which asserted that all people were possessed of the light of Christ within, which was sufficient to save them if they obeyed it and drew upon its power; that God's saving grace is universal and not confined to nominal, or outward Christians; that human beings are under an obligation to seek perfection; and that God's revelation of himself is not limited to nature or the printed word, but continues directly down the centuries, informing both individuals and the Church.

These are the enduring principles which emerged from the great period of Quaker expansion. In the following century they were protected, nourished and developed. It is one of the tragedies of English religious history that this took place behind the facade of Quaker denominationalism and exclusiveness. In the eighteenth century, Friends created a beautiful religious culture of great refinement. Unhappily it stood apart from the world. The Quakers still had a great message to give, but so stringent were the conditions they placed on its reception that few people hearkened. Friends were trusted, respected and admired, but they were not followed. The Letter to Titus speaks of Christ redeeming and purifying from all iniquity a peculiar people zealous of good works. This was the self-image the Quakers took into the eighteenth century, and it was not quite what their founders had intended.

Quakerism in the Classical Period

THE EIGHTEENTH CENTURY WAS OUTWARDLY AN AGE OF ELEGANCE, enlightenment and restraint. It was the period in which the Quakers developed the style of life, the public reputation and the character which many see as their finest achievement. The pressures of colonial expansion abroad and industrial and agrarian change at home took time to come to the surface of national life. The tone of religious intercourse, no less than that of philosophical, scientific and historical discussion, avoided the contrasts, the enthusiasms, the savagery of the previous century. It was the merit (if that is the word) of the wars of the eighteenth century that their ostensible purpose was diplomatic rather than religious.

There was scarcely any part of English national life untouched by these developments and the Society of Friends was certainly not a rock of abiding truth in a swirling tide of change. As the English people as a whole adapted to new patterns of life and economic opportunities, so did the Quakers. The characteristic figures of the yeoman farmer and small businessman of the first Quaker century gave way to the well-to-do merchant and manufacturer of the second. Though we must not underestimate the importance of purely religious factors, we cannot avoid viewing this period with a sociologist's eye and asking who the Friends of the second and third generations were. To some degree we will arrive at different conclusions for England and America, but the general principles of our approach are probably applicable to both.

Church and Sect

The sociology of religion continues to explore the related terms 'church', 'sect' and 'denomination', as applied to types of Christian religious organisation. What follows is a broad indication of the distinctions that can be drawn. It is important to remember that the use of the words in this context is intended solely to point to certain social factors in religious life, and these terms are used much more freely in the ordinary way.

A church is content to embrace saints and sinners alike, and is an essential part of social life. Babies are baptised into it automatically, civic authority professes its values, the state sanctions its activities and protects its privileges. It is therefore large, and most of the population tends to identify with it. There are potential conflicts between the interests of the church and the state, and crises sometimes occur. Broadly, though, churches accept the social order provided their position is not too seriously compromised, so they tend to be conservative, and often appear to be agents of social control.

Thus, a church has the problem of achieving a balance between its religious and social functions. If it leans too far in the latter direction, individuals and groups appear who argue that it has subordinated itself to worldly power. The claim is usually made that this would not have happened if standards of personal discipleship had been higher, and if the church itself had been prepared to exercise its authority instead of compromising. Movements like this tend to split off from churches, and become sects.

A sect, therefore, arises out of protest. Its first members are self-selected, for it is a voluntary association based on some kind of personal conviction or conversion experience. It is exclusive, and denies membership to those unwilling to make its affirmations or accept its standards, so it tends to have an attitude of hostility or indifference to outside society. Moreover, its ideology will tend to dictate a member's whole outlook on life and it usually has a system of controls designed to ensure uniformity with its collective testimonies. Sects tend to appeal to the economically or politically disfranchised and to take the form of protest against what is seen as the excesses of institutional religion.

In some, this takes the form of aggressive evangelism designed to change the world by changing people; others see the world as being under an imminent catastrophe and seek to warn or prepare people for it; yet others reject the values of the world and offer alternative principles for life here and now. There are other types, but what they all have in common is a rejection of what we have called the 'church' type of Christianity. Many sects are short-lived – they tend to mellow into denominations, keeping their habits of thought and in-group vocabulary – but being open to a much wider range of members, not often expelling people and admitting a certain imprecision of doctrine and conviction that would have been intolerable to their founders. The eighteenth century sees the Quakers as a sect; the nineteenth century finds them in process of becoming a denomination, at any rate among pastoral Friends in the United States.

At one time it was customary to regard Friends as having come from the lowest ranks of society, 'the dregs of the common people' as one hostile witness put it. In recent years, however, a more balanced view has emerged as researchers have worked on monthly and quarterly meeting minute books and the Society's births, deaths and marriages registers. Detailed studies have been made of a number of counties and the three most populous cities of the period, London, Norwich and Bristol. Generalisations about the Society's social composition at the start of the eighteenth century must therefore rest on the assumption that these areas are reasonably representative. The results within this sample are consistent enough for us to guess that they are. So let us see what is revealed.

Who the Quakers Were

Debate continues over the social origins and subsequent character of Friends in the seventeenth century. To start with, Quakerism did not appeal greatly to the nobility and gentry. Among the first leaders there are exceptions to this rule, such as Thomas Ellwood, William Penn and Margaret Fell, but they are a tiny minority. At the other end of the scale the percentage of servants or labouring men also seems to be small, but no one is quite sure about the character of the middling sort of folk who appear to make up the majority. One of the difficulties is our natural tendency to look for a consistent pattern in the country as a whole. It is more likely that there are significant variations from county to county, depending on local occupational and social structures.

An interesting feature of the evidence is that there were proportionately fewer Friends engaged in agriculture than might have been expected. In Lancashire, for example, they amount to about a third of the total whereas most of the Valiant Sixty were connected with farming in one way or another. Buckinghamshire was certainly a more predominantly agricultural area at the time, but even there the figure is almost exactly the same. The largest single occupational group represented is that connected with textiles, and there seems to be a firm connection between radical religion and this occupational group. When we look at the population at large we find reason to believe that Friends were over-represented in commerce and industry, both in trades and handicrafts.

When we have attempted to be as accurate as we can, it begins to look as if the Society that entered the eighteenth century was strongly populated by established farmers and wholesale traders – a class in the community that was independent, expanding and linked with the anti-Royalist tradition. So, on social as well as religious grounds, we should expect to find clear evidence of the development of the Quakers into a classical sect type of the second generation. It is customary to think of social or economic deprivation as encouraging the development of the sectarian mentality, but the social composition of Friends was quite broad, and those in business and other professions did not sever their connections with the wider world when they adopted the new faith.

In the eighty years before 1760, geographical and social mobility had made English Quakerism a mainly urban, middle-class phenomenon. It was also a period of decline in both numbers and devotion and, again, probably with considerable regional variation. Plain speech and dress had lost their power to shock, and dissent had become acceptable in many places, though there was also some niggardly and debilitating persecution. At first Friends adopted a posture of resistance, but in the 1670s began the long process of using negotiation and legal manoeuvre to ameliorate their condition. It also has to be said that at various times Yearly Meeting had to face the fact that there was considerable compromise over the testimonies. Paradoxically, it might have been toleration which encouraged this. When the social tensions caused by persecution abated, there was a much diminished need for personal loyalty within the group.

Before the dawn of toleration, many Friends concluded that the old country could no longer provide a peaceable habitation and they sought a new home in the American colonies, where there were many to make them welcome. In 1682, as we have seen, over two thousand Friends arrived in Philadelphia alone, and the starting dates of the new yearly meetings give a good indication of the 'prospering of truth' across the Atlantic – New England (1661), Baltimore (1672), Virginia (1673), Maryland (1677), Philadelphia (1681) and New York (1696).

Merchants and Manufacturers

An English Friend whose life illustrates the question of Quaker wealth was Richard Reynolds (1735–1816). His grandfather was one of the first Friends and his father a successful iron dealer in Bristol. Soon after finishing his apprenticeship he was sent on a business trip to Coalbrookdale in Shropshire, where he met, and later, married, Hannah, daughter of the Quaker ironmaster, Abraham Darby II. He became a partner in the ironworks at Ketley, and after the deaths of his first wife and his father-in-law in quick succession he stepped in to manage the Coalbrookdale works during the minority of the Darby sons. His own business prospered and he became extremely wealthy.

Reynolds was an innovator – he is credited with being the first man to use cast iron instead of wood for railway wheels, and to use inclined planes for getting canal barges from one level to another. He was just – he helped his workmen to take out a patent for a process they developed in his works. He held to Friends' testimonies – he refused government contracts to manufacture iron cannon and he was an early supporter of the anti-slavery campaign. He greatly improved his employees' housing and living conditions and even paid them to send their children to a school which he provided. He had a cat called 'Myrtle' that sat by him at table and a horse that outran that of Lord Chancellor Thurlow in what was ostensibly an exercise but was jovially regarded as a race by the statesman.

Reynolds had a calm authority and piety and his portrait shows him holding a Bible open at Romans 5:1, 'Therefore, being justified by faith, we have peace with God through our Lord Jesus Christ'. On retirement to Bristol in 1783, he devoted himself to the use of his wealth for the public good, and endless stories of his generosity grew up. On one occasion he cleared a debtors' prison of all its inmates and is reputed to have given away over £10,000 a year. He made an anonymous gift of £1,000 to the Bristol Royal Infirmary and remarked, when he was thanked, 'Thou hast no authority for saying that I sent the money, but thou seemest determined I should give it.' He duly sent another £1,000 in his own name.

John Bellers (1654–1725), another Friend whose reputation lies in his activities outside the Society, was a solid Quaker bourgeois of the

City of London. He married into the Quaker gentry of Gloucestershire, where his father-in-law used habitually to drive to meeting from Coln St Aldwyn to Cirencester in a coach-and-six. His father, a grocer, had been one of the earliest London Friends, and John remained a devoted adherent of the Society. He was the representative for Yorkshire on Meeting for Sufferings, was arrested for religious offences on three occasions, belonged to the Royal Society and was a friend of Hans Sloane. He wrote a number of books and pamphlets on spiritual, economic and political issues. His influence leapt a century, for he was one of the sources of inspiration for such diverse nineteenth-century radicals as Francis Place, Robert Owen and Karl Marx.

This many-sided man sought to bring reason and humanity into the operation of economic forces. It was said of him later that he formed 'a most interesting link between the high pressure prophets of the first generation of Quakerism and the philanthropists of its quieter period'. We are now in a position to qualify that statement. Whereas the social testimony of early Friends had been directed to the pride of the wealthy, Bellers' activity was devoted to the amelioration of the conditions of the poor. This most certainly arose from his spiritual convictions, but at the same time extended the primarily political concerns of people such as William Penn into the field of economic and social policy. Bellers the businessman was no mean economist.

According to a number of economists, the basic factors of production are human labour and the raw materials, food and energy provided by the earth. What we know as capital is not a factor of production in its own right, but simply some form of stored up, or saved, labour or 'land'. This line of reasoning, or some variant of it, is called the labour theory of value. Socialists take the step of arguing that therefore incomes derived from the ownership of capital should be abolished, since they represent the theft of the product of other people's work.

However, the socialist response to the labour theory of value is not compelling, for some of the apologists of laissez-faire capitalism adopted it too. Bellers was not one of the classical economists, but in 1696 he laid before the public his proposals for a scheme to diminish want, idleness and lewdness among the poor, relieve the financial burdens on the community imposed by the existence of poverty, and also (though he did not use the words) bring about growth in the economy through the stimulation of demand.

Bellers proposed the creation of a network of 'Colleges of Industry', working communities of perhaps 300 people of various trades. Though some were to be specialised, like those on the sea coast with nautical concerns, they were to be self-supporting. The economics and statistics of the time were used to support the proposition that the efforts of two thirds of the college would be devoted to covering the overheads (including a reasonable standard of living, proper education and health care for the inmates), while the work of the other third would produce a profit for the promoters. It was a subtle blend of altruism and self-interest. Welfare would be provided by the communities, structural unemployment would become manageable, and it would be easier to take up the slack in the economy created by seasonal unemployment.

Though these plans did not receive the public attention Bellers had hoped for, he continued to advocate the scheme throughout his life. Bristol Friends started a workhouse along these lines in 1696, but the colleges plan was really a blueprint for an economy, rather than a private philanthropic effort. Nevertheless in 1702, London Friends bought a workhouse at Clerkenwell which was to be used to accommodate elderly people and children together in a community.

The venture proved satisfactory, and the London monthly meetings maintained their support, Southwark Monthly Meeting finding it far more economic to maintain their old people in an institution than at home. By 1786, London was expanding and conditions had changed. The children were moved to a new school nearby, and the elderly went out to another home at Plaistow. London and Middlesex Quarterly Meeting was now becoming aware that competition from the newly-founded Ackworth School was hampering the recruitment of children, so in 1811 the enterprise was reorganised. What now became one of the officially sponsored Quaker schools was removed to Croydon in 1825, and thence to Saffron Walden in 1879, where it remains.

The forward-looking schemes of John Bellers were not confined to matters such as this. We have already seen how he sensed the link between economic and social policy that did not become widely recognised till the twentieth century. He seems to have been the first person to advocate the abolition of the death penalty. He proposed a solution to the rivalries of the European states that looks like a United States of Europe. He adopted with enthusiasm the scheme of Henry IV of France for a Senate of the Christian Commonwealths, which foreshadows the World Council of Churches and the United Nations together. John Bellers had a wholeness of vision which his native shrewdness did not allow to become so alluring that it was detached from life. What he had to say was practical and progressive, from the need to abolish poverty for the individual, to the need to stop warfare between nations. He was a new kind of Quaker, whose philanthropy was inspired by his faith, but was the stronger, because it could stand independent of it.

Slightly later, the Coalbrookdale Company began in the activities of Abraham Darby, who was born at Dudley, apprenticed in Birmingham and domiciled for a while in Bristol. In 1708 he came to Coalbrookdale in Shropshire to open up a derelict blast furnace, and carry on the trade of iron founder. At a time of wood famine and escalating energy costs, he found a way of smelting iron by using coke rather than charcoal, a process that was initially more expensive, but created a higher temperature in the furnace. This produced greater fluidity in the molten iron, so that thinner-walled castings could be made, and the pots and cylinders manufactured at Coalbrookdale became lighter, and therefore cheaper.

The process was doubly economic, for when the price of charcoal climbed permanently above that of mined coal, the technology was already there to take advantage of changed circumstances. How the discovery was made is now conjecture, but Abraham Darby must have conducted a number of his own experiments. We know that Shropshire coal had a very low sulphur content and that was a favourable factor. We know, however, that the Quaker entrepreneur had worked in the brass and malt trades in Bristol, and his sister-in-law's account of his life tells us significantly that he used coke 'as is done for drying malt' – a case of discovery arising out of a breadth of experience. This is a principle that Friends have now made part of their spiritual discipline too.

The Darby interests prospered, and wise management preserved them from danger during the minority of two of the heirs. Nor did the genius for invention depart. It was in the valley that steam pumps were introduced to recycle water from the furnaces and give all-year-round production; that the technology for casting cylinders for ever-improving steam engines was developed; that the first iron rails and railway wheels were cast, and where, finally, the gracious span of the Iron Bridge (the first large structure in the world to show the potential of iron in civil engineering) was designed and erected. Foundry practice is an unglamorous side of history, but nonetheless vital, for the skills of Coalbrookdale enabled the development of the mighty Birmingham steam engines that propelled Britain into the Industrial Revolution.

Confectioners and Bankers

Many people are under the impression that because the British cocoa and chocolate industry is almost entirely of Quaker origin, the explanation of this must lie with the Quaker testimonies somewhere, since cocoa is not intoxicating, and it has no military uses. Friends must have chosen to make it because they could do so without compromising their principles. This would be a nice moral tale, if true, but the reasons are largely coincidental.

The story of the Rowntrees of York has to begin with the Tuke family. In 1725, a redoubtable woman Quaker, Mary Tuke, won the right to be a Freeman and member of the York Merchant Adventurers' Company and to trade as a grocer. Her nephew William was later apprenticed to her and in 1752 he inherited her shop. In 1785 he was joined in partnership by his son, Henry, and these two men enjoyed a remarkably creative association.

William achieved fame as one of the pioneers of his age. Perhaps the fact that he encouraged his son to train as a doctor gives an indication of his interests, for he was the founder of The Retreat, a mental hospital at York, still in existence, which opened its doors to patients in 1796, and proposed to take mental illness seriously. In those days, the insane were often hidden away, chained or otherwise restrained, punished savagely, or displayed for callous amusement. William Tuke believed that the Inward Light shone in them as well as in the sane, and was convinced that in a loving atmosphere serious attempts at remedial training could be undertaken.

Henry was the Tuke with scientific training, and under his management the firm flourished. As an adjunct to the grocery, a chocolate factory was set up and this was to be the family's industrial legacy. In the next sixty years, members of the family were responsible for initiating or encouraging a number of things, including the promotion of the campaign to have William Wilberforce elected MP for the County of York in 1807. In the city itself, the Mount School for girls was set up with Tuke support, as was also Bootham School for boys. So was the Friends' Provident Institution, today out of Quaker control, but one of the big insurance groups on the London money market. Two sons moved out into banking and in 1849 the tea business was transferred to London. Fame was waiting for Henry Isaac Rowntree. He bought the cocoa and chocolate department that he had hitherto managed. The name of Tuke is now known only to the cognoscenti; Rowntree is a household name.

Meanwhile, Dr Joseph Fry had come to Bristol and entered the soap trade, as one might expect of a man with scientific inclinations. He made a lot of money. He lost some of it in a china works in Bristol, but one of the firms in which he and his son had an interest, the type-founders, Fry & Pyne, produced one of the loveliest books in existence. In 1798, they brought out *Pantographia*, which purported to be an accurate copy of every known alphabet. The cocoa and chocolate business developed out of the general merchandising business Joseph had set up and which was the ballast of the family's financial ship. The third son, Joseph Storrs Fry, was the man who emphasised this side of their affairs. In 1795, he adventurously installed a Watt steam engine for the sole purpose of manufacturing cocoa and chocolate. By 1822, the firm was secure, and he brought his sons into partnership. It was not for another forty years that the Cadbury brothers were to make their mark on the trade, and, again, they took the chocolate and cocoa part of a dividing business.

As we have seen, the Quakers were deeply involved in the iron trade in the West Midlands, and one of the families with extensive interests in the area was called Lloyd. They were gentry, and originally came from Dolobran in Montgomeryshire, now Powys. In 1765, there was, surprisingly, no bank in Birmingham, which was rapidly developing into the regional centre. Sampson Lloyd II entered partnership with a non-Friend, John Taylor, to provide one, and achieved immediate success. The firm pioneered the use of the inland bill of exchange for small traders, and did so well overall, that Sampson Lloyd III, to facilitate the growing London business, set up another banking partnership in Lombard Street. His business principle was succinct – 'We do nothing for nothing for nobody.' In 1889 these two separate firms amalgamated, and they now trade as Lloyds Bank in virtually every high street in England.

Lloyds is alone as a country bank that extended its contacts in the city of London. The many other Quaker banks of the period remained local or regional institutions, such as the Pease family enterprises in the north-east, founded at various times, G. Fox & Co. (1754) in Cornwall, and two banks based on the extension of credit in the textile trade, John and Henry Gurney & Co. of Norwich (1775), and J. & J. Backhouse (1778) of Darlington. There were many similar institutions, and, over a period, the families which owned them became linked in a strong network of marriage and business arrangements, quite apart from their common membership of the Society of Friends. In 1866 there was a tragedy, when the failure of Overend and Gurney caused a financial crisis in the City. In 1896, however, over twenty separate concerns amalgamated, and, as Barclays Bank, stepped overnight into the leading position in joint stock banking in England, remaining there ever since.

Richard Reynolds was an example of integrity in business as well as success, but as the century wore on, the Society at large became uneasy. Great wealth seemed to many to be available only at the expense of compromise with the ancient testimonies and the Quaker posture of withdrawal from 'the World'. Samuel Galton of Birmingham was disowned for manufacturing arms, but continued to attend meeting and eventually sold his interests. John Wakefield of Kendal eventually suffered the same fate, as did William Fawcett of Liverpool. William Stout of Lancaster found that a godly life led shrewdly to a good bank balance, but Friends of substance such as Thomas Shillitoe, Daniel Wheeler, Sampson Lloyd III and Joseph John Gurney had doubts. Some managed to live with them and it is not for us to criticise. Others, however, heeding their consciences, abandoned or limited their activities.

John Woolman

This was the course adopted by John Woolman (1720–1772) of Mount Holly, New Jersey, a quietist Quaker whose personal courage, purity of life and perceptive social criticism have attracted admirers and disciples far beyond the Society of Friends. Grandson of an immigrant, and fourth child of a family of thirteen, he came from what he called 'a middle station' in life. As a young man, he moved naturally and easily in the cultivated and well-to-do Quaker society on the Jersey side of the Delaware River from Philadelphia, but in his late teens he experienced a serious call to the religious life.

He had to make his own way and had been trained by his father in legal work, particularly the conveyancing of property. Like George Fox, he had a good head for business, and worked first as a book-keeper and assistant in a general store at Mount Holly. Then he set up on his own, having acquired some skill as a tailor, and thereafter supported himself variously by his shop, legal matters, his tailoring, and 'hoeing, grafting, trimming and inoculating' in his eleven-acre nursery of apple trees. There is a calm assumption that material prosperity could have been his, for he tells us that in 1756, 'the road to large business appeared open; but

I felt a stop in my mind'. He saw clearly that his business was to become a means for service to Truth, not for the accumulation of superfluities.

Woolman was not an isolated figure, but a member of a widespread Quaker network in the Delaware Valley. He was faithful in his attendance at the Society's public worship and meetings for business. He was recorded as a minister very early in life, and his application of the testimony of simplicity to his own affairs enabled him to undertake a large number of pastoral and missionary journeys, always with a travelling companion, and never without the blessing of the meeting's travelling minute,* which on one occasion he produced lovingly to the Wyalusing Indians to show that his visit was on behalf of his community and not just for himself.

The general pattern of his trips seemed to be that in winter he would go to Friends who could be reached conveniently in a few days. His concern for his own Jersey Friends is notable. But on his longer travels, usually in the early summer, he went as far afield as New England and the Southern colonies of Delaware, Maryland, Virginia and North Carolina. Always, he was under concern. He was always totally resigned to whatever God should have in store for him, but nevertheless sought every opportunity to talk to Friends about the things that concerned him. Not far in the future lay the War of Independence. Not so far beyond that lay the War between the States. Woolman saw deeply into the dynamics of human society and discerned the roots of these conflicts. He spoke God's will as he understood it, about war, about slavery, about economic aggrandisement. Woolman was an unusual combination – saint and prophet in one.

There are many parallels between English and American Quakerism in this period. The years down to 1756 were ones of peace and prosperity for Pennsylvania. A wealthy merchant class grew up in Philadelphia, and though Friends were proportionately fewer in the total population, they still played an important part in the government of the colony. As in the case of London, an increasing number of voices in the Yearly Meeting were to be heard recalling Friends to their testimonies, notably those of John Churchman, Anthony Benezet and Woolman.

Woolman had long been convinced of the wickedness of slavery, but chose to campaign against it in his own characteristic manner. He viewed the institution as a whole, and argued that it was as harmful to

* See pages 162–3

the slave-owner as to the slave. He travelled in the South and had first-hand experience of what he was talking about. He visited slave-owning Friends, and sought to reason with them. He did not argue from the worst case, nor under-emphasise or explain away considerations that did not fit neatly with his own views. He relied always on principle. He worked within the Society, used its ministry, its business methods and its procedures. He and his Friends set out to convince America through Philadelphia Yearly Meeting.

Gradually success came. Anti-slavery feeling grew. In 1754, Woolman's *Some Considerations on the keeping of Negroes* was published. In 1758 the Yearly Meeting finally directed the visitation of all slave-holders with a view to the complete abolition of slavery and the following year published Anthony Benezet's *Observations on the Enslaving, importing and Purchasing Negroes*. By 1774 slave owning or trading became a matter of disownment. It is worth noting that as far back as 1727 London Yearly Meeting had cautioned Friends strongly against dealing in, or importing, slaves. It clarified its own view, but was not yet in a position to campaign.

The steadfastness of American Friends towards their peace testimony was severely tested during the Seven Years' War (1756–63), appropriately known in America as the French and Indian War. There was the question of war taxes, and the effect of hostilities on trade and the political position of the Quakers in Pennsylvania. Friends had to work out a position on enlistment and the billeting of soldiers on civilians, and many Friends in the back country suffered from the incursions of the French and their Indian allies. This testing was sadly opportune. Already in 1747 the Philadelphia Yearly Meeting had decreed a general visitation by elders and ministers to prevent 'many growing inconsistencies and customs amongst us' and we can discern the growth of a strong spiritual renewal movement, which included a tightening of the peace testimony amongst its objects.

The year before the outbreak of the war the Discipline was toughened to provide disownment for marrying out, and the Queries were altered to include a strong statement on 'bearing arms, training or military service'. This was supported by *An Epistle of Tender Love and Caution to Friends in Pennsylvania* against the payment of war taxes, by an unofficial group of twenty-one weighty Friends, including Woolman. It turned out that many Friends paid the taxes, but, equally, many refused and suffered distraint. Few fought, but there was bloodshed among Friends on the frontier. To alleviate the distress of these two groups of testifying Friends, the Philadelphia Meeting for Sufferings came into existence.

Some were reluctant to lose the political and social influence the Society enjoyed, but other important Friends had to accept the logic of their position and left the Pennsylvania Assembly, on which Friends never again held majority control. Eleven years after the Peace of Paris (1763), America was at war again, this time with the mother country, and the same problems resurfaced. This time Friends were in a cleft stick, for the peace testimony could easily be seen either as a refusal to accept the burden of a struggle for liberty or else a traitorous loyalist posture. It was neither, but this did not prevent the persecution of Friends generally, and for some a disorientation of identity in a new world where the old certainties no longer held.

On the corner of Fifth and Arch Streets, Philadelphia, there still stands the meeting house of the 'Free Quakers', a breakaway group of Friends, who, unwilling to observe the strict discipline, and sympathetic to the war, flourished between 1781 and 1836, when they died out. It is estimated that over a thousand Friends were disowned for various offences in connection with the maintenance of the peace testimony during the War of Independence, but on the other hand, very many Friends suffered heavy fines and distraints for maintaining their witness.

The consequences of Friends' withdrawal from public life in Pennsylvania are historically interesting. From a dominant social position they gradually became a minority and needed to relate to society in a new way. Under the leadership of a small group of Friends which included Woolman, a thoroughgoing reformation in faith and morals occurred over the latter half of the eighteenth century. Steps were taken to ensure that the Discipline was observed over a whole range of matters, and the task of enforcement fell upon the body of elders. But they wielded a two-edged sword. When Philadelphia Yearly Meeting made slave-owning a disownable offence the way was clear for a corporate testimony which had immense historical consequences. On the other hand, the power of the elders was one of the main causes of the Philadelphia Separation fifty years later, from which, ultimately, most of the divisions in contemporary world Quakerism derive.

So this is the background to John Woolman's creative life. Though a member of this influential reform group in his own yearly meeting, he is still admired – and imitated – by Friends the world over for the way he testified to the power of his beliefs by the quality of his personal life. He could not write a bill of sale for a slave. When soldiers were billeted on him he refused payment. Believing that the light of Christ was in all, he sought and found it among the Indians, to whom he made a special journey in the ministry. Devoted to the art of persuasion rather than debate, he sought to move Friends to free their slaves by enlisting their consent, again making special journeys in the ministry for the purpose.

He avoided the temptations of wealth by avoiding wealth when it could have been his, seeking holy sufficiency rather than holy poverty. He felt what we would call the environmental damage of the dyeing industry, so he wore undyed clothes as a personal testimony. In the last year of his life he made a journey to England, travelling steerage in a ship captained by a Friend. His deep sympathy for the creation extended alike to the seamen's conditions of work and the poor bedraggled fowls brought along for fresh food, which he describes sorrowfully in his *Journal*.

Woolman arrived in London on 8 June 1772, wearing his white hat and undyed clothes. There were no stock or bands at his neck, and he had simple woollen buttons. He had no lapels, and his shoes were made of undyed leather. The traditional account of the occasion (which has been questioned) records that he was just in time for the Meeting of Ministers and Elders that preceded Yearly Meeting and it is clear that his weird appearance induced an immediate state of shock in the assembled Friends. After his travelling minute had been read there was silence. John Fothergill rose and said that his concern was accepted, but he might feel free to return home without further labour. After further silence, Woolman rose and said in measured terms that he could not feel himself released, but without the meeting's endorsement felt unable to travel in the ministry. So he would not accept hospitality as was the custom, but would set to work in his trade in the hope that Friends would be able to assist him in getting started. In continued silence the meeting repented and his minute was endorsed.

He set off to travel through his ancestral country, impressing and inspiring Friends everywhere, again testifying by his life. In America he rode, but here, observing the condition of the ostlers and horses employed in the trade, he preferred to walk rather than use the stage coach. In September 1772 he reached York. After a brief illness he died of smallpox and was buried there, at Bishophill, possibly the greatest Quaker of all and an adornment of the period of quietism.

There is little doubt that a great change came over Quakerism after the first generation had died. While struggling to establish the Society, Friends had been rebellious, self-confident, truculent and fiercely evangelistic. A century later, they had become inhibited, authoritarian and inward-looking, concerned not so much to transform the world as to avoid contamination by it. People are expelled for social failures of various kinds, such as bankruptcy. Marriage to non-Quakers is forbidden. Schools are started which preserve sectarian values in the children. Plain dress becomes a uniform. Plain speech becomes an obsession and a whole new technical religious vocabulary is developed. Friends go the way of every other cohesive but alienated religious group that has been studied.

To some degree modern social science would lead us to expect such developments but it would be a mistake to regard them as the outcome of purely secular causes. Eighteenth-century Quakerism has come to be called 'quietism' because its beliefs, practices and characteristic mood were later understood to resemble the continental spiritual movement of the same name, associated with the names of Miguel de Molinos, François Fénelon and Mme de Guyon. Caution is necessary here, for eighteenth-century Friends did not apply the word 'quietist' to themselves. That came later. It is, however, convenient, so long as we remain aware that it may not be the description they would have chosen to apply to themselves.

Quaker Quietism

In spite of this similarity between Friends and the continental quietists, it is probably going too far to see these as responsible for the changed emphasis in Quakerism in the later eighteenth century. Certainly their works were widely read among Friends, who drew inspiration and encouragement from them, but there were also important differences of principle between the two groups.

Continental quietism was a mystical attitude, but it came very close to a doctrine of justification by pure faith, a view which Friends have always strongly rejected. Moreover, it was antinomian, and the Quakers were ever forthright moralists. This was because their experience of God was primarily one of leading and vocation, not of stillness and contemplation. Friends shared the quietists' distrust of human nature, but this was common across the whole of Christendom. Rather than encouraging each Friend to cultivate his or her spiritual garden in isolation, the Society of Friends understood itself to have a collective responsibility. So the origins of Quaker quietism probably do not lie here.

There is a paradox in Quakerism, and in each period in their history, Friends have tried to resolve it in a different way. The main symptom of this tension in the eighteenth century was the increasing importance of silence in worship as time went by. Underlying it was an ambivalence about ministry. Some Friends felt that other Friends were too dependent on sermons and vocal ministry for their spiritual nourishment. Other Friends complained that too often the ministry was not 'in the life', that is to say, they thought it arose from human concern rather than from divine impulses. Ministers themselves experienced great difficulties with their vocation, and in the absence of any other outward expression of its spiritual life many parts of the Society of Friends went cold. The early Friends had bequeathed a theological problem which had implications they had never needed to consider. It now had to be picked up.

Early Friends distinguished a spiritual dimension in human affairs which they opposed to the 'worldly' or anti-spiritual dimension. 'Truth' belonged to God, not the world, so the only place where Truth could be learned was within, where God imparted it directly to every soul that was prepared to listen. Truth was not communicable by human agency. They therefore saw the reliance on authority in matters of faith as the worst aspect of the 'worldly' attitude, and castigated formal and intellectual religion.

On the other hand, they were quite clear that preaching, example and persuasion could point people to the source of Truth within themselves. People were open to convincement, and thereafter to a growth in grace, by the ministry of *other* people. This is why George Fox said, '. . . be patterns, be examples in all countries, places, islands, nations, wherever you come; that your carriage and life may preach among all sorts of people, and to them. Then you will come to walk cheerfully over the world, answering that of God in everyone . . .' So the knowledge of spiritual truth was something other people could point you towards, but you had to get it yourself, direct from God. Anything else was illusory. This was a very practical way of looking at things, and no wonder it appealed to large numbers of the religiously disinherited.

The impulse of quietism, however, was to devalue this element of mutual help in religious discovery, and to emphasise the principle of direct revelation by God beyond its proper importance. Quietism was therefore a personal, private and retiring form of religion and bore little comparison with the 'Lamb's War' of the first Friends. It was analogous to the thought of René Descartes, the founder of modern philosophy, who taught that the senses could only be relied upon if the evidence they provided was validated by God, because otherwise they might be a source of deception. Of course, Descartes belonged to an earlier period, but the similarity of this principle of systematic doubt to quietism is worth noticing.

The quietists reasoned that whatever is ultimately sensory or of the world – logic, reason, conscience, intellect, emotion, personality – is incapable of providing a certain knowledge of God. Indeed, such outward means, tainted as they are by human weakness, ignorance and sin are positive obstacles to a true knowledge of the divine. So we should seek to escape the influence of all symbols by avoiding outward means of expression and communication, relying instead on achieving a pure passivity or openness to God, wherein he will transmit a sense of his presence and a knowledge of his truth.

It is plain to see how this kind of mentality could be acceptable to Friends, and many aspects of contemporary Quakerism in the un-programmed tradition can be seen to derive from it – the distrust of theology, the suspicion of doctrine, the neglect of the Bible, and irritation with ministry which disturbs the silence, the absence of a teaching ministry and the scrupulous avoidance of anything resembling preaching or evangelism. What happened when the Quakers began to adopt a variant of quietism, was a subtle change in the distinction between inward and outward. Henceforth inwardness of religion was seen as the place of origin of religious truth rather than the place of its verification. The consequences were profound and are often ascribed to the influence of one man.

The Influence of Robert Barclay

Robert Barclay (1648–1690) was the only systematic theologian the Society of Friends has produced. He was born in Scotland of an aristocratic family, and educated at the Scots College in Paris and at home, being convinced at Ury near Aberdeen in 1667. His account of this event has impressed countless Friends. '. . . when I came into the silent assemblies of God's people, I felt a secret power among them, which touched my heart, and as I gave way unto it I found the evil weakening in me and the good raised up; and so I became thus knit and united unto them, hungering more and more after the increase of this power and life whereby I might feel myself perfectly redeemed.'

In 1676, when he was twenty-seven, he published his great work, *An Apology for the True Christian Divinity* in Latin, the first English edition appearing in 1678. A contemporary Anglican said of him, 'Mr Barclay is a very great Man, and were it not for that common Prejudice that lies against him as being a Quaker, would be as sure not to fail of that character in the World as any of the finest Wits this age has produced.' Throughout the subsequent century and a half, Barclay's *Apology* became the standard exposition of the Quaker faith. If we can come to terms with its central ideas we shall see how Barclay unintentionally expressed the central ambiguity of Quakerism and posed a problem which the evangelical and liberal traditions were later to solve in characteristically different ways.

In the first place, Barclay takes a traditional view of the work of the historical Jesus. He was the Christ, and therefore his death and resurrection brought about a permanent change in the relationship between God and the human creation. These events are historical, not merely symbolic, and forgiveness of sins, communion with God and entry to eternal life (i.e. 'salvation') are possible only on the basis that they occurred. They are the standard by which history, and thereby the possibilities of every individual human life, are defined. But in the second place there is a prior question as to why people should need to be saved at all. What is wrong with them? Why can they not approach God directly? Barclay's answer is simply that they are sinful.

'Sin' is not erroneous, inappropriate or morally reprehensible behaviour, a hapless or occasional missing of the mark set by some ennobling ethical code. Rather it is a description of the power which imprisons every human being, a corruption which makes us incapable of experiencing or obeying God. Our own unaided powers are insufficient to obtain release from its bondage. Hence the need for divine initiative. Only God can release us from the power of sin, and the way he has chosen to do it is through the work of Christ.

Thus far, Barclay is perfectly orthodox and argues strongly from scripture, reinforcing his case from the Fathers, as one would expect from one who had been a Protestant educated in a Catholic seminary.

As well as putting the Quaker position he is also concerned to block off what he sees as dangerous errors. Against the Presbyterians he rejects predestination. Against Catholics he rejects the imputation of sin to infants. Against the Unitarians and Rationalists of his day he denies that there is some spark of pure reason in us that remains uncorrupted by sin. Redemption, then, is the work of God alone.

We have seen how early Quakerism contained a distinctive and radical theory of the Church. We are now in a position to see how Barclay develops an equally radical and distinctive theory of the atonement, that branch of Christian theology that seeks to describe the way in which Christ's sacrifice of himself actually brings about salvation. Central to Barclay's exposition is a twofold analysis of the operation of the Holy Spirit. (In this connection it will be helpful to remember that, while disowning the word 'Trinity' and the wilder extremes of theological hair-splitting, Barclay used 'Father', 'Son' and 'Holy Spirit' with their normally accepted New Testament connotations.)

The first aspect of the Spirit's work is connected with our salvation, or redemption from the power of sin. To be saved we need 'knowledge' of God and this can only come through his own direct revelation to us. So when, like Barclay, we feel the secret power touching our hearts, and give way to it, when we feel the evil weakening in us and the good raised up, and when we feel knit and united to our fellow worshippers and hunger after an increase of this power and life, we are feeling the operation of the Spirit in us and we are experiencing this kind of knowledge. It comes to us directly and not through book, priest, doctrine, symbol, ceremony or other communication from outside ourselves.

The second aspect of the Spirit's work is to reveal Truth through the scriptures. They contain a faithful account of God's dealings with humanity in history; prophecies of various kinds; a full and ample account of Christian doctrine. Barclay quotes 2 Timothy 3:16–17 with approval: 'All scripture is given by inspiration of God and is profitable for doctrine, for reproof, for correction, for instruction in righteousness: that the man of God may be perfect, thoroughly furnished unto all good works.' Barclay asserts that the scriptures must be interpreted by the Spirit, not *vice versa*, but emphasises that while the Spirit will give new revelations of the gospel and Christian teaching, it will certainly not reveal a new gospel or new teachings. This, he says, is no part of the Quaker's faith.

So, therefore, in the 'true Christian Divinity' it is the direct inspiration of the Spirit that saves, not the secondary authority of scripture, for that is simply another expression of the Spirit to which we have direct access independently of it. Scripture witnesses to salvation but is not its origin. The true inward experience of God, and the outward expression of God's will in the Bible, must be in harmony, for both proceed from the Spirit. Where there is disharmony between the two there can be no proper understanding of the things of God, no firm faith, and no true Christianity.

Barclay then goes on to draw the logical consequence of universalism out of his own reasoning. He has to, of course, for the kind of knowledge he is talking about is not an intellectual grasp of matters of fact, but the genuine experience of divine grace, however it is described or whatever name it is given. We could call it a power in people coming from beyond themselves which challenges and consoles them. It leads to repentance and spiritual rebirth. It produces the fruits of love, goodness, meekness and perseverance. Barclay is bound by his premises to deny that these experiences come from anywhere but the direct and unmediated activity of God. Since they arise exclusively within, they are available to those with no knowledge of the outward facts of the Christian faith as reported in scripture. He asserts that those to whom a knowledge of Christ's death has been withheld may be made 'partakers of the mystery . . . , though ignorant of the History'. If they turn to what he calls the 'light', they can nevertheless enjoy 'Communion with the Father and the Son'. Hence, Christ's death can save those who have no outward knowledge of it whatever.

This is a pretty radical doctrine, and it is the outcome of an impressive systematic theology. But tight systematic theologies often have one or two central assumptions, and if these become seriously open to criticism, the system grinds to a halt. Barclay's first controlling assumption is that scripture is neither the principal basis of knowledge nor the main standard of faith. You can deny this assumption either because you think it wrong, or because the small print of his argument makes it an overstatement. If you are right, the way is clear for the development of evangelical Quakerism.

Barclay's second controlling assumption is the unity, or indissoluble link, between the spiritual reality he calls the light, and Jesus the Christ as an historical figure. If you take the view that modern biblical and theological scholarship renders the traditional Christian doctrines obsolete, and you are right, the way is clear for mystical universalist

Quakerism. Either of these courses can be taken, but each is in turn vulnerable to the criticism that it tends to fragment the Quaker tradition as Barclay develops it, by concentrating on one aspect of a balanced whole. If the work of Barclay was instrumental in stimulating divergence, a re-examination of the issues he raises might also be instrumental in recovering that wholeness.

The links between Fox's thought and Barclay's are the subject of lively debate, though on many matters like the above there is considerable identity of view. Some critics see Barclay as having all too pessimistic a view of human nature. He was probably no more pessimistic than Fox, but George was scarcely a systematic thinker, unlike his younger follower, and Barclay builds his conviction of total depravity too tightly into his general framework. Then again, Fox clearly sees the light as ready to operate whenever people are persuaded to turn to it. Barclay displays a narrower conception – for everyone there is a 'day of visitation', a period in which the opportunity of repentance and response to the light was on offer. It could be at any time, but it was temporary; once lost the opportunity was gone, never to recur.

Then there is a tantalising difference in atmosphere between the two men. Barclay is obviously a scholar, at home with the Fathers as well as the Bible, capable of taking nice points and making fine distinctions. Fox breathes the air of an Amos or Paul, and sees the whole sweep of God's covenant relationship with his Church in a far more dramatic and concrete way. Basically, Barclay has put Quakerism into a quietist kind of straitjacket by his philosophical dualism and distrust of the powers of the human mind. Fox's profoundly scriptural faith contains so many counterweights to enthusiasm in one direction that there is a diversity and comprehensiveness there that Barclay has not quite caught. But the die was cast. For the eighteenth century, when Friends needed theology it was to the Scotsman that they turned.

The Creation of a Quaker Culture

Q UAKERS LIVE A HAND TO MOUTH KIND OF RELIGIOUS LIFE, plain and with no nonsense, so they seldom need to express their faith at any length. Accepting implicitly the kind of theology Barclay offered, they got on with the business of living, so if we look for the influence of quietism in their lives, we will have to look at their habitual forms of expression and the institutions they developed. Many Friends today are perhaps unaware of the depth of theology underlying those well-known lines of John Greenleaf Whittier.

> Drop Thy still dews of quietness,
> Till all our strivings cease;
> Take from our souls the strain and stress,
> And let our ordered lives confess
> The beauty of Thy peace.
>
> Breathe through the heats of our desire
> Thy coolness and Thy balm;
> Let sense be dumb, let flesh retire;
> Speak through the earthquake, wind and fire,
> O still, small voice of calm!

This was written over a century after Barclay, but the quietist distinction between outward creaturely faculties, obstructive of divine communication, and the pure unbidden visitation is clearly preserved here. We contribute striving, strain and stress to the encounter – God supplies the still dews of quietness. We must not rely on sense or physical faculties or our own urges – we must deny them and listen instead for the still small voice of calm. It was in this spirit that the Quaker culture of the eighteenth century was built up.

The Quietist Way of Life

Out of a common religious outlook, a certain kind of meeting and a certain kind of ministry developed, and the practice arose of 'recording' those with the gift of verbal ministry. In turn the ministry was encouraged by the growth in status and influence of the elders, who also carried responsibility for pastoral care. What was, and what was not considered sound practice, was decided by the Yearly Meeting and laid down in the 'Discipline', the way of doing things endorsed by Yearly Meeting and recorded in the Book of Extracts. Public Friends, liberated by their monthly and yearly meetings, travelled the Quaker world. The establishment of a formal membership completed the framework, carrying with it the opportunity of securing compliance with collective testimonies by the sanction of disownment.

In this period some of the hallowed Quaker phrases and circumlocutions came into being, and many of them stemmed from its characteristic spirituality. In prayer and at meeting the 'creaturely' impulses had to be curbed and overcome. The soul needed to be made open and receptive to intimations of God. Thus, Friends were advised to 'centre down' or 'dwell deep' or simply 'be low' or wait for 'pure leadings'. 'Pure' is a key word, as it was much earlier with the Puritans, carrying connotations of experiences or messages untainted by human faculties. We must not search – purity comes through waiting.

The writings of Woolman are full of this kind of expression – pure Truth, pure Wisdom, pure guidance of the Holy Spirit, pure flowings of divine Love. New expressions for 'God' abound, adding greatly to the power of ministry – the Author of our Being, The Inward Teacher, the Inward Monitor, the Source of Unerring Wisdom, pure Principle. Satan was not forgotten – he became the enemy of all Righteousness or the author of all Evil. These phrases are interesting because the ministers combined them with a highly biblical imagery. If they were originally devised out of a feeling of reverence, they served a different kind of spirituality also. Impersonal phraseology allowed rationalists and others to construe them as referring to some other entity than the God and Father of our Lord Jesus Christ, which was not the intention at all. It is possible that they helped to promote that looseness toward scripture which prevented Quakerism from renewing its original theology when faced with the challenge of precise biblical forms of expression as it came under the influence of the evangelical revival.

Ministers were apprehensive lest they speak for themselves rather than God. If they tried to decide whether they were called to speak, they 'turned the fleece' as Gideon did to ascertain God's will. Alternatively they dug for springs. If they were not moved, the cloud remained on the tabernacle. When they were on their feet they had two fears, outrunning the guide by saying too much, or withholding more than was meet by not saying enough. The effect of this fastidious separation of creaturely activity from divine leadings was an exaltation of silence, and the trend to silence rather than ministry as the basis of meeting. In 1770, for example, Dr John Rutty records that in Dublin there were twenty-two successive silent meetings with only one break for spoken ministry.

These principles were expressed in the pattern of Friends' daily life also, for the testimonies of the Society were in deep harmony with its manner of worship. The heathen names of the days of the week and the months were naturally avoided as they had been by the radical Puritans, and as they still are in more scrupulous Quaker circles. Plain speech carried important implications about the relative importance of divine and human values. Plain dress likewise, and this is perhaps the most outwardly attractive side of traditional Quakerism. Friends contrasted simplicity, which was natural, with the dictates of fashion, which was worldly, and therefore to be avoided. Thus, they wore clothes that became a costume, a uniform, even, in dull colours such as grey, without lapels or unnecessary frills and buttons. As the eighteenth century progressed, their appearance became distinctive.

As Charles Lamb observed later, 'The very garments of a Quaker seem incapable of receiving a soil; and cleanliness in them to be something more than the absence of its contrary. Every Quakeress is a lily; and when they come up in bands to their Whitsun conferences, whitening the easterly streets of the metropolis from all parts of the United Kingdom, they show like troops of the shining ones.' One suspects that the simplicity and harmony of Quaker dress was more attractive to some observers than to some who were obliged to wear it – and it is clear that numbers did not.

In 1718 Yearly Meeting cautioned parents that clothing their children with 'gaudy apparel' may well lead to such a 'habitual devotion to vanity and finery that it may be found very difficult to restrain them.' One sympathises, and reflects that modern Quaker parents often have the same problem of restraint without the additional burden of plain dress.

Nor was every Quakeress a lily. Too many women, thundered the Advice, were going about 'with gold chains, lockets, necklaces and gold watches exposed to open view which shows more of pride and ostentation than for use and service, besides their vain imitation of that immodest fashion of going with naked necks and breasts, and wearing of hooped petticoats.'

The most risible offence was male: 'But to our grief we find too many of our young men, instead of observing that gospel exhortation to be sober minded, have given way to lightness and vanity and the pernicious effects thereof have led them into pride so that some have cut off good heads of hair and put on long extravagant and gay wigs which they that are not in profession with us see as a mark of declension from our primitive plainness.'

By 1798 the declension had proceeded so far as to allow two new words to be added to the Quaker vocabulary to take account of the fact. Friends who observed the regulations with punctiliousness came to be known as 'plain Friends' and to adopt the dress was a sign of seriousness of purpose in the religious life. On the other hand there were many who were unprepared to accept the consequences of disownment for marrying out, but were willing to flout the plainness rules, which did not carry that penalty. Such people were known as 'gay Friends', and in the year in question would seem to have been in a majority, at any rate in the staunch Quaker town of Norwich.

Recalling his visit, the American travelling minister William Savery remarks, 'I thought it the gayest Meeting of Friends I ever sat in, and was grieved to see it . . . The marks of wealth and grandeur are too obvious in several families of Friends in this place, which made me sorrowful . . .' Yet Savery's preaching had an effect he had not realised. In front of him, resplendent in purple boots laced with scarlet, defiant but troubled, sat the daughter of one of these eminent families, Betsy Gurney of Earlham Hall, known later to the world as Elizabeth Fry, who was destined to be converted, and turned into a plain Friend by this same melancholy evangelist. We shall see how she and her brother came to occupy important places in the early Victorian Society of Friends.

Life at Earlham was congenial. The old house was low, rambling and stately, full of interesting corners. A great avenue of lime trees threw cool green light through the windows. Nearby flowed a river where Betsy's brother, Joseph John Gurney, made the acquaintance of George Borrow, who was later to portray him in the pages of *Lavengro* as the Quaker who quotes scripture against the gentle pleasures of angling. It was natural that Friends, including the Quaker gentry such as the Gurneys, with their broad acres, should refuse to take part in field sports. This departure from the common pattern of enjoyment included cards and other games of chance, and extended to milder recreations, too, notably the practice and enjoyment of the arts.

Denial of the Arts

If the gay Friends were as numerous as Savery implies that they were, the prohibitions were more honoured in the breach than the observance. One could probably quietly but not notoriously offend against Friends' undoubted testimonies in these matters. Reading between the lines one can compare the personalities of the woman whose appeal to Yearly Meeting against her disownment for giving her children music lessons was turned down, and the elderly convinced Friend who, unable to bear life entirely without his flute, climbed the Monument once a year to play it as his concession to his own weakness and an unintended tribute to the watchfulness of elders.

It might seem perverse of Friends to take these attitudes, but they did not do so out of a misplaced sense of self-denial or a shallow philistinism. They did not object to singing as such, but thought that what you sang affected you by stirring up your emotions. Since the contemporary repertoire contained many old favourites concerned with the adventures and misadventures of love, feats of arms, alcoholic conviviality or the exhilarations of the field (e.g. 'Just as the Sun was rising', 'The British Grenadiers', 'John Barleycorn', 'A-hunting we will go') they quite reasonably concluded that such things were unsuitable for Friends.

They were equally strict with instrumental music. They recognised that it could excite pleasant, benevolent, tranquil and sociable sentiments and very rarely the reverse. Nevertheless, they thought that mastery of an instrument required more time than was justified, at the expense of more important sides of life, and that the desire for excellence placed one in spiritual danger. They also, oddly, argued that sitting down for long periods instead of getting exercise was harmful.

The other arts were to be avoided too. The theatre, particularly, was considered to have the capacity to harm the personality. The art of acting is based on impersonation. Friends were unhappy with this, for it could not be sincere to express a grief or happiness one did not feel and one only had to look at the lives of actors and actresses to see the sort of damage such insincerity could do. Actually, this is very close to the testimony against oaths. The playhouse and the courthouse are not so very far apart.

Since tragedy was usually martial, and comedy hurtful, the morality of the theatre was not considered strictly conformable enough to the standards of the gospel. The visual arts were open to the same objections. It was said that there were only three pictures you might encounter if you moved among Friends, Benjamin West's engraving of William Penn's treaty with the Indians, the *Interior of a Slave Ship*, and the *Plan of the Building of Ackworth School*. You often saw one. You sometimes saw two. You never saw three. And novels were out.

Friends tended to justify their position by the argument from the extreme case – that because a habit can lead to seriously harmful consequences, it should be avoided completely. This sort of view tends to become entangled with a position that is absolutist on principle and avoids all niceties of moral judgement. However, Friends were not making rules for society at large, but for their own Society, and they treated the question of the arts with great seriousness.

They recognised that artistic expression is not neutral in the world of values, and if it has good effects, it can have bad effects too. It is the power to move and change people that distinguishes art from trivia. If they were right in this judgement, they were half way to justifying their position. It follows, therefore, that some sort of critical standards will have to be applied to reach a balanced judgement as to the goodness or badness of artistic output. One might follow them that far too. But the question was, what standards? Friends with a 'high religious profession' would only tolerate the standards of the gospel as they understood them, and in a licentious age found that the arts did not meet those standards. We may not share the reasoning of our spiritual ancestors, but if we are serious about our Quakerism we can appreciate why they thought as they did, and perhaps even grant that they had a very good case.

But this is to put their philosophy in a purely negative way. Underlying their attitudes to the arts and also education and the moral life was a view of how you should occupy your time, a fundamental conviction about what you are here for and how your life should be lived. Perhaps only the old really know how short the span of a human life is; it is certain the young do not. Those in middle years are usually in process of learning and it was to this process that the Discipline was ideally addressed. To be sure of eternity, one should rest in God. One could rest in God by inward retirement with Friends in Meeting or alone in prayer.

Inward retirement was not a knack or a trick, it was an experience and a discipline built up over years of practice and it was what distinguished the Quakers of the eighteenth century. Some non-Friends have seen the Society with its peculiarities and its testimonies as an 'order' within the Church to which one has a vocation, and which expresses such vocations in its distinctive ways. If that is the case, the quietist Quaker attitude to the arts falls into its true perspective. It was not a prohibition to be endured, but a privilege to be enjoyed, the better to worship the Lord in the beauty of holiness to be found in silent communion within.

Birthright Membership and the Book of Extracts

The Society of Friends has always regarded inward experience of God as the only true religion and has always sought to distinguish the reality of the experience from its outward form of expression. That is the basis of the Quaker suspicion of sacraments. On the other hand, convincement has always been seen as a spiritual baptism, and joining oneself to the body of Friends means accepting responsibilities, for membership arises when the individual and the group recognise that they belong together. In the earliest period there was no problem. The test of your convincement was your willingness to accept the penalties of nonconformity – imprisonment, impoverishment, conceivably death – if they came your way. This was mitigated after 1689, but adoption of the testimonies of plainness, peace and tithe-refusal could still mean hardship. People knew by your behaviour, or conversation (as it was called) whether or not you were a Quaker.

For the first eighty years of its existence, the Society of Friends saw no particular need for a formal membership to say who was *in*, though a procedure of disownment existed that could be operated to say who was *out*. Actually, both Friends and 'the World' had a pretty clear understanding of what was what. In the times of persecution it was important to know who were Friends in good standing, for there were important testimonies to be witnessed to, and the whole society by its pastoral care and financial contributions supported those who were suffering on its behalf. Clearly they had to know who were the eccentrics or the carpet-baggers, and it is highly likely that many monthly meetings had records indicating who was entitled to support, and therefore, *ipso facto*, who belonged. Things were far less clear as the religious temper cooled after toleration, and formal membership was instituted to deal with a pastoral, not a doctrinal, emergency.

The origins of the word 'disownment' will help us to see how this came about. The earliest Friends were anxious to maintain the purity of their own standards against 'the World' and were vigilant lest any known Quaker depart from them. There are instances of Quaker drunkenness, lying, fornication, marriage to 'one of the World' or 'by the Priest' and sundry other malefactions. If the Friend repented, the procedure was for the offender to publish a paper in the community making it clear that the misdeeds were offensive to Friends' principles. This procedure was entirely similar to that of the other dissenting churches, who also faced these problems.

This was done to 'clear Truth' not to humiliate the offender. It provided an opportunity for the Society to 'disown' disorderly conduct. It is extremely rare for the record books to reveal any disciplinary proceeding about matters of doctrine. We are dealing with the ordinary pressures of life, and about the way some Friends found it impossible to resist them without compromising their profession of Truth. They accepted admonition not because they were on a list, but simply because they felt they belonged. At first that was good enough.

Later, though, the demands of organisation had to be faced. If a Friend died, there had to be a burial and that required land which had to be owned by somebody. The deceased Friend might have left a sum of money or some property to be administered, that could produce income for education, or to provide for the poor, or to support the travelling ministry. So necessarily trustees had to be appointed and the spiritual community of Friends developed into a corporate body. Trustees carried out their responsibilities on behalf of 'Friends' and the general law required to know, quite reasonably, who 'Friends' were. The answer that was given at first was in terms of the mutual recognition that underpinned the Discipline.

As time went by, problems arose, particularly where applications were received by poor Friends for financial assistance. Without a membership list or qualification, the question arose whether the person was sufficiently closely associated with Friends to qualify, bearing in mind that trustees, like executors under a will, commit a breach of trust to the other beneficiaries if they misapply the funds, by giving money intended for Friends to non-Friends. The other problem was what to do when needy Friends from one area moved to another. Which monthly meeting should be responsible? It was obviously possible for Friends in centres of population to bear a disproportionate financial burden unless these matters were cleared up.

A number of attempts to codify Friends' practice were made before Yearly Meeting in 1737 issued nine guidelines that effectively settled matters and inadvertently started the institution of birthright membership. It ruled that (*inter alia*): (1) all Friends were to be deemed members of the quarterly or two weeks meeting within the area of which they resided on 1 June 1737; (2) monthly meetings were to be responsible for the relief of Friends in want except those who were properly in the charge of some other meeting; (3) to minimise disagreement under the second head, Friends had to have a certificate before they moved, addressed to the monthly meeting of the area to which they were going; (4) if they were accepted (it seems) there had to be three years' residence before complete responsibility passed from the old to the new meeting; (5) wives and children were deemed members of their husband's or father's meeting. It is interesting to note that to this day the Discipline of Britain Yearly Meeting does not provide for automatic transfer. It would be in perfectly right ordering for one monthly meeting to grant a certificate of removal but for another with good reason to refuse it.

As Sir Henry Maitland remarked, substantive law is often secreted in the interstices of procedure, and the story of the development of the institutions of eighteenth-century Quakerism is as illustrative of that principle as is the medieval common law. The most important point to note about these rules is that they did not address themselves to the problem of who was a member, but to where membership was held. Failure to grasp this subtlety meant that in the subsequent generations Friends misread what had been done, and imagined that they had been bequeathed a certain kind of church organisation, when in fact they had not.

As we have seen, all sects have the problem of how to extend membership to children, who have not had the fiery convincement of the first generation. The Quakers simply sidestepped the problem by enrolling children by virtue of their birth in the same way that the Anglicans baptised all the infants of the parish. That cannot have been the intention in 1737, but it was certainly the effect. It shifted the whole basis of oversight and pastoral care to the family, rather than the individual, with everything that entailed.

The first and most obvious effect was that as time went by there grew up a class of habitual birthright Quakers, distinguished by adherence rather than commitment. It has been estimated from Yearly Meeting records that there were three disownments for every two convincements, and that by 1750 the overwhelming majority of Friends, perhaps eighty per cent, were birthright members. Accordingly, the Quaker engine went into reverse. The mighty rushing wind of the Methodist revival swept through the eighteenth century as the Quaker revival had shaken its predecessor. After an initial welcome, Friends came to perceive correctly that the evangelical zeal of the Methodists was inimical to their own principles and security. So they closed ranks behind their birthright membership and began to reassess their position as no longer an apostolic missionary church, but a peculiar people, kept apart from the world as a sort of spiritual aristocracy.

They thus missed the opportunity of a great influx of new life. Their positive response was to develop what they called the Quaker 'tradition', what they felt to be best in what they had inherited, and the work of ministers became largely an attempt to articulate what this tradition was, and to complain that people did not live up to it. That it could easily become purely habitual we can see in an incident recorded well before the 1737 regulations. At Brigflatts Meeting Anne Wilson stared accusingly at Sam Bownas and said, 'A traditional Quaker; thou comest to meeting as thou went from it, and goes from it as thou came to it, but art no better for thy coming; what wilt thou do in the end?' The reply might well have been, 'Form a majority' if we accept the implications of William Savery's words in 1798.

Throughout the century, ministers laid great stress on Friends' neglect of their tradition, and this can only be interpreted as the appropriate response to a lukewarm body. One of the favourite texts of the preachers of the period was Amos 6:1, 'Woe to those who are at ease in Zion'. The 'Tradition', then, is what gave the eighteenth-century Society its roots, its cohesion and its sense of identity. We have seen how it gained expression in a distinctive way of life and we now have to turn to the institutions which actually translated the tradition into a culture – the Discipline, the Ministry, and the corps of elders and overseers.

As the Society of Friends moved into its quietist phase, it acquired an outward unity it did not enjoy in its earlier, controversial years. The 'Discipline' was a generic name for the rules of Quaker church order and the religious principles to which Friends were expected to conform. The idea behind it was discipleship and in seeking to understand the institution one should lay aside any unpleasant connotations the word may now have.

From earliest times, Yearly Meeting had been accustomed to address 'Queries' to subordinate meetings. These were simply requests for information, originally largely statistical, about the number of deaths, convincements, imprisonments and distraints on property which had occurred since the previous such enquiry had been made. Gradually, this device was used to obtain information about the spiritual condition of the Society also, and meetings were expected to deliberate and return written answers to superior meetings all the way up to Yearly Meeting. Thus, the Queries became an instrument of control, for the questions implied what the acceptable answer was, and thus came to be a good indicator of what Quaker values were.

So the Yearly Meeting emerged as a curious legislative body which became more concerned with the internal management of the Society than its relations with the wider world. It had always issued advice to Friends, arbitrated their disputes, encouraged their concerns, warned them of their failings, reminded them of their responsibilities and sought to bring to their attention what it considered good Quaker practice to be. This was done partly by 'Epistle' – a specially composed collective letter – and partly by minute, but was never done systematically. Gradually, the spiritual aspect of these pronouncements came to be known as the 'Advices', although they were not collected separately and combined with the Queries till much later. The contemporary 'Advices and Queries' of Britain Yearly Meeting were first drafted in their present form in 1824, during the Society's evangelical period.

Feeling the need of regular, consistent and authoritative guidance in a comprehensive and accessible form, Yorkshire Friends petitioned Yearly Meeting in 1735 to prepare an abstract of minutes and rules issued at various times for the guidance of the whole Society, to be presented under the various appropriate headings. The matter was passed to Meeting for Sufferings, who appointed an inevitable committee which set to work to choose the necessary extracts from the records. The draft was returned to Yearly Meeting in 1738.

Agreement was reached, and copies were ordered to be made and sent to quarterly meetings at the expense of the counties in the then princely sum of fifty shillings. Yorkshire's suggestion of printing was passed over, presumably because so few copies were deemed to be required, and the book was put out in manuscript. Westmorland is recorded to have paid up promptly. Twelve years later Herefordshire was still procrastinating and there is no record that Friends there ever came across with their money. A number of these books are still in existence. They are written in a beautifully uniform copperplate hand and are arranged alphabetically under heads. There are blank pages for additions should Yearly Meeting direct, and they are commonly referred to in two ways. The title reads *Christian and Brotherly Advices given forth from time to time by the Yearly Meeting in London*, but they were commonly called the Book of Extracts for that is what they were.

The written book may have been an improvement on haphazard and personal collections of authoritative material, but it was not received with universal rapture, quite apart from meetings' reluctance to part with their cash. There was difficulty in making sure the books were kept up to date. Some minutes did not arrive and were therefore not included. Different counties inserted minutes under different heads. Essex tried to propose their own abstract as superior, and were turned down. Yearly Meeting of 1762 had to order the preparation of fresh volumes and the updating of existing ones, entering additional advices, fresh regulations and new queries. The clerks had the books and it was difficult, and in some places impossible, to get sight of them. They almost became *arcana* – 'the great green dragon of the ancients' as one Friend put it, referring to the green vellum that was one of the original bindings.

But the effect was achieved. The Book of Extracts contained the rules, and they were ascertainable. The next development was democracy. In competition with the 1762 issue John Fry issued a slightly more comprehensive pirate printed edition of his own, and followed it with a second edition in 1766. As Yorkshire Friends had earlier pushed for the issue of a book, Durham Friends now pressed for a printed book, emphasising the chancy and haphazard nature of the entry system.

Ultimately, in 1782 they got what they wanted. Yearly Meeting published the book (1) so that each subordinate meeting might have a complete and correct collection of the documents issued to regulate the affairs of the Society, (2) so that by being more generally known these regulations might be more uniformly observed, (3) so that young

Friends might be early and fully instructed in Friends' principles, and (4) 'That the unfaithful, the immoral and the libertine professors may be seasonably reminded of their danger and their duty'. In 1783 the Book was printed and available for purchase. In 1792 an appendix appeared, and in 1802 the second edition. By 1834 the Society was moving away from quietism, and one benchmark of this trend is the now evangelical tone of the third, 1834, edition.

Throughout the Quaker world Books of Discipline are still produced. They vary with the history and theology of the different yearly meetings but they still perform their traditional function of summarising and stating what Friends are committed to. There was a much greater uniformity of belief and practice in the eighteenth century, and if it was based on 'Truth' as articulated by Barclay, it was applied and developed by that extraordinary body of men and women, the 'Recorded' Ministers.

Public Friends and Recorded Ministry

There have always been Quaker ministers. Friends are no different from other Christians in believing that the ability to answer to the spiritual needs of others is a gift of the Holy Spirit, rather than a species of purely human sensitivity. Accordingly, they have always expected the call to preaching, teaching or pastoral care to emerge within their number, and again, like other denominations, have developed distinctive ways of nourishing it. The Quaker approach to ministry is most clearly illustrated in the many Journals, or spiritual autobiographies, that the great ministers left behind. So numerous are these works that we might almost call them a distinctive Quaker art-form.

Their influence was profound. In an age when the range of reading matter available to young Friends was severely limited by the Discipline, the need of even Friendly imaginations for adventure, romance, heroism and reassurance had to be met. The Journals, and the presence of the ministers themselves, set a pattern for what it meant to be a serious Friend. From the Journals we can build up a composite or characteristic picture of the way in which the ministerial vocation developed. Many writers report distinct childhood experiences of God – a spirit of love, not a censorious arbiter of fate, though this is not usually coupled with any feelings of intimacy or indulgence on God's part. It is as if the person became aware of a built-in confidence that in the end everything is all right.

Many of these experiences occurred out of doors or in solitude, and were shaped by the community's practice of silent and expectant waiting and its perspective on the Bible. William Penn, in *No Cross, No Crown* for example, emphasised Christ's habit of seeking refreshment and communion with his Heavenly Father 'in gardens, by the sea side and in lonely places'. One brought up on the stories of Elijah need only hide in a rocky place for the possibility of hearing a still small voice to be very real.

In adolescence, predictably, a period of doubt, temptation or despair was experienced and the pilgrim spirit came through to convincement with a knowledge of the mysterious and dreadful side of religious seeking, a disguise, as it were, of the soul's companion. Then a settled pattern of life emerged. The young Friend adopted plainness and the testimonies, became faithful in attendance at meetings, married, and entered fully into the life of the Society. Thus, the Quaker way came to be experienced in maturity as something infinitely precious, but at this stage a further highly unwelcome stage of turmoil might develop.

As we have seen, the quietist religious discipline was to still all creaturely thought and activity so that the voice of God could be heard in the soul. The effort of distinguishing the divine voice from the creaturely one was hard enough, but the prospect of being moved to speak in meeting was something most people viewed with little short of horror. So, as the call was faintly heard, the new Quaker ministers ran a whole gamut of highly uncomfortable emotions. They were afraid lest their call was not genuine, and some wrestled silently for years with this difficulty. They report occasions when they should have spoken and did not, and are filled with remorse and despair at what they considered to be their disobedience.

Eventually they rose to speak, and over a period of ministering they came to learn their own strengths and weaknesses, learned to match the appropriate length of time to the weight of what they had to say, learned, as far as they were able, to yield up all the abilities and accomplishments they possessed that might make Friends pay attention to them as people, rather than to the message of testimony, prophecy, preaching, exhortation, encouragement, comfort, inspiration or warning that they might deliver as ministers of Christ.

There is a famous Quaker painting entitled *The Presence in the Midst*. It portrays a silent meeting at Jordans, in Buckinghamshire, where William Penn and his family are buried. Friends in traditional plain dress worship peacefully, women and children on one side, men on the other. Elders preside from their gallery. On the facing bench, a dim figure emerges from the play of sunlight entering from the high windows. Christ stands, a real presence in the meeting, speaking to his gathered flock.

The scene is a vignette of the quietist understanding of ministry. Though there must be preaching of the word and opening of the scriptures, these things are not dependent on human will. Though articulated by human voice and understanding, the words must come from God alone. The present day finds it hard to make this sharp distinction between human and divine and seeks to assimilate the two in all kinds of ways. But the quietist conception was not translatable into contemporary idiom. The gift of ministry was dreaded, and those to whom it came became the acknowledged leaders of the Society.

Friends differ over the desirability of the direction the Society took in the eighteenth century. Some (*anti*) say that a movement hardened into an organisation and this is how the pristine power and fire of Quakerism was lost. Others (*pro*) say that it is largely the result of tendencies that had existed from the beginning, and that in any case the pristine power and fire was not totally desirable, and that Friends achieved maturity in their quietist phase. There is a little of the truth of both these viewpoints in the way the institution of ministry developed.

We saw earlier how the Society was built up by itinerant preachers called 'Public Friends' and how one of their tasks was the settlement of meetings that could release the gifts of ministry in others. Thus we can draw a loose distinction between Friends who travelled in the ministry and those who stayed at home to care for their local meetings. Members of both groups preached and spoke in meeting but at this time they also did other work that later came to be the specialised occupation of elders, and still later of overseers. When the century began the word 'minister' had a loose connotation. It gained in precision as the century wore on. Again, administrative chance was largely responsible.

Since 1673, all ministering Friends who happened to be in London were expected to attend the Second Day Morning Meeting, as we have already seen. In 1722, one William Gibson arrived and entered his name, as was the custom, in the book provided to record those attending. He was unacceptable to the meeting and the controversy that followed was

resolved by Yearly Meeting deciding that it was only the properly constituted monthly, quarterly and yearly meetings that could disown a
minister. No Friend was entitled thereafter to be entered in the book
as a minister unless he or she produced a certificate from a monthly or
quarterly meeting. Morning Meeting promptly requested lists of recognised ministers, and, as in the case of membership, the foundation had
been laid for an institution.

Ministry, then, was the recognition of a gift rather than the grant-
ing of an ecclesiastical status. In due course, granted sound doctrine,
a blameless life and a lengthy seasoning in Friends' ways, the name
of the person who had received the call was 'recorded', normally by
monthly meeting. Most ministers stopped in the line of development at
this point, belonging to their monthly meeting and attending monthly
and quarterly meetings of ministers and elders and possibly, after 1754,
the newly constituted Yearly Meeting of Ministers and Elders held on
a representative basis. Many, however, felt a further call to travel in the
ministry and this practice, universal in the Quaker world, provided
the means whereby a unity of practice and profession was maintained
wherever Friends settled, in the New World or the Old.

One well-travelled minister of the period was John Churchman
(1705–1777) of Nottingham, Pennsylvania, whom we have already
noticed as a fellow labourer with Woolman in stiffening the life and
witness of Philadelphia in the crisis years in the middle of the century.
He describes the call to travel: 'And one day, walking alone, I felt myself
so inwardly weak and feeble, that I stood still, and, by the reverence
that covered my mind, I knew that the hand of the Lord was on me, and
his presence round about: the earth was silent, and all flesh brought
into stillness, and light went forth with brightness and shone on Great
Britain, Ireland, and Holland, and my mind felt the gentle, yet strongly
drawing cords of that love which is stronger than death, which made
me say, "Lord! Go before, and strengthen me and I will follow whither-
soever thou leadest."'

As in the case of the original call to the ministry, the call to travel
could not be denied, and the Friend under concern first laid the matter
before monthly meeting, whose approval and blessing was expressed
in the travelling minute, a letter of recommendation to all Friends
and meetings the travelling minister might encounter, to be endorsed
by them and ultimately to be returned to the meeting. It was, and is,
the proudest passport a Quaker can carry. The specific objectives of a

journey were seldom clear, beyond the urge to meet and minister to whatever spiritual needs the Friend might come across in the people he or she encountered.

This involved addressing meetings among Friends or with 'the World'. It meant living with remote Quaker groups, and making pastoral visits to families in the congregation, or to prisons, or to political leaders. It involved, on occasion, hardship, danger and uncertainty. It involved travail of soul, for the minister was often obliged to forsake family, business and even country, to travel to far places with no certainty that, on arrival, the gift of words would be given. Above all it was for an uncertain season; as the call to go had come, the call to return would mysteriously only be heard when the work was accomplished in God's good time.

The world is sceptical of inner guidance of this kind. What is open-eyed dependence on Providence to one, is a blind and foolish faith to another. But however we view the psychology of the travelling ministers, they lived in total dependence on what they understood as God's will. Their support and maintenance was a charge on the communities among whom they travelled. They preserved the unity of Friends when it mattered, but, as we shall see, a later generation set in train the developments which fragmented the Society in America, and which in Britain preserved unity at the price of diversity.

Tightening the Discipline

The last piece of the jigsaw puzzle of classical Quakerism is the arrangements made by the Society for pastoral care. For many years it was the practice to appoint 'weighty and sensible Friends of unblameable conversation' to visit families whenever it was felt to be necessary. In America and Ireland, such Friends were known as elders at the turn of the century and they were distinguishable from ministers. John Churchman, for example, resigned his eldership when he felt the call to the ministry and was recorded. London Yearly Meeting in 1727 resolved to ask all monthly meetings to appoint serious, discreet and judicious Friends who were not ministers to accept responsibility for encouraging and helping young ministers and in due course to admit suitable Friends to meetings of ministers and elders.

Since sound ministry is the key to sound worship, this responsibility was clearly important to a general care for the spiritual life of the whole meeting, and these two things became the formal duties of elders and were the subject of suitable Advices. The elders were generally quietly authoritative – they did not minister, though they brought their considerable influence to bear on those who did. They guarded the traditions of the whole Society in the localities, and have been criticised for their conservative temper. This may be harsh, but the interaction of ministers and elders in the quietist phase produced harmony, continuity and a beautiful wholeness of life. It is perhaps a justifiable criticism that stillness can easily become inertia, and the Society was not properly equipped to deal with the epoch-making social and intellectual changes that were going on around it.

The position of elders as spiritual overseers of the ministry was strengthened in the middle of the century as other Friends were given moral oversight of the membership. Actually, the function of pastoral oversight had been carried on at least since the 1690s, but it had never been put on a formal basis.

In 1755, a Yearly Meeting minute considering answers to the Queries added a new one enquiring whether each particular meeting in fact had two or more Friends charged specifically with oversight, and in 1789 it was finally laid down that the offices of elder and overseer were distinct, and that overseers were not entitled to sit in meetings of ministers and elders. There was thus established a spiritual aristocracy within a wider spiritual aristocracy with a steadily declining membership. The effects were profound.

As we have seen, the Discipline was codified in 1738 and the responses to the Queries thereafter seem to have generated a continuous mood of disquiet about the state of the Society among leading Friends. Information about worldly activities in the country at large filtered through to Yearly Meeting, and a series of minutes and epistles exhorted Friends to return to their primitive plainness and piety. We know now that the Society was in numerical decline but this factor seems to have escaped contemporary Friends. They were far more concerned with what they conceived to be the widening gap between practice and profession, hence the quite rapid development of the tripartite system of elders, overseers and ministers and the application of the Discipline as a rule of church government.

By 1760 this pessimism had proceeded so far that a thoroughgoing review of the operation of the Discipline was carried out by Yearly Meeting. Indeed, so significant is this date, that some commentators see it as the watershed of the period, the time when the tendencies of the first part of the century came to maturity and the foundations were secured on which the classical institutions and spirituality of Quakerism were to rest. A committee was set up to undertake a widespread visitation. Fifty-eight Friends agreed to serve. Meetings were held with all the quarterly meetings and reports returned to Yearly Meeting. The importance of the procedures and the reasons for the Discipline were emphasised, and though there was a considerable tightening-up, the Yearly Meeting epistles continued their tone of lament over declining standards. It is interesting to speculate, therefore, whether the complaints really do reflect a low period in the Society's history, or whether (as some alleged) they proceeded from a spirit of intolerant misunderstanding. One book, written partly to support the official position, was criticised as containing 'maxims of ecclesiastical slavery'.

Similar conditions and attitudes existed in America. It is conceivable that many of the problems which beset the Society on both sides of the Atlantic during the nineteenth century have their origin at this time. The powers granted to the elders to enforce the Discipline proved to be a two-edged sword. On the one hand they were the mechanism whereby slave-owning ultimately became a disownable offence. On the other hand, supervision of personal conduct almost inevitably shades off into supervision of the beliefs that support that conduct. We shall see that with the passage of time the yearly meetings in both Britain and America were racked by a series of disownments, secessions and separations. Whatever the formal cause of these troubles, one very significant influence in all cases is resentment at the way elders carried out their duties.

John Fothergill and Others

It is strange that one of the Friends most closely involved with these moves was one of the most cultivated and liberal men of his time, Dr John Fothergill (1712–1780). He was born at Carr End, Wensleydale, son of a farmer who had travelled in the ministry to the American colonies on three occasions. John was apprenticed to an apothecary at Bradford and then went on to graduate in medicine from Edinburgh University. In 1740 he settled in London near Gracechurch Street Meeting House and began to practise as a physician.

Such were his talents that he made a large fortune. He was quick, shrewd and businesslike. Benjamin Franklin alleged that there were people who had crossed the Atlantic just to consult him, and it was enough to put 'Dr Fothergill, London' on a letter to have it delivered correctly. Fothergill was passionately devoted to the art of healing and to scientific enquiry. Though he did not make any long-term contribution to medicine at a theoretical level, he is remembered as a great practitioner.

He came to London at a time when there was a great interest in botany. As a trained apothecary he had an insight into the medical use of plants and herbs. Part of his success can be traced to his precise observations in an age when there were few other scientific techniques open to doctors. He began to base diagnosis on scientific principles and this led him to try to simplify current methods of treatment and prescription by the use of more straightforward remedies.

He became involved with importing exotic seeds and plants and moved in the society of others with similar interests, notably the great Quaker botanist Peter Collinson FRS, through whose introduction, presumably, he became a correspondent of Linnaeus. In 1762 he moved out to Essex, to Upton House, where he cultivated a magnificent garden, full of beautiful, curious and useful plants from all over the world. He tried many experiments, including that of trying to domesticate tea in England. Sir Joseph Banks is on record as saying that no other garden in Europe had so many rare and valuable plants. House and greenhouse have gone, but there is still a fine garden on the site which is now a part of West Ham Park.

The Royal College of Physicians was the leading professional body in medicine in Fothergill's time. The Test Acts confined fellowship of this body to members of the established church, and that came to mean graduates of Oxford and Cambridge. Others, mainly from the prestigious medical faculties of Leyden and Edinburgh were only licensed by the College to practise. The body of licentiates came to include many of the more eminent members of the medical profession, but their religious affiliation denied them a part in its management. Fothergill was involved in a long-running and ultimately unsuccessful attempt to reform this abuse. He eventually had to take the step of setting up a rival body, which, of course, had to remain unofficial. In 1767, the Society of Licentiate Physicians came into being for the purpose of reading papers and keeping up with the latest scientific and medical discoveries.

Fothergill made his reputation in 1748 through the publication of his account of the epidemic of scarlet fever the year before, and the means he used to combat it. He wrote a number of papers on topics such as influenza, the management of the menopause, obesity, angina pectoris, epilepsy, constipation and the use of emetics. His professional reputation was such that he became president of the Royal College of Physicians of Edinburgh in 1754, and a Fellow of the Royal Society in 1763. He was not only a writer in his own field, but an editor in others. He was personally responsible for seeing Anthony Purver's translation of the Bible through the press. He was also involved with the production of an edition of the select *Works* of William Penn, and the famous Baskerville edition of Barclay's *Apology*. These Quakerly books were quite apart from a number of botanic and other scientific works in which he had a hand.

As one would have expected, Fothergill was active in a variety of social concerns during this period. One of his wide circle of Friends was the prison reformer John Howard. To assist his campaigns, Fothergill gave evidence before the House of Commons on the health of prisoners. When he died, he was engaged in the supervision of an experiment to set up two penitentiaries in London on the most up-to-date principles. Though initially suspicious, Fothergill warmed to John Woolman on his appearance in London, and, naturally, took part in the anti-slavery agitation.

Through the three visits of his father, and the ministerial visit of his brother Samuel in 1754–6, Fothergill had a strong attachment to America. He served on the Pennsylvania Committee of Meeting for Sufferings, and his Quaker and scholarly interests combined to give him a wide knowledge of transatlantic affairs when ignorance of them was about to sever the connection of Britain with thirteen of her colonies. When the Seven Years' War broke out in 1756, Friends still controlled the Pennsylvania Assembly, and doggedly resisted attempts to defend the province. The non-Quaker population was united in its hostility to the Society, and a bill was prepared at Westminster to disqualify Friends from the Assembly entirely. Friends were privy to this proposal and Fothergill wrote to James Pemberton pointing out that retirement from the Assembly at this juncture might preserve Quaker influence in the province in the future, for insistence on remaining might mean the abolition of the Assembly as they knew it. This step meant the effective end of the Holy Experiment and, sadly, Friends had to take it.

Following the British victory in the war, which was concluded in 1763, the French threat was removed from the colonies, and independence became a realistic aim. One of its architects, Benjamin Franklin, came to London in 1757 as agent for the Pennsylvania Assembly in its negotiations with the Proprietors, the heirs of William Penn. Fothergill had already corresponded with him about his experiments with electricity. The two men had a great deal in common, and became great friends. This association provided the opportunity for one of the great historical might-have-beens. In 1774, as the Revolutionary War was about to break out, a proposal, probably emanating from the highest quarters in London, reached Fothergill, enquiring whether there was a possibility of working out a durable scheme of agreement between Britain and the colonies which would avert the war. Franklin was thus drawn into negotiations by the Quaker doctor, and a serious attempt made to work out an acceptable compromise. It was unsuccessful, but it shows another side of the character of this extraordinary Friend.

As a concerned Friend, John Fothergill played an active part in the affairs of the Society. Though he never felt the call to the ministry, unlike his brother, he was an elder, and one of the most influential Yearly Meeting Friends of his time. He was clerk of Yearly Meeting in 1749, 1764 and 1779, and was noted for the succinctness and weight of his minutes. He served on the Visitation Committee that attempted to strengthen the Discipline in the years after 1760 and he and Samuel contributed the article on Quakerism for the first edition of the *Encyclopaedia Britannica*.

The attempt to revive the Society did not confine itself to organisational matters and an inquisition into the spiritual lives of Friends. On the constructive side, it led to an increasing concern for education. For some years the Yearly Meeting had sought to impress upon Friends the value and importance of their schools, and the need for better educational provision. In 1777 Yearly Meeting began to look seriously at proposals for a national boarding school 'for the education of children whose parents are not in affluence'. It was John Fothergill who proposed the purchase of some vacant buildings near Pontefract, Yorkshire, which had previously been the home of the Foundling Hospital from London. He, William Tuke and others took the matter further, and in 1779 Ackworth School opened, taking children between the ages of seven and thirteen, and charging £8 per annum.

The success of so many Friends in the world outside their little Society was having long term effects. John Fothergill was part of what we might call the scientific establishment of his day, which included a number of other eminent Friends, many of whom were also fellows of the Royal Society. Jeremiah Dixon FRS is immortal. He was one half of the surveying team which drew the Mason–Dixon line, which settled the boundary between Maryland and Pennsylvania. South of this line, you all are in Dixie. George Graham FRS made important contributions to the equipment at Greenwich observatory.

In chemistry, a man of the next generation made a lasting contribution to scientific progress. John Dalton, a highly gifted child and autodidact, became Professor of Mathematics and Natural Philosophy (i.e. science) at the New College, Manchester, in 1793, when he was twenty-seven. From ancient times, it had been believed that there were fundamental constituents of matter which were conventionally called 'atoms'. It fell to John Dalton to demonstrate this mathematically, and to turn chemistry into an exact science. To him we owe our conceptions of the unalterable atomic weight of each element, and the principles according to which elements combine precisely to form compounds. There is a famous mural in Manchester Town Hall depicting Dalton siphoning marsh gas off a bog watched by a group of curious children.

Through science, medicine, trade and banking, Friends were achieving eminence, and enjoying stimulating professional lives outside the Society. It is ironic that in the second half of the eighteenth century an increasing internal rigidity in the Society of Friends should coincide with a much more relaxed social atmosphere outside it.

To some degree, Friends were suffering a natural reaction to their beginnings. As persecution lessened, so did ardour. As the founders slipped deeper into history, it became easier to live a life of outward conformity to the testimonies without an inward commitment; Quakerism had ceased to be experimental. So-called 'nominal Quakers' began to be noticed, and the problem of getting Friends to Meeting emerged.

The testimonies themselves had many ragged edges in an increasingly complex world, and Friends tended to use plain speech to each other, and the world's forms of address to everybody else. They saw no reason to avoid the innocent pleasures of entertainment and the arts. The convinced, and the leaders of the Society would easily see these things as a departure from tradition, which they were, but would never be able to face the possibility that perhaps they did not matter very much.

Methodism and Revival

To the outsider, there are many parallels between the emergence of Quakerism as a force in the seventeenth century, and the rise of Methodism in the eighteenth. Each is due in considerable measure to the work of one tough, energetic man of vision and deep spiritual experience. George Fox and John Wesley came from different stations in life, but each found, ultimately, that the church of his birth was too narrow to contain him. Each spent his life in bringing other people to Christ. Each in his way emulated Paul. Wesley was a great traveller for the faith, Fox was a great prisoner for it.

We have already seen how the older dissenting churches, including Friends, slipped into quietude at the end of the seventeenth century. Their main concern was for themselves rather than the world, and the mood of the times was against any display of emotion or enthusiasm in religion. The response of the churches to deism was to strengthen the rational and moral aspects of Christianity as against faith. This found expression in two ways. Parts of Dissent, including the Quakers, sought to cling on to their traditional worship as a safeguard against the confusion of change. They also came to feel that personal commitment and a lively concern for the salvation of one's soul was just a trifle vulgar.

The Augustan calm was shattered by the eighteenth-century evangelical revival and the rise of Methodism within the British Atlantic culture. Though it is most closely associated with John Wesley and George Whitefield, the first stirrings of revival occurred in the English colonies in America, in the work of Count Zinzendorf and the Moravians in Saxony, and in south and west Wales. Emotion and faith came flooding back into organised religion. As evangelical vigour created first the Methodist movement, and then the Methodist churches, the Church of England and Dissent could not remain unaffected. In each of the older denominations revival occurred and was contained within the tradition, often awkwardly. It came later to the Quakers and in a different form, but it was the same thing. Evangelicalism passed like a wave through the whole religious culture, and nothing remained undisturbed.

Undeniably, the Methodists and the early Quakers took the Great Commission more seriously than the other churches of Dissent and the national church itself. It was their *raison d' être*. As Friends began their period of withdrawal, the newer force took over as missionaries to the poor and builders of a religious fraternity of the outcast. Like their Quaker predecessors, the Methodists sent out travelling preachers to gather the harvest – they preached anywhere, in fields, on heaths, inside or outside with equal alacrity. The Methodists were noted for outbursts of emotionalism at their meetings and for a parallel we need look no further than the name 'Quaker'. Moreover, like the first publishers of Truth, the early Methodist preachers were often subjected to physical and verbal abuse. The religion they preached was, like the Quakers', based on personal experience and the inward witness of the Holy Spirit. The Methodist converts, like the early Friends, were possessed of an irrepressible joy. At first there was a minimum of organisation, and the institution of the class meeting and the lay preacher drew out and utilised the talents of those who would have remained passive members in a more formally structured church. The most distinctive feature the two movements had in common was that both George Fox and John Wesley taught a doctrine of Christian perfection.

There were also differences in doctrine between the two groups. Both preached the need for salvation, but they differed as to how it could be obtained. Friends had revolted against the strict Calvinism that prevailed at their beginnings and they had been forced to clarify their position in furious controversy with a mature Puritanism that was now very much a thing of the past. John Wesley was a non-Calvinist Anglican, and had a more balanced and traditional outlook, not needing to adopt such things as the extreme Quaker view on the scriptures. He was not a radical in the same sense that they were, and the fundamental distinction between Methodism and Quakerism should probably be drawn here.

In the period from 1739 to 1748 the Methodists began to make converts on a large scale, some from Friends. In turn, some Methodists became Quakers. There are a number of accounts of cordial relations between members of the two groups but gradually co-operation turned into rivalry. In 1748 Wesley published a pamphlet, *A Letter to a Person lately join'd with the People call'd Quakers*, which is largely an attack on Barclay's *Apology*, the standard exposition of Quakerism at the time. Later editions end with a summary that shows that Wesley understood clearly the basic incompatibility of his kind of evangelicalism and traditional Quakerism, singling out Barclay's treatment of scripture, justification, baptism and the Lord's Supper as taking Quakers outside what he understood Christianity to be. While attacking what he considered the weaknesses and dangers of Quakerism, Wesley maintained cordial relations with individual Friends, and in the period down to 1800 there was considerable mutual influence between the two groups.

The Friends' quarterly meeting and lay ministry has clear parallels among the Methodists, and it has been suggested that the emergence of the separate function of overseer among Friends owes something to the Methodist institution of class leader. At one time there was a group of congregations around Warrington who were actually called the 'Quaker Methodists'. While rejecting the testimonies of speech and dress as superficial, certainly in their regulatory form under the Discipline, many Methodists doubtless sympathised with what lay behind them. Wesley took an interest in the Quaker arrangements for children and the poor. He visited the institution at Bristol set up earlier under the inspiration of John Bellers, and was informed on the subject of the Quaker schools. It was largely the influence of Anthony Benezet of Philadelphia which brought him into the anti-slavery camp, and this fact may have had a considerable later influence on the course of the evangelical revival in its politically active phase in England.

The long-term effect of Methodism on the Quakers is hard to assess. Possibly the most obvious point is that had Friends remained an outward-looking evangelistic community, they would have appealed to the group which found its home in the newer spiritual movement. The marriage rules had already caused a significant decline in Quaker membership in the 1760s, and the trend continued. The policy of the Discipline was exclusive and not inclusive and it was to Methodism that the Quakers lost their chance to be a mass movement.

Then there is the vexed question of evangelicalism itself, which will be discussed in detail later. It should not be confused with Methodism, which is nevertheless the best example of the eighteenth-century revival. Of the influential ministers of the second half of the century who came into the Society of Friends from outside and helped to steer it in an evangelical direction, only one, Mary Dudley, had actually had formal links with the developing new church. The other great English minister in the first generation of evangelical Friends was Thomas Shillitoe, who had been an Anglican. In America, Rebecca Jones had also been an Episcopalian (Anglican), David Sands a Presbyterian, and Stephen Grellet a Catholic and a free-thinker. Perhaps American Quakerism was more dependent on the ministry for the transmission of evangelical principles than elsewhere. In England, where social conditions were different, Friends had a whole range of contacts with members of other denominations whose assumptions and attitudes were pretty similar to their own. Evangelicalism developed more by osmosis than transmission, and to dismiss it as an external influence deflecting Quakerism from its true course is a judgement of value rather than history.

If we are to listen to the official voice of eighteenth-century Quakerism, we shall hear that Friends in the period had lost the fervour and commitment of the founders of the Society, and were unwilling to be guided in the right paths. Meetings were considered to be lifeless, and the ministry uninspiring. The regulation of Quaker life by Yearly Meeting became stricter as time passed by, and owing to the obtuse operation of the rule against marrying out, and the unwillingness to seek converts, numbers began to decline sharply.

It is tempting, however, to take official pronouncements with a pinch of salt. It is true that many Friends drifted away from the Society, or were driven out by the marriage rules. Nevertheless, it seems that many Friends simply ignored the Discipline and were perfectly contented and fulfilled in their religious lives. The eighteenth-century Quaker culture had something that was deeply satisfying, and to regard it as burdensome is to apply the standards of another age.

Certainly it can be said that Friends in this period were very different from George Fox and his companions. So they were. They lived in a different world and different demands were made on them. To regard them as epigoni is unfair, for they produced a form of Quakerism, which, if it is distinct, is more enduring than the original. Within it grew up several generations which have greatly benefited humanity – inventors, manufacturers, bankers, scientists, social reformers, men of affairs, philanthropists and prophets. The problem was, they were so busy that they forgot to nourish the spiritual life of their community. As the Society of Friends was about to enter the nineteenth century, it was in desperate need of religious renewal, and its own resources were not equal to the task.

A Divided Inheritance

ONE OF THE ADVANTAGES HISTORIANS ENJOY OVER CHRONICLERS is that they can stretch the beginning or end of a period beyond the strict limits permitted by the calendar. It makes much more sense to define the nineteenth century as the period between the French and Russian Revolutions than to insist that nothing shall be admitted to consideration that did not occur between 1800 and 1899. In this way, while recognising the risks of any generalisation about the past, it is possible to emphasise what appear to be the main, or characteristic features of a period. For good or ill, the nineteenth century has come to be known as a century of revolutions, and the Quakers, like many other groups and nations, experienced fundamental and traumatic change.

In the United States, Friends followed the frontier westwards and came up against the limitations of the traditional system of leadership and pastoral care. The uncertainties of the age led to a reappraisal of the traditional faith in the light of new needs, and the unity of quietism was broken as Friends on both sides of the Atlantic wrestled with the challenges, first of evangelical, and then of liberal theology. These two movements both originated outside the Society, but swept forcefully into it to fill the void that was left when the Quakers sensed finally that their original quasi-Anabaptism was finished as a tenable theological position.

In this period the second main numerical expansion of the Society of Friends occurred. Changes in the membership posed entirely new problems and new solutions were devised. The two clearest examples, perhaps, lie in the fields of ministry and the peace testimony. Many

American Quakers have developed what are called 'programmed meetings', in which the period of silent, or 'open', worship is put in a devotional setting of music and scriptural readings, and many call a Quaker pastor to serve the congregation. As the scale of warfare and the preparation for war have reached unprecedented heights, Quaker pacifism has become a positive and dynamic witness of far wider scope than its earlier, more spiritual, and less politically committed form.

Uprising and Separation in Ireland

A suitable figure to illustrate the trials of nineteenth-century Quakerism is Abraham Shackleton of Ballitore, County Kildare, Ireland. In 1726, Shackleton's grandfather, also called Abraham, opened a boarding school which prospered and enjoyed the distinction of including the future statesman Edmund Burke among its pupils, although it later confined itself to educating the sons of Friends. Mary Leadbeater, younger Abraham's sister, has left a fascinating anecdotal account of life among the Quakers of Ballitore. The narrative is absorbing in its own right, but tantalising in that there are many matters which we would like to pursue further than the author was perhaps able to go.

The picture emerges of a group of well-read, well-connected Friends of confident simplicity, who were in close touch with the Society in Dublin and were regularly visited by travelling ministers such as Job Scott, who died of smallpox at Ballitore in 1793. One side of the picture is of Ireland in the age of enlightenment, cool, rational, elegant, epitomised by the grace of the Georgian squares of its capital city. The other side of the picture cannot be veiled. It is the age of the French Revolution and rising tension. As Pitt's policy of conciliation was frustrated, Protestant radicals and alienated Catholics combined into an important political force committed to the objective of an Irish republic independent of Great Britain. The nation divided, and we learn from Friend Mary Leadbeater how the squire of Ballitore raised a regiment of militia for the French war, but how, simultaneously, there began to develop ominous signs of civil conflict as well.

By 1796 matters were sufficiently serious for the National Meeting of Friends in Ireland to endorse a policy, already in operation in many quarterly and monthly meetings, for all Friends to be visited so they might be encouraged to destroy any guns or other weapons they might have in their household. In that year a French invasion fleet had been prevented from landing an expeditionary force by contrary winds.

A gun in Quaker hands might be nothing more than a tool for the farm, but to an officer of the government, or to a loyalist mob it might be taken as a sign of insurrectionary intent. To a rebel, it might be an asset worth robbery or even murder to acquire.

So as the crisis deepened, Friends took the paths of prudence and principle. It had been intended that in 1798 a French army should invade Ireland and there should be a simultaneous uprising organised and led by the United Irishmen. In the spring of the year, as one Friend wrote, the air was full of wild rumours of risings and attempted risings. Privy to the invasion plans, the government instituted a campaign to search out and destroy the opposition, and pursued its aim with counter-productive severity. In the south-east of Ireland, where Friends were numerous, the unrest grew so strong that the insurrection started independently of the plan when the Munster mail coach was ambushed and burned outside Dublin. A bitter localised civil war ensued, carried on with unspeakable ferocity, and the Quaker communities at Ferns, Ballitore and Enniscorthy were in the eye of the storm.

How well Irish Friends maintained their integrity is well known. Many lost all they possessed; they refused to be intimidated into taking arms or assisting the military preparations of one side or the other; they gave food and shelter to all who were in need; they faced situations of acute personal danger from mobs and violent individuals. Such was the strength given to them that it is said that in the whole period only one Friend lost his life.

Abraham Shackleton saw the worst of the uprising. His sister's narrative describes how he was carried off by the rebels, who presumably tried to impress him into their force. At one point he was informed that if he chose not to discharge a bullet for the cause, he would be put in the front of the firing line so he might have the privilege of stopping one for the same. He avoided this fate, however, and managed to get back to his own house, which we are told was regarded as a place of safety and security. For the insurgents, their prisoners and wounded, for the wives and daughters of rebels and soldiery alike, the Shackleton home gave food, kindness and an all too brief respite from the horrors of the uprising.

Abraham was a man of physical and moral courage and was more open than most Friends to the intellectual climate of the time. One indication of the family's interests is the friendship and correspondence between his father, Richard Shackleton, and Burke. Abraham became principal of the school in due course, and maintained a deep concern for what his father Richard had called 'the religious prosperity of the rising generation'. He came to the conclusion that a classical education, with its dominant themes of glory and heroism, was inimical to the cultivation of that meekness and gentleness he saw at the heart of Christianity. The judgement is sound evidence of Abraham's quietist temper; so was his decision that the school should therefore cease to teach the classics. At a time when these studies were essential to anyone hoping to progress to higher education, it was to be expected that he would lose pupils, and so it turned out. The number of enrolments declined and the school closed, though it was reopened later by others.

Parallel to his convictions about education were his views on religion, notably in connection with the nature of God, and the less congenial parts of the Old Testament, which were to bring him into conflict with the collective leadership of which he was part. For many years he had been active in the Yearly Meeting, serving on a number of committees that had periodically considered the state of the Society, and was in unity with the view that all was not well among Friends.

As the jargon had it, Friends were in a 'low state'. Such opinions were not confined to Ireland. They were voiced generally, for they arose out of the internal tensions, created by the institutions of Quakerism, which were being felt all over the Quaker world. The 'Tradition' was scarcely a century old and was beginning to display its weaknesses, the greatest being the impossibility of holding aloof from 'the World'. The enthusiasm of the first generation had waned. The pained tones of yearly meeting epistles and the reports of travelling ministers reflect the indifference they encountered on their pastoral visits and the slumbering formality of many meetings for worship. Friends forsook frugality and simplicity as they prospered in business. They connived at tithe-avoidance. They neglected the testimonies. They married outside the Society. They failed to read the Bible or to provide a religious education for their children.

For many, Quakerism was a nominal allegiance rather than a way of life. A typical report to London Yearly Meeting in 1778 reads, 'In divers places we had sorrowful occasion to lament the low and languid state of many in profession with us, finding Meetings for Worship, more especially on Weekdays much neglected, a great remissness in Religious Education of our Youth, many instances of unfaithfulness and painful defection in various branches of that Christian Testimony which we as a people are most assuredly required to maintain . . .'

There is reason to doubt the blackness of this view, but it was clearly the view of the dominant party among Friends. If it signalled the social difficulties inherent in quietist Quakerism, it indicated its religious drawbacks too. Great stress was laid on external conformity at a time when ideas of personal and political liberty were spreading rapidly. Conversely, within this spiritual walled garden, very little guidance, let alone instruction, found a place, and there was widespread ignorance of the doctrinal and biblical basis of Quakerism. The world had changed since the Tradition had been laid down about a century before, but there had been little innovation or constructive thought among Friends. But it is theology that provides the vocabulary, the concepts, the methods of accommodating abiding truth to changed circumstances. Failure to take part in the common theological enterprise may mean losing the means of communicating with other Christians, and also with formative movements of ideas outside the Church.

To a considerable degree this was the case with Friends in the years around 1800. The body of the Society either strove to preserve its traditional separation, or ignored it as irrelevant. The leadership of the Society wanted a renewal but was unclear about how it should be promoted. The enterprising souls were going outside their inheritance and were trying to express what they thought to be central Quaker tenets in a new way. The result was a series of sharp differences of opinion, followed almost inevitably by divisions. Abraham Shackleton was one of the first heroes, and first casualties, of this conflict.

By 1791, London Yearly Meeting had more or less permanently satisfied itself that the appropriate response to slackness among Friends was to tighten up the operation of the Discipline and to ensure a closer conformity with what they considered Friends' doctrine to be. Accordingly a supplement to the Book of Extracts was issued to give effect to this conclusion. The Advices and Queries were revised and Friends were reminded that they were not just requests for information, but were also intended to promote self-examination. Directions were given as to how meetings should consider them, and elders were reminded that they were obliged to report clearly and in good time as to their use.

Though Ireland adopted them, Abraham Shackleton made no secret of his dissatisfaction with the whole approach, and said so in writing to a number of Friends. Matters came to a head in 1797 when it was his turn to clerk the Carlow Monthly Meeting of Ministers and Elders. He refused to read the Advices and Queries and somebody else had to do it. Quarterly Meeting was not satisfied with the minute of reply and, on enquiry, discovered that objection had been taken to the use of the word 'Holy' as applied to 'Scripture' in Query IV as inconsistent with Friends' traditional position. There were precedents for this usage dating back to 1728 at least, so this view, which was Shackleton's, rested on shaky ground historically, whatever else might be said in favour of it.

Almost simultaneously, he entered into a public controversy with a fellow elder, Samuel Woodcock, over the wars and acts of violence portrayed in the Old Testament, apparently by divine command. He argued that it was not in the nature of a loving God to order the performance of deeds that were 'perfidious, cruel and unjust'. If they appeared on the record they could best be accounted for as rationalisations by contemporary or subsequent writers to justify their own actions, and could in no way be claimed as part of a divine revelation. These differences of opinion caused considerable distress to the Quarterly Meeting, which perceived a breach in the unity of Friends and made visits to each under pastoral concern.

Early in 1798, William Savery visited Ireland and Abraham Shackleton travelled forty miles to confer with him. William's resolute mind was unable to minister to Abraham's difficulties as it had to Elizabeth Gurney's, and he summarised their unhappy encounter with the celebrated and dramatic comment that Shackleton and his sympathisers were caught in the 'vortex of deism'. Shackleton began to absent himself from meeting and informed Ballitore Friends through third parties that he was no longer able to keep their records. In the following year his deep convictions were rebuffed by a Yearly Meeting which deplored the prevalence of unsound doctrines and called for watchfulness to prevent the dissemination of 'sentiments of a dangerous tendency', i.e. *his*.

Friends remained concerned for him but his position was impossible. In 1799 he was removed as an elder, possibly with justification. In 1801 he was disowned, without justification. The new approach to discipline was intended to produce concord and renewal, but it merely stimulated dissent. In Ireland, a number of influential Friends were disowned or withdrew from the Society. At one point only one recorded minister remained in Ulster Quarterly Meeting and only two monthly meetings in the province continued to report to Yearly Meeting in Dublin. The size of the Irish separation was unprecedented, and it was the first of a series of such separations which are perhaps the most obvious feature of nineteenth-century Quakerism.

The Challenge of New Thinking

The particular issue that divided Friends was the authority of scripture. Robert Barclay's statement of the Quaker view in Proposition III of his *Apology* was usually considered a perfectly adequate account, but like many apparently authoritative pronouncements in religion, it could be interpreted in different ways. Barclay asserts that the scriptures are a 'secondary' authority in the sense that we recognise their truth not on their own merits, but by the direct inward testimony of the Spirit in our hearts. Nevertheless, he does not deduce from this the individualistic conclusion that the meaning of scripture is a matter for private interpretation. He draws some practical limitations to his principle by asserting that since they also were written under the inspiration of the Spirit, the errors that might have 'slipt in' are not sufficient to destroy their clear testimony to the essentials of the Christian faith.

He continues by saying that they are the only suitable outward standard by which controversies among Christians may be settled, and that Friends are willing for all their doctrines and practices to be tested against them. Actually he goes further, and says that if anybody claiming the direct inspiration of the Spirit does anything contrary to scripture, he is under a 'delusion of the Devil', and that while Friends confidently assert a new revelation of the old gospel, they utterly deny that they are claiming a new revelation.

The authorities of the Society of Friends, at the beginning of the nineteenth century, were content to include the warlike God of the Old Testament as part of the testimony of the Spirit. Abraham Shackleton would have said that the objectionable passages were examples of the errors that had slipped in. The Irish separation and the subsequent divisions in America and Great Britain can in part be traced back to the failure of Friends to reach an agreed understanding of Barclay's principle in a totally different intellectual climate.

Looking back, we can see that Friends were faced with a crisis of identity. They came into existence at the confluence of a number of spiritual streams that bubbled out of the manifold strata of the

Reformation. During the first century-and-a-half they had tried to maintain themselves as far as possible as they were, and their insistence on their traditional beliefs and ways of doing things expresses this. But the world had changed, and they were coming under new pressures that their isolation prevented them from understanding. Their response was therefore a defensive one, and all they could do about Abraham Shackleton was (almost literally) to throw the book at him.

The two main forces that were at work on Friends were the rationalistic temper of the Enlightenment, and the evangelical revival. There seems to have been no attempt to synthesise these movements comprehensively with Quakerism as a Barclay or a Penn might have undertaken, and new ideas from each direction tended to dribble into the Society haphazardly. Consequently, the anti-evangelicals sought to portray their opponents as having departed from a true understanding of the forerunners, while the evangelicals thought that they were in fact recovering the intentions of the founders of the Society, and preventing the spread of ideas ultimately inimical to true religion. There was grave mutual misunderstanding complicated by the fact that the ascendant party, the evangelicals, had their hands on the levers of power in the main yearly meetings. As we have seen in the Shackleton case, the manner in which that power was exercised tended in itself to preclude the sort of dialogue that just might have prevented the separations.

In the earlier part of the eighteenth century, there had been widespread speculation about the nature of God and his relation with the cosmos, and many advanced thinkers took the position known as 'deism'. This was the doctrine that God is quite other than the cosmos and entirely transcends it. Having created it as a closed system, he remains aloof from its operations and lets it go its own way. This obviously denies totally the pantheist view that God and the universe are one entity, and that the divine is wholly immanent in the creation.

It also denies the theist position taken by Christianity. This is an interim view that accepts the transcendence of the divine being, but claims that God is nevertheless immanent in the creation so that at least some direct relations with him are possible. According to the deists, God presides over a largely autonomous universe from outside. Contemporary developments in experimental science had led to the view that there was a regularity and order in the phenomena of the universe which could best be explored by the new techniques of physics, chemistry and mathematics. These enquiries produced standards of truth and rationality which were certain, and should therefore be used to judge all other claims to knowledge, including religion.

This was the genesis of the Enlightenment, the Age of Reason. Theology was removed from her throne as the Queen of Sciences and relegated, Cinderella-like, to the intellectual scullery. A distinction could be drawn between the truths of natural religion, which could be verified by reason, and the claims of revealed religion which were true only in so far as they coincided with what could be discovered anyway. It followed that providence and particular revelation were impossible.

This carried with it certain implications which received wide acceptance outside deist circles, and attracted a number of Quakers because of similarities with many of their traditional positions. Deism provided a comprehensive critique of the authority and inspiration of scripture. Since the Bible portrayed a divinity that was arbitrary and frequently failed to measure up to the highest ethical standards, reason required the rejection of that sort of God. If reason showed the universe to be a system of regularities, miracles were impossible because they were an interruption of these regularities. They were either misunderstandings or superstitions, though they were capable of a symbolic meaning. Into this category fell many of the events of the life of Christ, notably the Virgin Birth, the Transfiguration, the Resurrection and the Ascension. It is easy to see how Quakers who were not accustomed to place too much emphasis on the outward facts of their faith, and possessed a doctrine of scripture as a secondary authority, could see these deist conclusions as quite congruent with their own tradition.

Moreover, if this line of reasoning be accepted, the traditional doctrine of God is untenable. Jesus becomes no more than a spirit-filled human and the whole question of Unitarianism is opened up, as indeed, it was. The Society of Friends has never formally adopted Unitarianism (which in its modern form denies the divinity of Christ), but its refusal to employ the technical term 'trinity', with all the theological nuances it carries, has often led its critics and some of its members to mistake the nature of its corporate objection to the use of that word.

Deism saw the discovery of truth as the object of reason, and this, paradoxically, is its closest approximation to, and departure from, Quakerism. In deist terminology, truth is an intellectual category, its object the knowledge of God that is accessible to the mind. Quakers, on the other hand, have always seen truth as a spiritual category, its reality only accessible to the worshipping soul. They were also accustomed, as the deists were, to employ the word 'light' to mean that by which truth is apprehended. For deists, the light was the inherent rational capacity of the mind. For Quakers, light was the direct operation of God upon the soul, something which the deist cosmology in principle refused to admit.

The deist world-view certainly had an effect on some Friends, usually, one suspects, the more intelligent members of the prosperous and well-connected branches of the Society. In France, the attack on the pretensions of an established church supported by an undemocratic political system which culminated in the Revolution was the product, to a considerable degree, of English ideas, and involved religious as well as political issues. It is not surprising that as the desire for freedom from whatever forces were oppressing mankind grew in strength there were Quakers, dissatisfied with an antique and repetitious 'tradition' and an onerous 'discipline', who would look for new ways of thinking to express their inherited values.

Deist conceptions, coincidentally rather than causally, entered their speculations, but this did not prevent them from being misunderstood by the dominant party in the Society. Deism found no room for a continuing expression of divine love toward the creation. It removed the mystery and emotion as elements of religious experience. It was strongly anti-mystical and emphatically intellectual. All these things are at variance with Quakerism of whatever kind.

On the other hand, it had aspects which were very much in harmony with the Quaker outlook. It required honesty and personal responsibility, and would not allow authoritative scriptures to provide sanction for irrational or obscurantist opinions. It required a reliance upon reason, and probably generated the modern view that if God really is the creator of the universe, religion and science cannot conflict. As men such as Abraham Shackleton, William Rathbone and John Hancock, and women such as Hannah Barnard strove to open Quakerism to the new ideas it desperately needed, they were profoundly misunderstood, and they paid a penalty exacted by Quaker intolerance and theological naiveté.

The Great Migration in America

While Irish Friends were passing through the fires of the Uprising and their subsequent separation, American Friends were on the move. In 1787 the Continental Congress decided that the Northwest Territory would be permanently free of the institution of slavery, and opened up the valley of the Ohio River for settlement. Friends had already arrived in Western Pennsylvania, Tennessee, Kentucky and Upper Canada, some from the south, some from New England, but the trend now accelerated sharply. The Ordinance of 1787 opening up the Northwest provided an opportunity. Drawn by the rich farming land of what are now the states of Ohio and Indiana, and driven by the desire to escape from the stresses of maintaining their testimony against slavery in Georgia, Virginia and the Carolinas, large numbers of Friends, sometimes whole meetings, took to the precipitous, winding mountain trails and crossed the Appalachian range.

Once over the Ohio River they were in a new land. They faced the problems of survival as they wrested their farms from the wilderness, and sought to live peaceably with the Indians. Hardship and joy came hand in hand, and all they had to sustain themselves with were their skills and their faith. Redstone Quarterly Meeting in western Pennsylvania, astride the beautifully named Monongahela River was the place where many of the migrating Friends deposited their removal certificates until meetings were settled in the country to which they were going. Redstone was a unit of Baltimore Yearly Meeting, and so quickly did its western appendage develop that in 1812 Ohio Yearly Meeting came into existence, and in 1821 Ohio set up Indiana Yearly Meeting.

One of the trail-blazers of this Quaker migration was Thomas Beals, who made regular visits to the Indians under religious concern. In 1775 he visited the redoubtable Shawnee nation with three companions. On returning home to North Carolina he is reported to have said that he had seen with his spiritual eye the seed of Friends scattered all over that goodly land, and that one day there would be a greater gathering of Friends there than any place in the world. His monthly meeting did not feel able to consent to his removal for some time, but it is known that before 1782 he and his family went to the Ohio country. They moved from place to place for a while and then in 1801 Thomas died and was buried on a hilltop in the then primeval forest.

There is a monument to his memory in the yard of the meeting house at Londonderry, Ohio, which is inscribed, 'Thomas Beals, First Quaker Missionary to the Indians in the Northwest Territory'. His biographer closes with a summary of his character as a man and an American, '... this humble man, noble and brave and good, who carried the message of love to his brother man of whatever race or station, and who carried that message through the gateway into the heartland of a great new Republic.' His prediction came close to the truth. For many years it could truthfully be said that one third of the Friends in America could be found within the limits of the old Northwest Territory. We shall see that in due course this region became the heartland of the pastoral expression of Quakerism.

There is a Quaker folklore of the area. On one occasion at East Fork, a small child sitting next to her mother in meeting saw a huge snake curled up among the rafters. So deep and peaceful was the meeting that snake and child were both undisturbed. A mother of Chester Meeting left her baby in its cradle outside her cabin one day and came out again to find the child gone. Terrified, she could find no trace of it, but next morning an aged Indian emerged from the forest and replaced the baby in the cradle. 'No want him,' he said, 'Him cry-baby.'

We can take Thomas Beals' spiritual vision of a gathering of Friends in the Ohio country with some degree of licence. Nevertheless it remains true that to this day it is one of the great Quaker centres of the world, worthy to rank among equals with London and Philadelphia. How it came to be such is part of the story of Friends and the evangelical revival, that great spiritual movement of the eighteenth century associated with the names of John Wesley and George Whitefield which, by the dawning of the nineteenth century, was becoming the orthodoxy of Quakerism.

Evangelical Quakerism

Any passing observer of the Christian scene will soon notice that evangelicalism is a very powerful and durable expression of the faith. Uncompromising in doctrine and spirituality, it incurs the hostility of church authorities which like an ordered and quiet life, and the scorn of those who like their religion sunlit, rational and bland. Non-evangelicals tend to think that its appeal lies in the simplicity of its theology (which they believe to be mistaken), and tend to overlook the deep and vibrant personal experience that gives rise to it (which they often fail to comprehend).

The evangelical movement of the mid-eighteenth century coalesced round the leaders of Methodism and soon spread through the churches. Though it produced outstanding leaders, it seems to have been the simultaneous intuition of a large number of people who discovered that they were thinking about religion along similar lines. They were dissatisfied with the complacency, formality and rationalism that was too often the spiritual diet of the day. Instead, they developed an intense religion of personal commitment. It had some very unpleasant features, to be sure, but it led to a great deal that was remarkable and noble in the achievements of the Victorian age.

Basic to the evangelical outlook is the conviction of personal sin, the idea that the nature of humanity is to be disobedient to the divine will, and the conclusion that this is the cause of what is wrong with the world. Social systems, economic conditions, historical circumstances are in the last analysis the collective actions of individuals. Acts of neglect, cruelty, injustice, selfishness cannot be blamed on 'the system'. The system consists of the avoidable, and therefore sinful, acts of the individuals who belong to it. So people are naturally in a state of alienation from God. It is a common observation that nobody is perfect, and the evangelical vision of the utter goodness of God requires the view that, unaided, we are not capable of entering into communion with him. So we encounter the paradox Barclay tried to solve – how can the love of God operate to draw us into this communion if by nature we are incapable of it?

The answer was seen to lie in God's love. If justice is to be more than a hollow gesture to those who have been wronged, punishment must be imposed on those who have no remorse for any wickedness they may have committed. So in a natural state, humanity deserves no more than Hell. But if some human being were loving enough, brave enough, self-sacrificing enough to offer to accept the penalty, justice would be secured, and so would love, for no obstacle would remain to an indiscriminate and unconditional forgiveness.

However, a loving God could never act through a representative or deputy, for the ultimate perversion in the moral universe is to use someone else for your own purposes. Thus, by entering human life in the person of Jesus Christ, God accepts on the cross the consequences of the sins of the whole world, and brings release from the power of sin. You cannot enter the evangelical experience if you see the cross as a symbol of vengeance rather than love.

Around this central diagnosis of the human condition, certain more characteristic evangelical doctrines arrange themselves. First, sin, or disobedience, is seen as a total distortion of the human personality affecting the intellect and the imagination as well as the will, to which certain other Christian traditions confine it. Second, the Bible is crucially important as the divinely-appointed method of conveying the revelation of God's loving actions and purposes for us. It is therefore inspired and infallible, so the idea that it should be interpreted by the standards of secular learning is a grave mistake. Third, saving faith must be a matter of conscious choice. You must be converted by acknowledging your sin and asking for forgiveness. There can be no accidental, absent-minded, habitual or half-hearted Christians. Fourth, since the consequence of rejecting or ignoring God's offer of forgiveness in Christ is the torment of Hell, love requires mission as one of the very highest priorities of the Christian life. Every Christian is a missionary. Fifth, saving faith has to be doctrinally sound. You have to appreciate the nature of the reconciliation Christ offers you. You are justified before God for one reason only – that Christ has accepted the penalty for your sin, and without a clear appreciation of this vital fact, this demonstration of God's love, the Kingdom of Heaven is closed to you.

If we are justified by our faith alone (a good Reformation principle), is that all? Can the Christian sit back in the complacent security of knowing that all is forgiven and continue as before? Indeed not, for conversion is the beginning of a new life as well as the end of an old one. Traditionally, we receive the gift of the Holy Spirit to work in us and help us overcome our continuing proneness to sin. This is the work of sanctification. Though we can never overcome our sinful disposition entirely, we can nevertheless go some way towards it.

Some contemporary evangelicals and Pentecostals speak of a baptism of the Spirit as a second work of grace, with a clearly definable experience to go with it. It can be argued that this was the nature of the early Quaker convincements, since most of the early Friends were already converted. Though not a final proof, good works were seen by the evangelicals as a sure sign of grace operating in the person doing them. For a group with such an austere and inward conception of the gospel, the evangelicals were astonishingly busy in the struggle against the evils of the world. In many ways they were the original do-gooders.

Evangelicalism entered the Society of Friends in the late eighteenth century. It reached its peak of influence in London Yearly Meeting towards the 1870s, and is still the official persuasion of at least half the Quaker world, notably in the United States and in the Third World countries which were once mission fields of some of the American yearly meetings. The story of the reception of evangelical principles is a complex one, involving the nature of quietist Quakerism, the changing social structure of the big cities of Britain and America, a number of outstanding personalities, an intellectual climate that was receptive to this revived theology, and, last, its congruence at many points with the original Quaker message.

We can only lightly sketch these influences here, but it is important to do so, for evangelicalism is a feature of all denominations and something all thoughtful non-evangelical Christians have to come to terms with, including Friends. Thus, we shall approach it as a necessary movement for the renewal of the churches of the day, most of which, including the Quakers, were going through a period of lethargy and indolence. Friends were by no means unique in this respect and to see evangelicalism as a foreign import is to mistake it, for it cut (and cuts) across all denominational boundaries. Among Friends it was attracted by two deficiencies, and two institutions facilitated its growth.

The first deficiency which cleared the way for evangelicalism was the conservative temper of quietism. Though this nourished spirits like Woolman and Job Scott, it had a deep suspicion of Bible study and co-operation with outsiders under religious concern. It maintained its strict discipline, its reliance on the charisma of the travelling ministry, the conceptions and phraseology of the Tradition and its separation from the world. Thus, it became progressively antique, so that many people, if they did not leave the Society, sought spiritual refreshment elsewhere.

The second deficiency, another expression of quietism, was the isolation of the body of the Society, which was nevertheless breaking down at the upper end of the social scale. A number of Friends, of whom the Gurneys of Earlham are the best example, were moving in the company of earnest evangelical Anglicans and were coming to adopt their characteristic attitudes.

The institutions which facilitated the growth of evangelicalism were, ironically, the characteristic products of quietism – the travelling ministry and the primacy of London Yearly Meeting. By 1820 London had entertained a quartet of powerful American evangelical ministers – Rebecca Jones, David Sands, William Savery and Stephen Grellet, the first two convinced Friends from other denominations, the latter two of French extraction, Huguenot and Catholic respectively. To lay the growth of evangelicalism at their door is greatly to overstate the matter, but without doubt they strengthened and confirmed what was already the dominant trend.

London Yearly Meeting was at that time a collective Quaker papacy. Its Discipline set the pattern for the Quaker world; its pronouncements were received with respectful attention everywhere; it controlled its ministry through the Morning Meeting and its endorsement was necessary for any Friend wishing to travel within its borders under religious concern. The same went for Friends travelling abroad. Between 1810 and 1840 a group of strong British evangelical Friends visited America – William Forster, Anna Braithwaite, Thomas Shillitoe and Joseph John Gurney. They carried the prestige of the parent body with them and are held by some to have contributed materially to the separations of 1827–8 in the United States.

Philanthropy and Philanthropists

It is in social action, however, that we can see the most characteristic effect of evangelicalism on British Friends. Quietism was benevolent, to be sure, but quietly benevolent. The maintenance of spiritual purity required that Friends did not give undue attention to organising to counteract social evils, for that would be creaturely activity. Nor might they work in co-operation with members of other denominations, for that would have involved a possible contamination by the world. At the beginning of the nineteenth century though, we can discern the emergence of two groups of Friends – the rich, such as Richard Reynolds, Joseph Storrs Fry, John Horniman, and later, the Cadburys, whose generosity became a by-word, and concerned and prosperous people such as William Allen and Joseph Sturge, who not only gave their own money to their own causes, but enlisted other people's money as well.

William Allen (1770–1843) of Spitalfields in East London was apprenticed to his father's business as a silk weaver but soon gave this up to join the pharmaceutical firm that, as Allen and Hanbury, still trades under his name. He was one of a long line of Quaker scientists, becoming a Fellow and member of the Council of the Royal Society and one of the leading theoretical chemists of his day. He was passionately interested in philanthropic activities, editing the monthly The Philanthropist, travelling widely, becoming an intimate of Tsar Alexander I, writing, advising, encouraging. He found time to act as overseer, elder and minister. He was clerk of monthly meeting and Meeting for Sufferings and assisted in the revisions of the Book of Discipline, as the Book of Extracts was coming to be known, in 1800 and 1832. He married three times and was three times widowed and his only child died giving birth to his grandson, the one member of his family to survive him. His love transcended the harshness of his private life and he is remembered for his humility, his tenderness and his generosity.

The Anti-Slavery Society, one of William Allen's lifelong concerns, typifies the Victorian movement for voluntary social reform in a number of ways, though it began at the end of the eighteenth century. Interdenominational philanthropic committees were the usual medium for promoting such concerns. Generally operating from London, they comprised those who were willing to devote their time to the promotion of the case. Generally members were either wealthy and willing to contribute their cash, or well-connected and willing to use their influence.

Having constituted themselves, the philanthropic societies then set about what is now called 'consciousness raising', or, less politely, publicity, by conducting research and discussion on which to base a series of books, pamphlets and tracts. Meetings were held, and the endorsement of the great and the good solicited. It was necessary, too, to enlist the help of supporters in the country, to spread the word, to raise money, and to use local influence. Because of their small, educated, well-to-do and intimately interconnected Society, Friends were usually of great assistance in this regard. Friends possessed intelligence in both senses, and their numbers on the Committee of the Anti-Slavery Society can partly be put down to this.

As time passed, many of the societies achieved their objectives and they either laid themselves down or widened their sphere of activities into related matters. Often, with the passage of time, subtle changes of emphasis occurred as social conditions changed and they became institutions, in some cases even with a Royal Charter. For example, the Society of Friends set up a committee to promote the abolition of the slave trade in 1783. It was widened to include non-Friends in 1787, and joined forces with the Anglican evangelicals of the Clapham Sect, including William Wilberforce, Thomas Clarkson, Zachary Macaulay and others. In 1807 the slave trade was abolished in the British dominions. In 1833 slavery itself was abolished, but so intractable were the problems that followed that the Society continued its work, notably by including the 'protection of aborigines' among its aims. It remains active to this day, more than two centuries after its beginnings.

A number of the non-Friends active in the campaign to abolish slavery are met with under other hats in the work of the British and Foreign Bible Society, founded in 1804 and numbering three Friends on its foundation committee of fifteen. These included the father of the journalist and meteorologist Luke Howard, who was succeeded by his son when he died, and (for it was a small world) the first husband of William Allen's third wife. In his account of the beginnings of the Bible Society, its first secretary writes that it may have had a vital role in drawing Friends out of their quietist seclusion into the mainstream of national life. He goes on to say that so close were the relationships between the various philanthropic societies of the day, that the connections made there may well have influenced that pattern of good works for which the Friends subsequently became noted.

The ability to read the Bible obviously requires literacy. In 1798 Friend Joseph Lancaster opened a school for poor children in Southwark. He is known in educational history as one of the founders (with Dr Andrew Bell of Madras) of the monitorial system, by which the teacher teaches a small group of 'monitors', who then each proceed to teach another group of less advanced pupils. Joseph Lancaster was an inspired educator but an awful businessman. In 1808, in spite of royal patronage, he had contracted immense debts of over £6,000, and William Allen had to step in to help him out. With a committee of six, half of them Friends, he constituted a trust known as the Royal Lancasterian Society for Promoting the Education of Children of the Poor.

This was probably the main concern of William Allen's life, and he strove to protect Lancaster's work from the effects of an erratic temperament. When Joseph resigned from the organisation in 1814, it was renamed the British and Foreign Schools Society. It ran schools, trained teachers, spread to many parts of the world, within and outside the British Empire. In the following half century, until the Education Act of 1870 began the era of public elementary education, it was the mainstay of nonconformist educational provision in England.

If the desire to spread the gospel led to the Bible Society, and the need for literacy to the Schools Society, the degradation of the lives of the poor led to more direct schemes of relief. William Allen worked closely with a neighbouring Spitalfields Friend, Peter Bedford, in association with the Bettering Society, more properly the Society for Bettering the Condition and Increasing the Comforts of the Poor. Allen conducted a survey of the conditions in Spitalfields and published his results in 1812. On the basis of what he found, he set up a soup committee for immediate relief of poverty and an association for more long-term relief. He was perhaps too busy for the sort of visionary schemes John Bellers had, or too early for the sort of public works promoted by George Cadbury in the East End in 1904–5. But he was aware he was dealing with symptoms not causes. 'There is certainly some radical error, either in the system of parochial relief, or the administration of it, which loudly calls for investigation,' he wrote.

He later returned to the matter. With two other zealous Friends he joined the group that provided finance for the experiments of Robert Owen at the New Lanark Mills. What went for industry should also go for the land. He saw the potential of the co-operative form of enterprise in the cotton trade, and his visits to Ireland in the 1820s led to the rural colonies at Lindfield in Sussex which were intended to provide similar opportunities for agricultural labourers.

The links in the chain of Quaker acquaintance go further. William Allen's friend, William Forster visited Newgate prison in London in the winter of 1812 in the company of Stephen Grellet and Peter Bedford. The three men were under religious concern, but Peter Bedford certainly took the opportunity to underline the need for a radical change in penal policy and the contemporary criminal code. They visited the women's ward of the prison and were so appalled by what they saw that one of them went straight to Elizabeth Fry and laid the whole matter before her, thus opening the way for what has become one of the favourite Quaker romances.

Elizabeth Fry was gracious and talented, and belonged to a rich family, the Gurneys, who were aristocrats of the world of banking and finance no less than the world of Quakerism. Having been converted to the evangelical faith by William Savery and adopted the plain dress, Elizabeth now found her vocation. Her first visit to Newgate was in 1813, but for a while she was unable to pursue her work for family reasons. But she collected information about the conditions of prisons throughout England and in 1816 she went back to Newgate to begin the work that lasted till her death in 1845. She clothed the inmates and comforted the condemned. She visited every possible convict ship bound for Australia. She ran a school and a Bible class. She enlisted the support of an association of sympathisers, including the Lord Mayor of London. She appeared before a committee of the House of Commons and entertained visiting royalty. She sought new directions in correctional policy, struggling against severe punishments and solitary confinement and worked for the introduction of proper after-care for released prisoners. Outside her Society she is probably the best known of all Quakers.

Friends remained active in this kind of voluntary social work throughout the nineteenth century, although methods, and to some extent objectives, changed as time went by. The anti-slavery agitation promoted an interest in Africa, and this in turn led to schemes for settlement and colonisation by emancipated slaves, the development of mission work and the opening of schools. Friends were active individually in all these fields though the undertow of quietism prevented a wholehearted corporate involvement.

At home there were the usual enemies to be fought – social deprivation, drink, gambling and vice, and then, as always, Quakers turned to education as their weapon. It is noteworthy that the one great evangelical campaign which they did not take part in to any noticeable degree was the agitation to reform the conditions of work in the factories. Indeed, it was the common gibe against Friends that they cared more for the welfare of the West India slaves than they did for the industrial workers in their own country.

So the legacy of evangelicalism in Britain was to bring the Society of Friends back into the life of the nation from its self-imposed exile, and to teach it that individual benevolence cannot change the world unless it is harnessed to an organisation. Its theological impact on Quakerism was far less dramatic in England than in the United States. In America the Society of Friends was neither as close-knit nor as all-of-a-piece socially as it was in Britain, so it was, in one sense, more open to outside influences. There was a freer traffic in ideas in the United States, and the fact of having thrown off British rule made the intellectual climate different. The struggle against arbitrary authority now gave way to the exercise of personal freedom and the nation had to stake out its place in the international community. If the Revolution were to be seen as more than an act of economic or political opportunism, it had to be justified at the bar of reason, and it was to the ideas of the Enlightenment that leading thinkers turned.

Rationalism as applied to religion was seen as a danger by many Friends and there was an increasing insistence on sound doctrine as speculative thought began to affect the Society. As we have already noticed, this was the period when the 'low' state of the Society was thought to be amenable to revival by a tightening of the Discipline. At this time, moreover, leadership in American yearly meetings was passing into the hands of the wealthier and more cultivated Friends in the big cities who were better educated and more cosmopolitan in outlook than their fellows, so there grew up a tension between city and country Quakerism. The last ingredient in a potentially explosive mixture was the evangelical theology that many Friends were coming to espouse, and the differences between quietist and evangelical spirituality were becoming too obvious to be ignored.

The 1827 Separation in Philadelphia

The nineteenth century opened with a conflict that presaged what was to come. In 1801, after considerable commotion, London Yearly Meeting refused to endorse a visiting American minister, Hannah Barnard, for further service in Europe, because she was considered to have unsound views, taking essentially the same position as Abraham Shackleton on the authority of scripture. She went home and, following a report from London, her monthly meeting disowned her, their action being confirmed on appeal by New York Yearly Meeting. The case became a focus for the disagreements among American Friends, as the tide of evangelical 'orthodoxy' began to flow strongly to the detriment of those who did not accept it. Books and tracts began to appear to square the evangelical emphasis with the views of early Friends, notably Henry Tuke's *Principles of Religion* (1805), which achieved a vast circulation and set the pattern for subsequent expositions of evangelical Quakerism such as those of Joseph John Gurney of England and Elisha Bates of Ohio.

Then, in 1806, Philadelphia Yearly Meeting revised its Discipline to make it a matter of disownment to deny the divinity of Christ, the immediate revelation of the Holy Spirit, or the authenticity of scripture. By now, opposition was beginning to form, and it came from the ranks of both quietist, or conservatively inclined, Friends and those who were coming to share the more rational attitude to matters of faith. The suggestion was aired for a single uniform Discipline to be devised for all the American yearly meetings. Friends who opposed this proposal correctly discerned that this would have meant the enforcement of evangelical theology and managed to prevent its going any further.

Another scandal to Friends was the connection of some in New England with Micah Ruggles and the 'New Lights', a group that professed an individualistic Unitarianism that most Friends of whatever persuasion found no difficulty in rejecting. Nevertheless, the issues of doctrine and discipline that were exercising the main body were present here too, for the New Lights, like the Ranters before them, mark an extreme at which a recognisable Quakerism shades off into something else.

The individual who eventually found himself at the centre of all these tensions was Elias Hicks (1748–1830) of Jericho, New York. Elias was a Long Island farmer and one of the greatest travelling ministers of the period, though he never came to Britain. He received an irregular education, much like any other farm boy, though he had a logical mind and an eloquence that was able to draw thousands to hear him preach. He was a surveyor of sorts, and was well read in the Bible and some of the early Quaker journals and histories. He had a striking, if somewhat traditional appearance, and had been preaching and ministering acceptably for half a century before he became the focus of Friends' internecine quarrels. Elias Hicks, like Fox, was no man's copy, and in trying to arrive at an estimate of his effect on the Society of Friends' subsequent history, it is essential to distinguish between what he himself taught, and the conclusions other people drew from what he said.

Elias was a man of deep personal religious experience in the quietist tradition. Central to his life was an awareness of that of God within which he describes in a number of ways without using a consistent terminology, though he uses many of the familiar quietist synonyms and circumlocutions. He was not concerned with descriptions; he wished to emphasise a fact. He believed that by giving heed to the divine principle within us we can come to an infallible knowledge of God, and it is this alone which can save us. Thus, our whole spiritual life should be given over to opening ourselves to this inward light, for it is the only reality.

In his system of thought he sharpened the dualism that is always latent in Quakerism by denying that human instrumentality can bring us to the light. The only path is to be purely passive and wait for the revelation to be given. Hence, neither teaching nor preaching, nor Bible study nor reason, nor example nor precept nor discipline can lead us in this path. These things belong to the outward or external world of reason, intellect and human contrivance. All they can do is act as signposts – we travel the path alone. So there is a fundamental cleavage between the world of our ordinary experience and this supra-sensible saving reality. Things which happen in the ordinary world are communicable through the normal channels of sense perception, but they are not in the same order of reality as the light. They may reflect or symbolise spiritual reality, but in no sense can they be part of it.

On this analysis, then, the grounds for traditional Christian belief are considerably weakened. The atonement may be deeply symbolic, but it cannot be objective, because the crucifixion is an event in the external, temporal order. Likewise, the union of human and divine in the person of Christ offends the principle of the absolute separation and is equally unacceptable. Particular evangelical doctrines are also incompatible with a thoroughgoing inner light theology of Elias Hicks' kind. Scripture itself cannot be ultimately authoritative because it is not part of the inward reality. Saving faith cannot include beliefs because these also have their object in the outward world rather than the inward reality. If the atonement itself is unreal, then the particular evangelical statement of it must be, and the grounds for evangelicalism's distinctive doctrine of human depravity taken away.

The irony of the whole situation was that, while his opponents saw the logical consequences of Elias Hicks' position, he himself did not assert them. The party that became known as the 'Orthodox' took the view that evangelical doctrines were both true and also the correct understanding of what early Friends had taught. They believed that Friends' fundamental doctrines had not come under scrutiny and challenge from within the Society till their own times, so to preserve essential Quakerism it was necessary to insist on doctrinal soundness. The non-Orthodox included a much wider variety of opinion, including those who broadly agreed with Elias, and many more who did not. But attitudes were hardening. To be non-Orthodox was taken to be anti-Orthodox, and this group, much against their wishes, were lumped together under the eponymous misnomer, 'Hicksites'.

In the Hicksite, as in the Orthodox party, there was a fair range of opinion so that in any given case the labels are liable to mislead. In general, though, the two groups differed over their approach to certain matters of Christian doctrine, notably the manner of the atonement, the nature of Christ's divinity, and the authority of scripture. Though certain quite general historical factors brought a strain into Quaker relationships, it was the growth of a mutual fear which translated strain into conflict.

The Hicksites were the main victims of a combination of assertive evangelical theology and rigid quietist discipline. They feared, with justification, that Friends would be disowned for matters of belief and that the doctrinal tolerance of the Society would be jeopardised. They thought, indeed, that Friends' doctrines on the points at issue were settled and strong enough to absorb deviations without undue trouble. Demurring, the Orthodox saw the inroads of rationalism in the Society, and considered that the untutored traditions of quietism would be unable to resist them. Both groups were, therefore, in reaction against each other.

We have seen that early Quaker theology was a delicately balanced system. Fox, Penn and Barclay could be heard to say that the scriptures are inspired, that our only salvation is through Christ, that his death on the cross atones for our sins and that the Christ of history and the Christ revealed to faith are one and the same. Equally, they laid total stress on the proviso that these truths can only be realised if God reveals them directly in the soul of the individual. It therefore follows that salvation occurs when the repentant individual turns to the light. Nothing can gainsay the absolute necessity for this inward experience, and reliance on the outward facts without it is futile. Unhappily, but perhaps inevitably, the two factions tore this seamless robe.

The Hicksites were deeply suspicious of the Orthodox emphasis on the authority of scripture. They saw it as an innovation that would destroy the first principle of Quakerism – the ultimate authority of the inward light. The Orthodox argued that this was a false antithesis, both were derived from the same source – another Quaker fundamental. The Orthodox argued that the atonement was a precondition for the availability of the light and should be a major item in Quaker spirituality. The Hicksites contended that this was an unjustifiable redirection of emphasis away from the spiritual to the intellectual, outward part of the original Quaker system, which was redundant in new circumstances. The Orthodox countered that without the atonement, the divinity of Christ was surrendered and the way was cleared for Unitarianism, a position vigorously opposed by the early Friends. Some of the Hicksites actually were Unitarians, but they pointed to the difficulties of definition and said that their position was no worse than the Orthodox tendency to adopt traditional Trinitarianism which was equally vigorously opposed by early Friends.

Matters came to a head at Philadelphia Yearly Meeting in April 1827 when it became quite obvious that there were two deeply divided bodies of opinion among the assembled Friends. The first intimation of difficulty was the failure of the proper committee to agree on a name for submission to the Yearly Meeting as clerk. After discussion, a minute was put before the meeting to follow the usual course in such circumstances and ask the former clerks to continue until new ones were appointed, and this was greeted with considerable dissent, since the sitting clerk was of the Orthodox party. There was really no alternative, and the

Yearly Meeting trundled on, veering between tumultuous disorder and graceless acquiescence.

At the final session, the women's meeting sent in a representative to report a proposal that a committee should be appointed to carry out a general visitation to quarterly and monthly meetings to restore 'harmony in the flock'. Again, considerable opposition was voiced, but at this point a Friend rose and said he thought he ought to announce that a number of those present had met the evening before to organise a separate meeting and had prepared an address which they intended to send down to all subordinate meetings. The die had been cast, and the action taken which fatally divided American, and therefore world, Quakerism.

The Philadelphia Hicksites separated quickly. There is argument over statistical detail, but it is clear that they substantially outnumbered the Orthodox. After holding two conferences, they established their own parallel yearly meeting. At first they looked for representatives to the existing structure of monthly and quarterly meetings but soon had to recognise that the consequence of separation had to be independence.

In 1828 New York Yearly Meeting divided, and again the Hicksites were in the majority, possibly in a proportion of two to one. The parties were more or less even when Ohio divided, but in Indiana the seceding Hicksites were considerably fewer. In Baltimore Yearly Meeting, on the other hand, the Hicksite Friends were the majority and the Orthodox seceded. New England, Virginia and North Carolina Yearly Meetings did not divide, but aligned themselves with the Orthodox group. However, a good case can be made to say that if there had been an unQuakerly head count, the Hicksites would have topped the poll.

Families were divided. In some places whole meetings separated, but elsewhere there was bitter dissension within meetings about what to do. Lawsuits followed. Questions arose as to whether the ownership of meeting houses, trust funds, burial grounds and schools could be appropriated by the separatists (of whichever kind) while a properly constituted Quaker structure existed. Accommodations were reached, but the process permanently soured relationships between the two groups.

In some ways, the Ohio separation was the most significant. The state (and the Yearly Meeting) lay at the gateway to the West, and its strategic position was bound to give it great influence as the westward movement of Friends flowed gradually through the Ohio Valley to the Great Plains and beyond. Had Ohio not divided as it did, the story of Quakerism in America might have been very different.

The rowdiest Yearly Meeting was held in the meeting house with the totally inappropriate name, Mount Pleasant, Ohio, with Elias Hicks in attendance. Some Friends see the disruptive influence of some English travelling ministers behind the crisis of 1827–8 and point to the London Friend Thomas Shillitoe as an example. He was present at the Ohio separation, and has left us an entertaining, if coloured, account of the proceedings. At meeting on the first day, according to Shillitoe, Elias Hicks and others are supposed to have 'occupied much time setting forth doctrines opposed to Christian principles'. On the second day, when their business was finished, the Committee on Indian Affairs remained in the meeting house and filled up the gallery and the front seats.

Notices from the trustees had been served on Elias and his companions and posted on the doors excluding them from Yearly Meeting sessions. When the time came for the meeting to gather, the doorkeepers tried to exclude them, but could not. It was pouring with rain and Friends struggled to get in. A crowd rushed forward and after a pause gathered round the clerks' table shouting for a clerk of their own persuasion to be appointed. At this point a great crash was heard. A cry went up that the gallery was collapsing. Exeunt Friends, by every available door and window. Shillitoe alleged it was a put-up job, designed by the separatists to get possession of the table. Misfortune was heaped on ridicule. If that were their purpose they were frustrated, for the table was smashed in the mêlée, and the clerk thought he ought to adjourn. How he got his minute accepted is not recorded.

Indian and Anti-Slavery Work in the USA

One of the few hard facts to emerge from all this was that the uproarious separation session was preceded by a meeting of the Committee on Indian Affairs. This is more significant than it sounds, for the original Quaker settlers in Ohio were frontiersmen, but they brought with them the attitude of responsibility for the Indians that Friends always adopted, apart of course from the scandal of the 'Walking Purchase'. (This is the name given to a dishonest acquisition of land from the Indians in 1737 by the Proprietor of the Pennsylvania colony, Thomas Penn. Allowed to annex such land as could be walked by a man in a day and a half, Penn hired trained walkers and cleared the ground, thus getting more than he was entitled to.) Friends always dealt squarely with the Indians apart from this and sought to prevent them being cheated, legally or illegally. They opposed the sale of liquor to the Indians and refused to rely on the hatchet and the musket as the means for adjusting relations between the two cultures. This was difficult, and all the yearly meetings maintained committees to co-ordinate Friends' official and unofficial activities.

Following the outbreak of war in 1756, Friends finally gave up control of the Pennsylvania Assembly. Part of their peace testimony was the foundation of the 'Friendly Association for gaining and preserving Peace with the Indians by pacific measures' and the 'New Jersey Association for helping the Indians'. For the four subsequent decades the frontier of settlement pressed against the Allegheny mountains and there were periodic Indian wars in which Friends sought to play a mediating role, apart from their continuing concern for the removal of the causes of wars.

By 1796 they had begun to set up mission stations to protect, educate and convert the Indians left in reservations as the frontier rolled westwards. Such work, undertaken for the best of motives, now appears as a minor amelioration of the process that led to the genocide of the aboriginal Americans. It is also a sad sidelight on John Woolman's visit to Wyalusing and his parting comment, 'and then I believed that a door remained open for the faithful disciples of Jesus Christ to labour amongst these people.'

By the early 1800s such a settlement was in operation on the Wabash River near the site of the present town of Fort Wayne, Indiana. After 1811, the yearly meetings of Baltimore and Indiana joined Ohio in opening a mission round a grist mill and a saw mill on the Auglaise River, to help the Indians to change from a hunting to a more secure agricultural economy. One of its leaders, Isaac Harvey, became a great friend of the Shawnee chief, We-as-se-ah. On one occasion, an Indian woman, accused of witchcraft, sought Isaac's help. He hid her, but his friend the chief, suspecting her hiding place, asked him to bring her to the tribal council, hoping to persuade the members to pardon her. Isaac went alone to plead, and when the pardon was refused, he offered his own life instead of hers. It was about to be accepted when We-as-se-ah intervened and pledged his life for his white friend's. Fortunately for both, the council relented, and the woman also was pardoned. She was called Polly and of mixed race, being the daughter of General Richard Butler and a Shawnee wife.

By 1832 the Shawnees had been resettled in Kansas and Friends continued their contacts with them. But the Indians could not escape the 'manifest destiny' of white America. In 1841 the Oregon Trail was opened, blazing a highway across the continent for the covered wagon trains. In 1849 the California gold rush released a further flood of white immigration and by the 1860s the majority of the Indian nations had been driven to the west of the Mississippi basin. They were about to make their last stand, tragically glorified in a thousand western films and novels.

President Ulysses S. Grant was the chief executive who had the task of pacifying the frontier after the Indian Wars of the 1850s and 1860s. In 1869 he took the imaginative step of calling on the Society of Friends to accept service under government appointment to supervise many of the Indian reservations and treaty areas. Prior to the General's inauguration he had been approached by a conference of Hicksite Friends, convened at Baltimore, which urged radical reforms in the conduct of Indian affairs. This was coincidental; Orthodox and Hicksite alike were already highly active in this field. Encouraged by the President's invitation, the Orthodox took over the Central Superintendency for the southern plains in Kansas and Oklahoma. Hicksite Friends took responsibility for the Northern Superintendency in Nebraska and South Dakota. Friends enjoyed a fairly free hand, distributing government supplies, allocating land, setting up a school system, encouraging agriculture and promoting religious meetings.

A decade later, President Hayes introduced a new and unacceptable policy. Friends remained at their posts but relinquished their government appointments. The All-Friends Committee is still at work with four congregations that include Indian Quaker members, including Friends from the Kickapoo, Osage, Wyandotte, Seneca and Cayuga tribes, while at Rough Rock Arizona, Rocky Mountain Yearly Meeting maintains its mission to the Navajo. Friends finally severed their official links with the government in 1885, but their influence on policy continued through a series of gatherings known as the Mohonk Conference on the Indians and other Dependent Peoples which met in New York State down to 1913 under the leadership of Albert K. Smiley, who was for forty years a Quaker member of the US Board of Indian Commissioners.

If the nineteenth century witnessed the extinction of the American Indian hope, it saw the beginnings of hope for the American Negro with the emancipation of the slaves in 1863. The part Friends played in this great movement illustrates the wide differences between the social and political situations in which Friends found themselves on either side of the Atlantic. Britain was still, to all intents and purposes, a narrowly aristocratic society and Quaker influence was thrown behind a group of rich, religiously motivated lobbyists who got slavery abolished almost incidentally, as part of a wide-ranging set of social reforms that permanently altered the national way of life. In the United States, however, a loose, democratic, federal state, the problem was quite different. It called for popular agitation, political clout and willingness to break the law.

In 1820, Missouri was admitted to the Union as a slave state. In St Louis during the struggle to avoid this outcome was Benjamin Lundy (1789–1839) from New Jersey by way of Ohio, journalist, agitator and traveller, one of the first men publicly to call for immediate and unconditional emancipation. Already a leader of the western abolitionists, and founder of the periodical *The Genius of Universal Emancipation*, he came back east and began to publish, to lecture and to organise anti-slavery societies whenever he found support. In Boston, Massachusetts, he found a firebrand, the uncompromising non-Quaker radical William Lloyd Garrison (1805–1879). Garrison was devoted to the struggle against what he considered to be the three greatest evils afflicting humanity, slavery, intemperance and war. He was himself intemperate in another sense. He shared Lundy's desire for immediate emancipation but was not as cautious in seeking it. His editorship of the *Genius* brought personal assault, threats and libel actions. In 1830, Lundy returned to Baltimore from a lecture tour and found Garrison in prison. He was released from both the prison and the *Genius*. He continued to campaign in the *National Enquirer*, a periodical which became the organ of the Pennsylvania Anti-Slavery Society, and his own paper, *The Liberator*.

In 1838 the name of the paper was changed to the *Pennsylvania Freeman* and Garrison's protégé, the Quaker poet John Greenleaf Whittier (1807–1892), became editor. His period in office opened with a bang, for Pennsylvania Hall, the anti-slavery headquarters in Philadelphia, was attacked and burned by a mob while a meeting was in progress. Under Whittier's editorship the paper excluded political, religious or reforming material not directly connected with its main concern, so he ruled out women's rights and debate over the use of physical force, adhering strictly to political action under the constitution and the preservation of the Union. At this time there occurred a division in the anti-slavery ranks between those who took Whittier's line and the radicals who went with Garrison, who were prepared to see an end of the Union if that would serve their ends. Strangely, it was Abraham Lincoln, who was prepared to compromise on slavery and go to war to preserve the Union, who ended up as the great emancipator.

At this point the fourth great Quaker abolitionist takes the stage, Lucretia Mott (1793–1880), one of the Coffin family from Nantucket, a Hicksite Friend, a great minister, a deeply spiritual woman, an enemy of humbug of all kinds. She learned the arts of public life in the Philadelphia Female Anti-Slavery Society, which came into being because women were barred from the conventions of the Anti-Slavery Society. With her husband she went to the general conference of the British and Foreign Anti-Slavery Society in London in 1840, but was excluded from its proceedings, largely because of her sex, but also because of the intolerance shown towards Hicksite Friends by the authorities in London Yearly Meeting. Thereafter she added women's rights to her concerns and became one of the most distinguished members of that movement in the United States.

The embers of quietism were warmer than might be supposed as the century approached its half-way mark, and having freed its own slaves, the Society was forced to take account of the need to get others to do the same. There was official resistance in both Orthodox and Hicksite branches to the use of political methods and association with non-Friends in the agitation. For many years Friends had been active in promoting colonies and manumission societies but the growth of the movement for outright abolition sometimes caused grave disquiet. Some meeting houses were closed to anti-slavery lecturers, and campaigners felt that the Society was lukewarm towards one of its most important testimonies. There were disownments and separations.

The main body of the Society, both Hicksite and Orthodox, earnestly supported the abolitionist campaign, as would have been expected. Understandably, feelings ran high, and there were strong disagreements over method. In the Indiana (Orthodox) Yearly Meeting in 1842–3, four quarterly meetings, comprising about two thousand Friends, some ten per cent of the total body, separated and set up Indiana Yearly Meeting of Anti-Slavery Friends. They advocated civil disobedience while the main body favoured education and other methods that stopped short of breaking the law.

There seems to have been no doctrinal issue in this separation, and though the new yearly meeting was never recognised elsewhere, it was received with some sympathy in London, and British Friends sent a committee to the United States to attempt to heal the breach. This attempt to reconcile the parties was a diplomatic disaster, however well-intentioned, for it concentrated almost entirely on organisational considerations rather than the matters of principle about which the anti-slavery Friends were exercised. But a sort of sanity prevailed on both sides, and by the outbreak of the Civil War most Friends had returned to the fold and the new yearly meeting had been disbanded.

By far the greatest of the Indiana anti-slavery Friends was Levi Coffin, a merchant of Cincinnati, whose service to the cause lay not in agitation but in law-breaking, defeating the Fugitive Slave Act by receiving runaway slaves in his home and arranging their safe transit onwards to freedom in Canada. There were many of these clandestine escape routes. Some were by sea to the New England coast. Some were lengthy, like the 'north star' route, up through Pennsylvania and New York to the Great Lakes. Others, like the one immortalised in Harriet Beecher Stowe's *Uncle Tom's Cabin*, came straight across the Ohio river at various points and through the states of the old Northwest Territory, of which Indiana was one. Having come from the South to escape a slave-holding society, Friends now found the old problem catching up with them again. Many of them joined with non-Friend abolitionists and opened 'stations' on the 'Underground Railroad'. Such were Levi Coffin's exploits that he became known as the President of the Underground Railroad. He and his wife are thinly disguised in the characters of Simeon and Rachel Halliday in the abolitionist classic. In twenty years of outwitting the authorities, Levi Coffin is credited with having helped two thousand fellow human beings to freedom.

The Civil War (1861–5) was a grave challenge to the Quaker conscience, willing the end but being denied approval of the means. As the armies of the Union engulfed the South the problem of free and destitute Negroes grew to major proportions, and American Friends began to develop a skill in dealing with refugees that became a major part of Quaker service in the following century. Aid Societies were set up, money raised, personnel recruited and educational work started. As the great republic returned to peaceful life the immediate needs passed, but the long-term problems remained. Friends have been concerned with race issues all along, and were in at the beginning when the twentieth century put civil rights back on the political agenda.

Victorian Recovery and the Rise of Pastoral Quakerism

O N THE SURFACE, BRITAIN SUFFERED FAR LESS POLITICAL stress than America during the nineteenth century. It was a remarkably cohesive society with definite ideas about its own position in the world – that of leadership. The Whig historians taught the nation that since the time of Magna Carta the English (and the British) political system had been characterised by a continuous movement towards the rule of law, representative institutions and democratic government. Its rewards had come in rising prosperity and commercial supremacy, and the nation thus acquired its destiny as an enlightened, civilising, colonising power on which rested the burden of keeping the world's peace. They called it, with a flourishing classical analogue, the 'Pax Britannica'.

Friends were part of this process, and their activities outside their own Society both reflected their nation's place in the world, and also its own estimate of itself. They had been part of the dissenters' struggle for a religious liberty that had attracted political freedom too. In the main, they belonged to the prosperous commercial classes and had wealth at their disposal. Their participation in the philanthropic movement at the beginning of the century had brought them a wide network of social and political contacts in the highest quarters. They had integrity, reputation, an undiminished zeal for peace and, above all, influence, which they set about using for its proper purpose – the relief of such suffering as it lay within their power to provide. It is not surprising, therefore, that as American Friends wrestled with the problems created by the internal colonisation of North America, British Friends turned their attentions to the effects of European wars.

Organising Relief

They began the century by taking part in the Committee for Relieving the Distressed Inhabitants of Germany, which operated between 1805, shortly after Napoleon's victory at Austerlitz, and 1807, when the Treaty of Tilsit closed the Continent to their ministrations. The Committee operated through a network of bankers and clergy and the Quakers contributed (apart from their cash) their links with European religious groups of a similar outlook to their own, notably those around Pyrmont and Minden who were later to become the core of modern German Quakerism. By 1814 the situation in Germany was nearly as bad as it had been at the height of the Thirty Years' War. The distress among the civilian population was calamitous and extended well beyond the end of hostilities. Over the period an enormous sum was raised at home, including grants from Parliament, and reports show that the Quakers tended to see beyond the immediate problem and reserve their money for the provision of tools for agriculture and handicraft.

The war that brought Byron to his death was fought between 1821 and 1828, and British sympathy with the cause of Greek Independence is well known. Whatever sympathy Friends had was tempered, as in the case of the American Civil War, by pacifist principles. Not for the first time were they put in a difficult position, and they now felt obliged to set up their own separate relief fund. This was a significant step. The evangelical dominance in philanthropic and relief work was generating resistance as denominational feathers were ruffled, not only among Friends, so relief work became more the product of a coalition than it had been at an earlier phase. Though raising money separately, Friends worked through the local committees of the larger relief fund scheme, and sent doctors and a dispensary out to Greece.

Part of the country had been a British protectorate since 1815 and the London Mission Societies were already in the field. Friends took the initiative in setting up schools on the Lancasterian pattern, but continuous political struggles restricted their effectiveness. Friends nevertheless came in for criticism from those who could only see a military solution to Greece's problems and considered the Quaker effort to have been unnecessarily limited and badly managed. These opinions may be justified on the facts, or they may stem from too ardent an admiration for the undoubted heroism of the Greek patriots.

The usual manner of Quaker support for international relief was informal encouragement. The Society tended not to be involved officially, but its leading members usually maintained links in three directions – with the particular relief committee(s) in the field, with their own Quaker supporters who may not have formed a committee for themselves, and with the Yearly Meeting through the Meeting for Sufferings, which preferred to give support indirectly. In Ireland, there was also a separate yearly meeting to be considered. We encounter another complication of relief work here, for as the century wore on, the question of Irish home rule came into increasing prominence in British party politics, though Friends' traditional dissent usually carried them into the Liberal camp. Throughout the period it slowly became apparent that the work of relieving poverty and distress required more than unofficial action by benevolent persons. It involved questions of economics and politics at a far higher level, and, as William Allen had surmised in Spitalfields, the whole system itself was thrown into question.

The Irish potato famine in the years around 1846 had a profound effect on Anglo-Irish relations. Emigration and starvation reduced the population by about a quarter within a decade, and it halved over the century. The extent and intensity of the impoverishment of Ireland turned its people permanently against the British connection. Most of the Irish people lived on the land. The poor law provided the workhouse but no dole or outdoor relief. In the earlier phase of the distress, the law forbade the import of cheap corn. The government in London, which was willing to organise some relief and some public works, nevertheless considered it was a problem for the Irish to solve.

This was not the view of large numbers of people, including Friends, and committees that had been active in the past revived themselves quickly, some under the aegis of landowners such as Lord Kildare, others through committees of the main religious denominations. Another part of the design of later Quaker relief organisations began to appear. Because of the political atmosphere of the time, Friends began to disengage from ecumenical effort. They were thus able to preserve the advantages which their reputation for disinterested humanitarianism brought them, and their connections in trading circles in Britain and America made sure they could act speedily when speed was required.

They utilised their experience by building up a network of trustworthy agents and organising soup-kitchens, the most effective and economical way of feeding large numbers of destitute people quickly, as William Allen had discovered in the slums of London. Free of political or journalistic bias, their reports could be relied on in London so that projects could be inaugurated where they were needed most, and plans altered as circumstances changed. Shoes and clothing were provided in the bitter winter of 1846–7.

Friends also tried long-term schemes to revive people's independence, distributing seeds to impoverished smallholders, redeeming nets and fishing boats from pawn to revive the fisheries and setting up model farms. It was a noble effort, but in retrospect the need was on a scale that could only be provided by government. The work gradually wound down, and the limits of private philanthropy on the old model had probably been reached.

The modern period of relief work is usually dated from the outbreak of the Franco-Prussian War in 1870. London Yearly Meeting became officially involved when Meeting for Sufferings set up the Friends' War Victims Relief Committee, one of the direct ancestors of the contemporary service organisation of that body. A group of just under sixty people met weekly during the emergency to support the work of a smaller group meeting more or less daily to service the pool of some forty 'commissioners' or field workers. This group, comprising unpaid volunteer men and women of mature years with responsibilities at home, and including a leaven of suitable non-Friends, went out for periods of about a month before being relieved in rotation.

They joined large numbers of others from all over Europe with the same concern and this was the first major conflict in which the Red Cross made its appearance. The scale of the Quaker response was as great as it had been in the Irish emergency a few years earlier, but at a personal level, more heroic. The destruction, the horrifying effects of modern war on the civilian population, the exposure to military operations, the difficulties of communication, the epidemics, all made entirely new demands on Friends' skills in mobilising in the struggle for peace, and on the spiritual resources they needed to see them through. It was as frustrating as Ireland, too, for once more the needs of the hour were far beyond the capacities of anyone to meet adequately. It was a watershed, and thereafter we can trace the development of that earnest dedication to peace work that is the most widely known characteristic of modern Friends.

A symbol still in use among Friends is the eight-pointed black and red Quaker star. It was originally the symbol pasted on relief goods sent out by a London newspaper, the *Daily News*, later to come into Quaker ownership, by a strange quirk of history. Friends were advised that their paper work would be speeded up if they could acquire an obvious symbol like the red cross, which was not theirs to use. The agent of the paper referred to his editorial office, which agreed to share the use of the star, and it has been used with effect ever since by British Friends and later by the American Friends Service Committee.

Three English Peacemakers

Throughout the century Friends played a full part in the campaign to remove the causes of wars as well as in undertaking relief work. They helped to set up peace societies in the United States in 1815 and in London the following year. The immediate aims were realistic. The societies campaigned for the use of arbitration in international disputes, with the insertion of an arbitration clause in all treaties; general reductions in the level of armaments and the setting up of an international court for the settlement of disputes. Among the Quakers contributing to this work were a writer, a publicist and a politician.

Jonathan Dymond (1796–1828) died perhaps before he could mature into one of the leading thinkers in the Society. Born in Exeter, he had the love of poetry and nature characteristic of the Romantic movement, and the Napoleonic wars had the effect of confirming his religious sentiments. His inquiry into the *Accordance of War with the Principles of Christianity* was very well received in Peace Society circles and his *Principles of Morality*, which contains a long essay on the light within, gives us a sad glimpse of an influence that might have been. The book went through nine editions before the end of the century.

Birmingham was a great radical centre in the nineteenth century. At the Five Ways road junction in that city stands the statue of a Quaker corn merchant, Joseph Sturge, who came from near Bristol in 1822 and stayed on to make a modest fortune and a great reputation. The American pacifist Elihu Burritt said that the site of his memorial was a happy coincidence, for 'Freedom, Peace, Temperance, Charity and Goodness were the five ways of his good and beautiful life.' We shall encounter Joseph again, through his influence on another eminent Birmingham Friend. He was active, like William Allen, in a wide range of reforming activities, including the Chartist movement for a while, but today his name is inseparably linked with the rise of the adult school movement in the latter half of the century, and his work for peace.

Joseph was an early advocate of the arbitration clause in treaties and he argued strongly for friendship with France and the United States during the mid-century period of diplomatic tension. He came to the centre of the stage in 1850 when he sought, unsuccessfully, to mediate in the dispute between Denmark and the Duchies of Schleswig and Holstein. Again, in 1854, when the Crimean War broke out, he went to St Petersburg with other Friends on a deputation to the Tsar with an address from Friends. Under this monarch's brother, another Friend, Daniel Wheeler, had been employed in agricultural improvements and draining marshes around the Russian capital, but whatever goodwill this may have created had gone, and the mission was unsuccessful. During the war, a British fleet ravaged the coasts of Finland and between the end of the war in 1856 and his death in 1859, Joseph was the instigator, and then supporter, of organised relief for Finland.

If Birmingham has a statue of Sturge, it also has a street named after another of its famous adopted sons, John Bright (1811–1889), cotton magnate, libertarian, democrat, orator, Liberal Party politician, conscience of the nation and the first Quaker cabinet minister. After Parliament had been opened to dissenters in 1832, Joseph Pease of Darlington sought election, and made history as the first MP to affirm rather than take the oath. Then, in 1843, Bright, who was to have a more distinguished career in the House, arrived for the neighbouring seat, Durham, though he was later to represent both Manchester and Birmingham.

Bright was spiritually deep. He did not talk about the fact, so it mostly passes unnoticed. He was a great advocate of laissez faire capitalism as the economic system most likely to create the conditions of peace. Trade, in his view, meant prosperity and interdependence, which in turn meant co-operation, fellowship and mutual advantage. Like Sturge and the other mercantile optimists of his time, he saw his own sphere of activity as contributing to the onward and upward movement of human progress. He saw no necessary conflict between politics and principle, but unflinchingly followed the latter when they diverged. His great speeches in opposition to the Crimean War are still remembered, particularly the words, 'The Angel of Death has been abroad throughout the land; you may almost hear the beating of his wings.'

In 1882 he was President of the Board of Trade in a Liberal government when British foreign policy was held to require the naval bombardment of the city of Alexandria in Egypt. His resignation as a matter of principle has been an example and an encouragement to Friends and others in succeeding generations who believe, as Bright did, that it is in political life, above all, that idealism must enter the engagement to outwit and outlast deceit.

During the middle years of Bright's life the Society which he loved and adorned finally moved out of its self-imposed isolation into the world. Its character did not change overnight, but a number of steps were taken which had important long-term effects on its discipline, its beliefs, its social composition and its temperament. Far reaching though they were, these changes did not give rise to the degree of strain which produced the separations in America. English Quakers remained a united body, but at the expense of losing the variety of emphasis that America retained. American Quakerism had diversified, British Quakerism remained far more homogeneous.

It is not quite correct to say that there were *no* divisions, rather it should be said that London experienced no long-lasting separations, for there were three splinter movements at various times, in an evangelical, a unitarian and a conservative direction. None has survived.

Mid-Century English Quakerism

In 1835, Isaac Crewdson of Manchester meeting issued a tract called *A Beacon to the Society of Friends* intended as a counterblast to suspected Hicksite sympathies among British Quakers. Crewdson adopted an extreme evangelical position, condemning the doctrine of the Light as a 'delusion' compared with the outward authority of scripture. In the row that followed, he and a large number of Friends around Manchester and Kendal resigned and set up on their own, taking the name, 'Evangelical Friends'. They were in an impossible position and rapidly declined as a community, most joining in fellowship with other churches, notably the Plymouth Brethren, who observed the ordinances of baptism and the Lord's Supper but, like Friends, did not have an ordained ministry. The best known member of the group was Luke Howard.

Underlying their secession was unhappiness about the absence of outward baptism and communion among Friends, which their strong biblical faith led them to see as a failure to carry out Christ's clear commands. Quakerism of the Anabaptist type can cope with this problem with little difficulty, as, perhaps, can quietism, but evangelicalism is in difficulty in contriving not to appear selective in its scriptural interpretation, while liberal Quakerism faces the problem of explaining why it accepts the parables as authoritative but not the institution of the supper. For a few years after the Beaconite secession, there was a move in London Yearly Meeting to adopt the two ordinances. It failed, but it shows up exactly the problem which exercised Ohio Yearly Meeting later, with a different result.

In the generation that followed the Beaconites, Manchester was again the centre of controversy. In 1858 Manchester Friends Institute had been set up as a social club for younger Friends. Its programme included lecture series and discussions, and it became an important feature of Quaker life in the Manchester area. A prominent member of the Institute was David Duncan, who has been described as 'an earnest and outspoken Victorian intellectual.' In 1861 he delivered a series of lectures on *Essays and Reviews*, that mid-Victorian theological time-bomb assembled by the Master of Balliol, Benjamin Jowett. David Duncan, and those who supported him, were willing to countenance the use of scholarship to elucidate the meaning of scripture, to break away from the doctrine of inerrancy, and to brave the disapproval of those in the yearly meeting who might object.

After some initial controversy, Duncan's opinions seemed to have been forgotten, but by 1866 the elders and ministers of Manchester meeting began to question the kind of books purchased for the library and sought to limit or prohibit discussion after lectures. David Duncan was accused of unsoundness and the matter found its way to Yearly Meeting. There were visitations to Manchester, and in 1871 David Duncan was disowned. Duncan was a harbinger of new things, though he died tragically of smallpox before his appeal to the Yearly Meeting could be heard.

Like the Beaconites, the Duncanites were wrestling with the strains that modern ways of thinking place on the traditional Quaker positions. In their case, the ambivalence of the Quaker doctrine of scriptural authority required replacement with something more rational, and this principle they resolutely stuck by. Beaconites and Duncanites were perhaps incompatible, but it is certain that each group was representative of opinions that continued to be found on the back benches of meeting houses throughout the period.

In times of turmoil there are always people who try to stick to familiar ways. Such were the Friends who followed John G. Sargent into schism in 1870. The General Meeting instituted at Fritchley in Derbyshire rejected evangelical theology, and sought to preserve the peculiarities of speech and dress that had been made optional in 1860. It was reported that they '. . . utterly resist being guided by Reason, except in matters of buying and selling, at which they are very sharp.' Socially they no longer attended or accepted the authority of London Yearly Meeting. Fritchley suffered its own secession when a group of Friends at Bournbrook, Birmingham, set up its own general meeting against Fritchley's wishes. The Bournbrook group died out, and the remaining Fritchley Friends were welcomed back into London Yearly Meeting in 1967.

So England experienced a few minor defections, but nothing remotely resembling the upheavals in the United States. There were strong personalities of a rationalist, conservative or evangelical turn of mind who came into conflict with the Society, but they seem never to have had a mass following. This is probably because of the peculiar circumstances of English Friends. John Bright thought they were 'the most tolerant people on earth' and the only church that could 'freely discuss and make great reforms without schism or something like dissolution'. He may correctly have interpreted the mood of the average meeting, but as a historical generalisation, or a statement about the international community of Friends, he was quite wrong.

It is to insularity rather than tolerance that we should look. Membership was still hard to come by and easy to lose, and for friends who cared about their Quaker identity belonging was very high on their list of priorities. This is because of the way of life rather than the Discipline, for the plain dress, and use of 'thee' and 'thou', the testimonies against war and titles, the training which produced the repose of silent worship and quiet decorum, were all meaningless outside Friends. Additionally, the Society was small and closely knit, to a considerable degree a system of kinship with intimate social and business connections superadded. Most members of the Society had been educated at one or other of the Quaker boarding schools and John Stephenson Rowntree acidly commented that Quakers prized the length of their Quaker descent as a nobleman prized the antiquity of his titles.

By 1860 it had become clear to Friends in London Yearly Meeting that their Society was possibly in terminal decline. It is estimated that the Quaker population in 1680 had stood at about 60,000. In 1840 an unofficial census numbered the Society at 16,227 in a greatly increased national population. There were very few convincements and the trend of membership was inexorably downwards. To many, the dress regulations were offensive and the prohibition on marrying out, intolerable. Quaker dissenters did not set up rival Quaker churches, they simply left and went elsewhere. The Society saw its danger in time. It both re-formed its Discipline and began a reappraisal of its role that brought it safely to the twentieth century.

The process began in 1856 when Yorkshire Quarterly Meeting proposed that Quakers should be free to marry non-members with-out facing the penalty of disownment. It took three successive Yearly Meetings before the change was agreed in 1859. The Society had finally thrown off the noose that had come close to strangling it. Perhaps en-couraged by these moves, Joseph Sturge had suggested in 1857 that the peculiarities of dress and speech be made optional. Similar difficulties were encountered in carrying Friends along with the proposed reform, but it came into effect in 1860. These *ad hoc* decisions persuaded the Society that a complete revision of the Discipline was now necessary and this was completed in 1861 without delay. Over fifty rules were abro-gated or removed. There was no immediate change in Friends' practice, but the air of freedom was circulating again, and a way was opening for a renewal of the Society of altogether different proportions.

The first symptoms of an intellectual awakening can be traced in the pages of new journals, the *British Friend* and *The Friend* (both founded in 1843), the epistles of Yearly Meetings, and the first appearance of the *Friends' Quarterly Examiner* in 1859. The most dramatic challenge to Quaker self-awareness came with the publication of *Quakerism Past and Present* by John Stephenson Rowntree in 1860. This book was the winning entry in an essay competition for a prize of 100 guineas put up by an anonymous 'gentleman' for an account of the causes of the Society's declension (which he both asserted and deplored), from the strength and influence of its original witness.

Rowntree offered what was in effect a critique of the way evan-gelicalism and quietism had combined to produce the character of the Society of his day. He emphasised the spiritual character of early Quakerism and criticised its subsequent failure to develop creatively its early preaching. He pointed to its disparagement of reason and the Bible, its neglect of prayer, its suspicion of enthusiasm and its elevation of silence above what he considered its proper place to be. He did not like the concentration of power in the hands of elders and overseers and the intolerance of dissent. He pointed to the significance of Methodism as a factor in Quaker decline.

We can see now that in the period that followed, Friends were grop-ing their way towards a new outlook and were much more receptive to the ideas being debated in the wider Church. Quakerism was no longer self-explanatory and the 'Tradition' was being scrutinised critically by a much larger body of Friends than had been able to support the Shackletons and the Rathbones of earlier years. The first great investigation of Quaker origins, *The Inner Life of the Religious Societies of the Commonwealth* by Robert Barclay of Reigate, appeared in 1876, and about a decade later came two books which heralded the arrival of the liberal theology which captured English Quakerism as quickly and as completely as evangelicalism had done – *A Reasonable Faith* by three unnamed Friends in 1886 and *The Gospel of Divine Help* by Edward Worsdell in the same year. The latter book caused such a scandal that it was actually attacked on the floor of London Yearly Meeting and cost its author the headship of Lancaster Friends' School.

London Avoids the Pastoral System

Further points of comparison with American Quakerism arise at this point. These are the years of the great revivals in the United States, and though there were revivals in Britain, the Society of Friends did not acquire the large infusions of new blood that came into the western yearly meetings of the Orthodox branch across the Atlantic. The reasons were partly theological, for English Friends were moving away from evangelicalism at a time when it was experiencing a new lease of life elsewhere. The main reason, however, probably lies in the social position and expectations of English Friends. They were in the upper reaches of a stratified society, and were paternal rather than comradely in their approaches to the unchurched.

We have seen that originally Friends' educational efforts on behalf of other people's children were concentrated on the British and Foreign Schools Society. This support continued, but in the middle of the century they began to move into adult education partly under the inspiration of William White, Joseph Sturge and the Severn Street Schools of Birmingham. By 1900 Friends were running 197 First Day Schools, as they were called. Run by volunteers, they were originally intended to teach basic literacy, but they also came to express the values of the Victorian philanthropists.

These institutions taught temperance and biblical knowledge. They encouraged self-help and thrift through savings banks and insurance schemes. They fostered personal improvement through physical and mental recreations and developed social responsibility through committee work and members' participation. Their usefulness declined after elementary education became compulsory in 1870 and the subsequent movement of population away from the city centres began. The problem was that though the organisers of the adult schools wanted to make people Christians, they were reluctant to encourage them to go to other churches and yet disinclined to make them Friends. So, *faute de mieux*, the adult schools became quasi-churches.

Thus, the Sunday evening programmed meeting with hymns, talks and scriptural readings, the so-called 'mission meetings', came into being. By 1875 it was estimated that there were as many members of mission meetings as there were Friends. Clearly this posed a problem which Friends could not cope with. A few mission members visited meetings and were discouraged by the silence or disappointed by the formality and reserve, which contrasted with the vigorous and friendly atmosphere of the schools. A few became Friends, but most did not.

Some mission meetings became to all intents and purposes independent, Quaker-inspired churches. Policy towards them varied across the country and it became clear to Friends and mission members alike that what was on offer was in fact a second-class Quakerism. A great opportunity had been missed. On the positive side, great educational work had undoubtedly been done in the schools, and the experience of crossing class barriers drew many Friends to consider for the first time the social implications of their faith.

In 1881, official recognition was given to a development that had been going on for some years, when the Home Mission Committee gained the reluctant endorsement of the Yearly Meeting. It sought to put missioners into the field to make converts, to provide Christian education and to begin such enterprises as Sunday schools and temperance societies such as the Band of Hope. Sometimes efforts were co-ordinated with the mission meetings in the cities, but the main task of the Committee was to support and revive small country meetings. By 1893 the Committee had forty-three missioners at work.

The heart of the Society of Friends was not really in it. The missioners were often evangelical and neither well-off nor well-educated. They preached, arranged services, gave pastoral care, were closely attached to meetings, unlike the mission meetings that were based on the adult schools, and they were paid. Moreover, they began to get results, and they faced Friends with the challenge of finding a place for a programmed and pastoral element in the life of their Society. The challenge was declined. The periodicals and conferences of the time contain erudite discussions of topics such as 'The Message of Quakerism' or 'Friends' Social Witness Today' without a terribly clear idea of who, apart from other Quakers, were to receive the message and the witness. Consequently, when Friends encountered a willing audience, they drew back in confusion, for it was not composed of their sort of people.

There were no such hesitations in the United States. In the western yearly meetings the grandchildren of the old Orthodox party rode a wave of religious revival that invigorated their meetings, greatly increased their numbers and made dramatic changes in the outward expression of their Quakerism. It was no part of their intention to preserve tender denominational purity or to struggle with the challenge of modern thought. They preached Christ crucified – and the converts came flocking in to a warm welcome.

How pastors and programmed meetings entered Quaker church life is part of the history of the Orthodox Friends who emerged as a clearly discernible sub-group early in the century. Their distinguishing feature at that time was not their manner of worship, which was as silent and traditional as the Hicksites', but their concern for sound doctrine. The Hicksites warned them that this attitude would have two consequences: first, a preoccupation with the finer points of doctrine would lead Friends away from spiritual religion to a more formal and intellectual faith; second, where faith is considered primarily in these terms, it would be impossible to preserve unity, and divisions would occur. On both counts, history shows the Hicksites to have been right.

The Hicksite yearly meetings of Philadelphia, New York, Baltimore, Ohio and Indiana originated in the desire for liberty and the refusal to accept what they considered to be the unwarranted use of authority in matters of faith. In the same way that the original Hicksites had been a collection of people with a wide variety of views, so now the Friends in this tradition are remarkable for the diversity of their views and witness.

In 1827 there was a fruitful combination of rationalism, liberalism and conservatism in the Hicksite branch, and these attitudes did them good service. These Friends steadfastly refused to adopt programmed meetings and the pastoral system, and are now the main bearers of the tradition of silent worship in America. Toleration of diversity meant laying stress on individual responsibility and Hicksite Friends have always seen philanthropy and social concern as more effective ways of inaugurating the Kingdom of Heaven than mission work. In 1844 they acquired a voice when the *Friends' Intelligencer* of Philadelphia made its first appearance. Once the original break had been made, the dramas of further separations and revivals passed the Hicksites by. In the latter half of the nineteenth century, there was probably not much difference in the pattern of life between London Friends and Friends of the Hicksite branch. We have seen how Hicksite and Orthodox alike took part in the anti-slavery agitation and the Underground Railroad. Following the war, both branches began to work in the related fields of education and race relations, and we have seen them both in the Indian Superintendencies on the Great Plains. The Hicksites began to develop their own schools, notably the George School near Philadelphia and Brooklyn Friends' School, and in 1869 they set up Swarthmore College, also in the vicinity of Philadelphia as their first venture into higher education. For the more specific purpose of the religious education of the children in the meeting, the various yearly meetings came together in 1868 to found the Friends' First Day School Conference for the sharing of ideas and the development of materials. In 1875 a new yearly meeting came into being in Illinois, set off by Indiana with none of the traumas of that body's origins.

The liberal strain in Hicksite Quakerism shows through most clearly in the concerns of its individual members for social progress on all fronts. In 1881, the Friends' Union for Philanthropic Labor was started, bringing together again numbers of Friends who had helped to run the Underground Railroad. As time went by, the matters taken up included child welfare and industrial conditions, prison reform and civil rights, temperance and peace. This body was an obvious precursor of the American Friends Service Committee.

Looking back, we can see a trend of closer co-operation as the nineteenth century progressed and communications became easier. In 1893 the Friends Religious Conference grew out of the interests of those who had taken part in the World Congress of Religions that year, and in 1894 the Friends Education Conference convened, intending to meet biennially for those Friends in the Hicksite tradition with concern and responsibility for Friends' schools.

These organisations frequently met at the same time and in the same place, and it seemed reasonable to combine them. Accordingly, between 1900 and 1902 the work was done to create the Friends General Conference. This body has a consultative and co-ordinating function and its membership now goes well beyond the old Hicksite yearly meetings, though it retains the qualities of tolerance, independence and resolution that originally gave rise to them.

The Influence of Joseph John Gurney

No sooner had the Philadelphia furore of 1827 died down than an English Friend, Joseph John Gurney (1788–1847), appeared on the scene. Though debarred from the university as a dissenter, Gurney went to Oxford and studied under private tutors, becoming a brilliant linguist and biblical scholar. He was a member of the rich Norwich banking family and was the brother of Elizabeth Fry. Dividing his time between residence at Earlham Hall and travel in pursuit of his many religious and philanthropic interests such as the Bible Society and the Schools Society, he became a renowned minister and an exponent of evangelical principles, which he combined with a deep and refined quietist spirituality.

In the early 1830s he caught the attention of John Wilbur (1774–1856), a New England Friend who, though Orthodox himself, conceived the view that Joseph John was departing on a number of points from what he considered Friends' true teaching to be. Wilbur was a representative of the more traditional strand in Orthodox thinking and is a good touchstone for the artificiality of drawing a sharp distinction between Orthodox and Hicksite on purely doctrinal grounds. He was as deeply suspicious of 'creaturely activity' as Elias Hicks and was strongly opposed to Friends' ecumenical involvement in philanthropy and Bible societies and anything that looked like preparation for worship. He was on a collision course with Gurney.

Gurney had already developed a clear and powerful exposition of evangelical Quakerism in his *Observations on the Religious Peculiarities of the Society of Friends* (1824) and *Essays on the Evidences, Doctrines and Practical Operations of Christianity* (1825). He presents Quakerism not as the Truth in opposition to others' errors, but as an expression of commonly held Christian principles which Friends have developed in a certain direction through their peculiarities and testimonies. Thus, evangelical theology became the vehicle whereby Friends, like members of other denominations, could break out of the circle of hostility and suspicion that had so often characterised interdenominational contacts since the Reformation, and concentrate on more important things such as mission work.

These ideas were revolutionary because they struck at Friends' image of themselves as a spiritual aristocracy and also undermined the traditional understanding of the authority of scripture. Evangelicalism provided an ideology for Quakerism that the educated could defend and the simple could understand. It was both puzzling and threatening because it used a different terminology from that of traditional Quakerism, causing Friends like John Wilbur to argue that the substance of the faith was thereby endangered and that Gurneyite evangelicalism would precipitate a further round of disownments and secessions. Friends had traditionally spoken about the light in an imprecise way as some divine spiritual energy or operative power that they knew they had experienced. It was terrible and gentle by turns but it was a safe guide through life. Gurney knew this power, of course, but in his mind he did not know how it was different from what he read in scripture about the Holy Spirit. So he tended to assimilate the two, and thus raised the whole question of whether it was possible to distinguish them. Was he right?

Also traditionally, Friends have taught that justification is the forgiveness of sins through the intercession of Christ subsequent to repentance, or turning to the light. Sanctification is the process of being moulded into the likeness of Christ that comes with growth in the spiritual life. Since the common denominator of both experiences is the light, they are both aspects of the same process. Gurney, however, taught the full evangelical doctrine of the atonement in which sanctification is logically entirely dependent on justification. Christ's death frees you, but the Holy Spirit sanctifies you. Here Gurney insisted on the distinction. Again, was he right?

John Wilbur did not think so, and when he was in Britain in 1831-3 he drew his misgivings about matters of this kind to Gurney's attention, both personally and in some letters to his Friend George Crosfield, which were published in a small book. Gurney epitomised all that Wilbur thought wrong with the direction the Society seemed to be taking, and he returned home without apparently having advanced his cause very much. However, in 1837 Gurney applied to the Ministers and Elders Meeting in London for a certificate to travel in the ministry in America. The liberating meeting was not clear that it should endorse the request and took some hours to decide finally that it should. This suggests that in spite of his scholarship and urbane presence, there was considerable suspicion of Joseph John Gurney in London Yearly Meeting.

His tour among Orthodox Friends was an immense success. Thousands came to his meetings, he preached to members of Congress and met the President. He promoted Bible societies and encouraged the school at Richmond, Indiana, which later adopted the name of his Norwich home and is now one of the distinguished Quaker academies – Earlham College. Friends might not have adopted his ideas so willingly had he not possessed such an appealing presence, and had John Wilbur not taken it upon himself to oppose him at every turn, writing to people and travelling to interview them to show up Gurney's doctrine as unsound. Slowly, as before 1827, battle lines were drawn up, and the Orthodox party divided into Gurneyite and Wilburite factions.

In 1843, John Wilbur was the victim of a scandalous piece of Quaker gerrymandering. Pressure was brought on his monthly meeting to disown him, and it was stoutly resisted. The quarterly meeting was then persuaded to abolish the monthly meeting outright and transfer all membership to a neighbouring and more pliant one, which promptly executed the disownment. There was uproar, and in 1845 New England Yearly Meeting separated into a larger (Gurneyite) body and a smaller (Wilburite) body, who immediately went to law over the ownership of property. It was 1827–8 all over again.

Though John Wilbur's views did not obtain a large following, or express widely held sentiments, they did prove capable of sustaining a small but permanently influential group now known as Conservative Friends. There are three Conservative yearly meetings – Iowa, North Carolina and Ohio – and they are an important part of the Quaker landscape. In the past, they survived because they rejected many of the Gurneyite innovations and drew together in close groups to maintain what they saw as the true traditions of the Society. Friends have great difficulty in describing what the Conservative attitude is, but they know that without it the Society would be lacking something distinctive and very important.

Friends now found that the existence of a dozen or so Orthodox yearly meetings tended to exaggerate differences, which proved to be exportable from one group to another. It was the practice to exchange Yearly Meeting epistles and to recognise other people's ministers. This was known as being 'in correspondence' and operated at the top level. Your own doctrinal posture could be read from whose epistles you accepted and whose you did not. London, for example, did not recognise yearly meetings of 'the other branch' as they called the Hicksites, until as late as 1908.

Without perhaps realising the implications of what was going on, London, Dublin, and North Carolina, Indiana, New York and Baltimore Orthodox Yearly Meetings immediately recognised the larger body in New England, and in the two latter yearly meetings, and soon after in Iowa, there was a secession of Wilburite Friends. Philadelphia Orthodox was more cautious. After concluding an investigation that in fact leaned towards the smaller body, it declined to go on corresponding with the other yearly meetings. (It should be noted that this was a development within the Orthodox tradition. The Hicksite yearly meetings were not involved in any way.) Though it continued to accept transfers of membership from both Gurneyite and Wilburite bodies, it declined to receive the minutes of travelling ministers or appoint meetings for them. It was thus well placed, when the fires of the nineteenth century died down, to lead the way in the growing reconciliation of the Orthodox and Hicksite traditions that is a dramatic feature of the second half of the twentieth century.

The Philadelphia compromise, which may have seemed suspiciously pragmatic to a serious Friend, shows up well in contrast to the story of the Orthodox body in Ohio. Having separated from the Hicksite Friends, it now lost the Wilburites too. It was probably the absence of counterbalancing views that prevented what became a vigorous and experimental evangelical Quakerism in Ohio from recognising the virtue of certain traditional positions, and in due course, brought some Friends to question both the testimony against sacraments and the principles of the Quaker business method.

The Pastoral System Emerges in America

In the decades from 1850 to 1880, Midwestern America was changing. As the railroads pushed westwards, subsistence farming gave way to grain production for the market. Friends became spread over a wide area, Iowa Yearly Meeting being set up in 1863 and Kansas in 1872. Friends settled with members of other denominations in small townships rather than predominantly with their own kind. It was a different kind of migration than that which had taken Friends across the Alleghenies to Ohio and Indiana. As the public (state) school system spread, Friends gave up one of the main institutions, the Friends' school, by which the outlook and peculiarities of the community were inculcated into its young. It was also a time of great religious revival, and, in co-operation with their neighbours, Friends found themselves taking part. On the other hand, this was the period in which Friends began to develop their present system of higher education. The origins of over half a dozen of their present undergraduate colleges lie in the second half of the century.

Making allowances for local circumstances, the activities of Indiana Yearly Meeting in the decade before the Civil War are a mirror image of what was going on in London. Friends went from house to house distributing Bibles and tracts. They ran Bible schools and First Day schools. They revised the Discipline, substituting 'simplicity' for the traditional 'plainness'. They sought to limit the influence of elders and to encourage more than just the 'weighty' to minister in meeting. They read the Gurneyite *Friends' Review* out of Philadelphia, which reported the revivals in the eastern cities, often led by lay people, often with a minimum of structure and programme, and always enthusiastic. As time went by, the younger and more active Friends came to think that there was no earthly reason why they should not do the same. They began to realise that this was how the Society of Friends itself began, and that was their revolution.

At Indiana Yearly Meeting in 1860 a petition that must have been highly embarrassing arrived at the clerks' table. It requested a special Sunday evening meeting for younger Friends. Ministers were not to preach or dominate proceedings and the whole congregation was to take part. Fifteen hundred people came and over a hundred testified or prayed, and for the first time in Friends' recorded history for a hundred and fifty years, *somebody sang a hymn.* This meeting had a long-term importance. Its moving spirits were young, and its mood not really acceptable to the establishment. It was enthusiastic and not over much concerned with the virtues of silence. It marks the real beginning of revivalism among Friends, and out of the results of revival came the first appointments of pastors among the Quaker congregations.

Revivals are the practical outcome of any kind of Christianity that takes seriously the salvation of the soul or the fear of its damnation. They have occurred periodically in both the Catholic and Protestant churches. The evangelical revival associated with Wesley and the Methodists in the eighteenth century was the first wave of revival in the modern world. The second came in the nineteenth century in Britain and America, and some have seen the Pentecostal movement as a third wave of the same phenomenon. British Friends were deeply affected by the first wave, and American Quakerism was irrevocably changed by the second.

Revivals are about preaching the gospel to the unchurched and producing a real commitment in the habitual Christian, so they depend on charismatic leaders. Meetings are emotional rather than intellectual occasions and are characterised by fervent enthusiasm. Atmosphere is created by songs and rhythmic choruses, often in a contemporary style to distinguish them sharply from the familiar hymns and music which enshrine the accepted religious values that revivalism is implicitly rejecting. Extempore prayer is essential, and at some point preachers ask for personal commitment to a new life in Christ from those whom the service has reached. Such converts often testify in dramatic terms and there may be a 'mourners' bench' which they may approach to make a public avowal of penitence and acceptance of salvation. There is no single pattern, but most revival meetings bear some resemblance to this.

There was at first considerable resistance to Orthodox Friends getting involved in this kind of thing. There were many who were, though firmly Gurneyite in their theology, still highly traditional in their suspicion of any pre-arrangement in a religious meeting and in their feeling that forces were released at revival meetings that Friends' habits and structures might find it difficult to accommodate to. But the pressure was too great. The periodical *Christian Worker* (founded in 1871) began to diverge from the *Friends' Review* and to support innovations that had no precedent in Quaker practice, and the two great Quaker evangelists, John Henry Douglas and David B. Updegraff, were in the prime of their ministry. The crucial decade was the 1870s.

Seeking to harness the new enthusiasm to more traditional ways, the Gurneyite yearly meetings turned in the years 1871-3 to the 'general meeting' which had been in use for extension purposes earlier in England. A wave of revivalism followed, and far from controlling the movement, the general meetings served only to give it added impetus. The vigour of the Quaker body increased visibly, but at the same time large numbers of converts appeared who had no particularly Quaker seasoning.

This was a considerable problem which had not really been thought through at the beginning – and it was too late to go back, even though that were thought desirable, which it was not. How were new Friends to be nourished spiritually when many were on a religious high? How were they to be shown the importance of the Society's distinguishing testimonies? How were they to be acclimatised to the silent worship when their door of entry to the Society of Friends had been a revival meeting? Who was to give an authoritative answer to the myriad questions on doctrine and biblical teaching that they brought with them? In other words, what would be the nature of the follow-up to revival? For follow-up there had to be, if the whole enterprise was to be more than a glorious sham.

At first, the traditional means were tried, and specially appointed yearly meeting committees experimented with combined monthly meeting support, or arrangements for unpaid resident ministers to undertake the responsibility. This was in effect an adaptation of the hallowed institution of the travelling ministry, and elders and recorded ministers both took part. Sometimes evangelists, not always Friends, were employed to carry out revival meetings, and the meeting itself, in consultation with Yearly Meeting, would contribute to their keep for a period of extended service after the original evangelistic campaign. Theoretically, the meeting itself should have undertaken the task, but three factors combined to prevent it, all connected with the circumstances of Midwestern rural life at that period.

First, there was simply the increasing size of meetings, and the wide areas over which the membership was spread. In more densely populated places a normal committee of ministry and oversight could cope with visiting and pastoral care, but where Friends were spread out over many miles, the cost in time alone of maintaining this system was proving prohibitive. Second, some Friends might have found such service possible, notwithstanding, but the farmer was now a single crop producer, vulnerable to market fluctuations which he could not insure himself against, so he would find it reasonable to contribute part of the upkeep of a pastoral Friend where he would be unable to contribute time to that service himself. Third, the ministerial vocation has always been understood among Friends of all persuasions to require a discipline of study and meditation in preparation for the exercise of the gift that Friends in the Midwest were simply too pressed by their economic circumstances to undertake.

The solution seemed obvious – to liberate some members of the body for full-time work. There was no ordination, no intention to compromise with the testimony against a hireling ministry, and the pastoral system entered the Society of Friends. As the pastoral system took root in the 1880s and 1890s certain strains appeared. The most noticeable was the changeover from meetings based on silence to worship services presided over by the pastor, which began to include the familiar elements of the worship of other denominations – hymns and music, readings from scripture and a prepared sermon. Silence, or open worship was retained but in an attenuated form, a shadow of what it had been a decade or two earlier. This added a layer to the differences that already existed between the various branches of the Society, for there was now a far more obvious symbol of division. In the Gurneyite yearly meetings, the meeting became the Friends' Church.

This development was historically rich in significance. Earlier in the century, one Quaker tradition began to bump into a rationalism that might have taken it outside Christianity altogether. Now, another branch bumped into the idea that what it had hitherto thought were its defining characteristics (silent worship, free ministry, rejection of sacraments, etc.), might be no more than the optional extras of a particular variant of the Reformation tradition. The question arose, and still requires an answer, are the Quakers Protestants-in-disguise, or something rather different?

The attempt to answer this question lies at the root of yet another division, when the matter that caused the Beaconite separation in England reared its head in the United States. The problem of taking scripture literally and still maintaining the testimony against sacraments has always caused trouble. In the early 1880s a large number of Friends in Ohio and elsewhere, the followers of David B. Updegraff, accepted baptism. In 1885, Ohio Yearly Meeting refused to make it a disciplinary matter for a minister to participate in, or advocate the necessity of, the outward ordinances (i e baptism and the Lord's Supper). The other Orthodox yearly meetings, including London and neighbouring Indiana, promptly issued statements reaffirming the traditional position and thus isolating Ohio.

Friends and the Holiness Revival

These developments need to be understood clearly if the evangelical form of Quakerism is to be put in its proper perspective. In the Midwestern heartland in the middle of the nineteenth century the holiness revival was bringing about irrevocable and far-reaching changes in American church life, while at the same time the sectarian character of the Society of Friends was breaking down under the pressures of economic and social change, as we have seen. On the frontier, there was a sparse population, a hostile environment, poverty and insecurity, no professional classes, little law and few institutions of social control. The positive side of these circumstances was the development of the virtues of generosity, neighbourliness, independence, frankness, optimism and the kind of resentment of government the British find difficult to comprehend. It is easy to see how the churches embodied, preached and practised these things. One of their instruments was the holiness revival.

The roots of the holiness revival lie in the so-called second Great Awakening, conventionally dated as beginning with the great revival meeting held at Cane Ridge, Kentucky, in 1801. From then on, on both sides of the Appalachian range, the periodic camp meeting became the main form of evangelism and the main means of church planting and growth. It was based on extravagant preaching, raw emotionalism and urgency in seeking conversions. Life was precarious and this might be one's last chance. So the importance of instantaneous conversion was emphasised, as was the quite unorthodox assumption that one was free to take one's own decision to turn to God. This might be closer to early Quaker threshing meetings than many might be comfortable in admitting. The camp meeting tradition lives on in the Billy Graham crusades.

The end of the Civil War in 1865 marks the beginning of a new era, as the frontier retreated across the Mississippi, leaving much more settled communities in the East. One of the doctrines that had animated the camp meeting tradition was that of the second blessing, or the second work of grace. The first work of grace is conversion, when one is saved from the consequences of one's past sins, empowered to struggle against present sin, and assured of a place in heaven. John Wesley had taught that it was possible to experience a second work of grace, that under the inspiration of the Holy Spirit it was possible to achieve a total victory over sin and lead a life of Christian perfection. The holiness movement, which was essentially Wesleyan in inspiration, took this doctrine and fashioned it into something different. The experience of entire or total sanctification subsequent to conversion became the focus of Christianity to the exclusion, it seemed to outsiders, of almost everything else.

The holiness movement proved divisive and troublesome to all the established denominations, including Friends. After the Civil War it became institutionalised and there were already holiness churches that had broken away from the mainstream. It was also subversive of order. It had its own publishing organisations independent of official control, many of its itinerant evangelists were freelances, answerable to no synod, bishop or yearly meeting, its doctrines became a full-blown ideology, and it set up a whole range of what would now be called para-church organisations from mission societies to presses which produced Sunday school materials and song-books. With the passage of time, tensions increased between loosely organised holiness associations and solidifying denominational bureaucracies at a time of rapid social change. This was the challenge that changed the face of the Orthodox tradition.

As we have already noted, there was a decline in traditional observances and practices before the Civil War. The Hicksite separations meant a renewed interest in theology and the growth of a 'Gurneyite' identity, critical of early Friends, more attached to the Bible and accepting of the view that justification and sanctification are names for distinct spiritual realities. Gurneyite Friends engaged in politics, took part in interdenominational philanthropic activity, read periodicals and books, and became interested in music. A movement for renewal grew up, concerned to find a new balance between the progressive evangelicalism of the times and what was best in the Quaker tradition. Unfortunately, it failed to inspire the body of Friends. Many of its leaders were people of standing in society as well as in the Society. Perhaps it lacked the common touch.

The renewal Friends were in fact upstaged by those who had been influenced by the holiness movement. The first ever Quaker revival meeting was held at Bear Creek, Iowa, in 1867 and was peremptorily closed down by elders. Much more celebrated was the series of revivals held at Walnut Ridge, Indiana, the same year. Quaker revivals tended to be organised by those who had been to Methodist ones, and though they were not infrequent in the next few years, they were sporadic and uncoordinated. Friends' attraction to the holiness movement has a number of causes. The development came at a time when sectarian Quakerism was in sharp decline, and young people were increasing in influence. There is not much difference in practical terms between an evangelist and a minister, and inevitably, as traditional practices declined, there was a reappraisal of the theology on which they were based. Most importantly, perhaps, foreshadowing the group which later took London Yearly Meeting in a liberal direction, there were Friends devoted to the promotion of the new ways, and determined to use their influence to bring them about.

Holiness teachings obviously met a deep need among Friends, as among Americans generally. There is a parallel to be drawn between itinerant evangelists and travelling ministers on the old pattern. The un-structured meeting for worship and the general-purpose general meeting, both traditional among Friends, lent themselves easily to new forms and new functions. Such was the influence of holiness elders and preachers that by the 1870s disciplines were being revised to include longer doctrinal sections. At the same time many of the old ways were being relinquished, and not only the old speech and dress codes. Significantly, marrying out became acceptable and marriage by the pastor the norm, instead of the reciprocal promises of the traditional Quaker marriage.

The holiness revival left an indelible imprint on the evangelical Quaker tradition, the most significant consequence being the entrench-ment of the pastoral system. Actually, it is hard to see what could have emerged apart from some sort of development of this kind. Indiana Yearly Meeting was 18,000 strong in 1881 and in the subsequent dec-ade received 9,000 applications for membership. The yearly meeting had many new members, many new churches and a plummeting pro-portion of birthright Friends. But Friends' whole tradition was against this kind of thing, and the performance did not live up to the promise. The educational standard of many pastors was poor and many were part-time. The twentieth century was to see a struggle to raise these standards, which succeeded magnificently, as the concomitant Quaker prejudice against book learning in religion was dissipated.

Many Friends, of course, were opposed to the changes taking place and the second major consequence of the revival was the secession of a sizeable number of Friends who set up new yearly meetings more in keeping with their convictions. One has to be careful when discuss-ing Conservative Quakerism because each of the Conservative yearly meetings has its own historical origins. When the process we are dis-cussing came about there were already 'conservative' Wilburite yearly meetings in New England and Ohio, to say nothing of the Philadelphia Orthodox. These would have had serious differences with the yearly meetings about to emerge, particularly over such matters as the na-ture of the atonement and the proper Quaker attitude to the scriptures, though all were in one sense evangelical.

The separation of Iowa Yearly Meeting took place in 1877, Western YM (Plainfield, Indiana) in 1878 and Kansas YM, barely seven years since it was set off, in 1879. Only Iowa remains. The Conservative sepa-rations which occurred in the 1870s were responses to the growth of revivalism and holiness doctrines rather than the continuing effects of the 1845 separations, thus arising within the larger body of the Orthodox Quaker tradition. Seceding Friends did not originally object to evangelism, but objected strongly to the methods used. They saw the introduction of the programmed meeting and the pastoral system as fatal compromises with the proper Quaker tradition.

This, of course, strengthened the hand of the revival party, who were drawn ever more closely towards the mainstream of the holiness movement, also being drawn into the controversies which marked the gradual supersession of holiness by fundamentalism and Pentecostalism as the twentieth century dawned. They were not unopposed, however, and a middle party emerged which was sufficiently strong to prevent evangelical Friends becoming another holiness or fundamentalist denomination. It is quite possible to believe the main tenets of the evangelical faith – outward atonement, personal conversion, permanent mission and the authority of scripture – without being a literalist or closing one's mind to the scholarly critique of the Bible, or even the theory of evolution, for that matter. There were, and are, many Friends of this kind, and they preserved the Quaker tradition in the evangelical branch. The line was drawn in the sand in two events in the 1880s, the Ordinance Crisis and the promulgation of the Richmond Declaration.

The Ordinance Crisis and the Richmond Declaration

The holiness revival and co-operation with Christians of other denominations weakened Friends' sectarian character in the Midwest. The harbinger of change was Elisha Bates (1780–1861), a printer, journalist and social reformer of ancient Quaker stock, who had moved when young from Tidewater, Virginia, to Mount Pleasant, Ohio. He was associated with all kinds of movements for social reform (then largely church-led) against such evils as war, duelling, capital punishment and drink. Like Joseph John Gurney, he regarded Friends as an evangelical church which shared a central corpus of agreed doctrine with other evangelical churches but had certain theological reservations that it wished to preserve, and which corresponded to similar reservations among others. The Presbyterians had predestination, the Methodists had the second blessing, and Friends had pacifism and the Inward Light. In 1836 he was baptised and left the Society, leaving behind a solid textbook, *Bates's Doctrines of Friends*, and a controversial reputation.

The question of the ordinances is a tricky one, and Friends who only know societies in which Quakers have had to define themselves against a state church often misunderstand what is at stake. The word 'ordinance' applies to ceremonies plainly taught in scripture, namely baptism and the Lord's Supper. The reason for observing them is that, as Christ's commands, it is one's duty as a disciple to obey. The rest is commentary. One of the things the ordinances are not is sacraments. Now the reasons that can be given for Quaker disuse of these ceremonies are historically not clear.

Originally, it seems, the reason was metaphysical and had to do with the millennial expectations of early Friends. If, in a spiritual second coming, Christ was already here, then memorials of his historical, earthly life were no longer necessary, since the reality to which they pointed symbolically was now present in reality. The ground shifted somewhat when it came to be argued that the historical church fell into apostasy a generation or two after the apostles, and misinterpreted the new covenant instituted by Christ. On this understanding, the outward observances were indeed instituted by Christ, but only as interim measures until the remnants of the old faith had passed away and the true spiritual meaning of washing and communion were properly understood as inward, not outward realities. In the one case the ordinances had been superseded, in the other, they remained essential to the Christian faith as understood by Friends, as the exposition in Barclay's *Apology* illustrates. But they could not be both. So which was it?

The evangelical solution was to adopt the second alternative and to see the Church as still living in the end-times, but awaiting the second coming. The imperative of faithfulness to scripture allowed this, but produced two further alternatives. One could argue that other churches were mistaken when they failed to see the ordinances as a temporary expedient in the first Christian century. On the other hand, one could accept that Friends took a minority view, but argue that participation in the ordinances is not necessary for salvation, and so Friends were entitled to maintain their testimony in its entirety, involving, as it does, a range of claims about reality in religion and the dangers of ritual observance.

These are not academic questions. To many Friends, compromise on the testimony against the ordinances would signal a radical departure from anything that might be called traditional or authoritative in the faith. Yet to some, the arguments did not seem to be conclusive. Bates had already accepted baptism and departed. In 1882, David Updegraff, a leading minister in Ohio Yearly Meeting accepted baptism, as did a number of other Friends who were in sympathy with him. This was not an insignificant matter. At this time Ohio was one of the most populous states in the Union, and what happened there was a good indication of the way things were going everywhere else. Updegraff was a recorded minister. Was that so inconsistent with Friends' testimonies that his recording should be rescinded? Should baptism be an absolute bar to recording in future? Should it be a disciplinary offence to recommend or preach the necessity of baptism?

The matter became public in 1885. New York and New England Yearly Meetings minuted that no minister who had been baptised or had partaken of the supper would be received as a minister among them. Other Orthodox (by now 'Gurneyite') yearly meetings took the same step, but Ohio was the exception. A recommendation to this effect by the Yearly Meeting of Ministers and Elders was turned down by the full Yearly Meeting. The 'water party' had achieved toleration. The other Orthodox yearly meetings, including London and neighbouring Indiana, promptly issued statements reaffirming the traditional position, thus isolating Ohio. The question then arose as to what should be done to plug the dyke the water party had opened up. To tolerate those who chose to be baptised would seriously compromise any corporate witness.

Realising that quick action and a strong response was called for, Indiana Yearly Meeting called a conference at Richmond in 1887 to be attended by representatives from all the yearly meetings in correspondence with London, that is to say, the whole Orthodox body, including Ohio itself. The conference lasted a week and discussed a range of matters including the pastoral system, peace work in the modern world and the ministry of women. After this lengthy consideration of the state of the Society, the conference resolved to issue a Declaration of Faith to clarify what it considered to be the correct attitude to matters then exercising Gurneyite Friends. One of the main authors of the Declaration is thought to have been J. Bevan Braithwaite, who attended as a representative of London Yearly Meeting.

The Declaration itself is a clear, scripturally-based statement of belief, and an examination of similar documents from the early period of Quakerism will show that it is a far more traditional statement than its critics often allow. The early Friends frequently wove words of scripture into their texts without quotation or attribution in the manner of the

Richmond Declaration, but the Declaration attaches the appropriate text as footnotes to each section. The differences tend to come in what the Declaration does not say, rather than what it does. Critics point justifiably to the absence of a section on the Light Within and its emphasis on outward atonement and the need for strict conformity to the written word. It is therefore a revisionist document. But unless one wishes to maintain the early Quaker message in all its fullness, which very, very few do, revision there will have to be.

The delegates at Richmond had originally hoped that their statement of Friends' doctrine would be acceptable 'to all the Yearly Meetings in the World', but this hope was quite forlorn. London and Philadelphia (Orthodox) distanced themselves from the conference; the Hicksite Friends were not even invited; the final form of the Declaration was unacceptable to Ohio because it did not permit the ordinances; London felt finally unable to grant its endorsement. The Richmond Declaration marks a significant stage in the development of modern Quakerism, providing a reasoned account of the beliefs of its evangelical wing. But it thereby made itself unacceptable to nascent liberal Quaker opinion. It was for this reason that it was viewed with suspicion by the younger members of London Yearly Meeting, who were about to launch their own revisionist revolution, going in a very different direction.

Though the Richmond Declaration failed to achieve its authors' ambitions, the conference itself had important consequences, and it is not to be supposed that in the Gurneyite tradition the breeze of change was not being felt. The experience of coming together at Richmond was so helpful that many delegates felt it would be wrong not to continue and further conferences were held. At Indianapolis in 1897, proposals were brought in for a federal body with a uniform discipline (as far as it could be obtained) for the Gurneyite yearly meetings, and Rufus Jones and others set to work to make this a reality. There were practical reasons for a larger grouping. It would be far easier to co-ordinate all kinds of activities which individual yearly meetings might find expensive or difficult, and to provide assistance for weaker parts of the body. There were geographical and other influences tending to separate Friends, and in principle some sort of federation would effectively close the ranks.

But there were more subtle considerations. Some felt that if the tendencies represented in the Richmond Declaration were not checked, the Gurneyite branch was in danger of losing its uniquely Quaker spirit.

It might thus become detached from the wider Society of Friends, from which it was, at that point, only separated. The 1890s were therefore a crucial decade, which might have taken the Gurneyite yearly meetings further along the trail being blazed by the Ohio Orthodox. These yearly meetings had it in their power to move away from common traditions, or to keep open a door by which they might return to them. Under the influence of Friends such as Rufus Jones, and not without cost, the Gurneyite tradition chose the door.

Ultimately, in 1902 the Five Years' Meeting, now known as Friends United Meeting, and originally named for the interval at which it was to meet, was set up with Richmond as its headquarters. Eleven yearly meetings signed the uniform discipline – although, as one would expect, some of them had reservations over one point or another – the Gurneyite bodies of New England, New York, Baltimore, Canada, Wilmington, Indiana, Western, Iowa, Kansas, California and Oregon. The organisation set up boards for evangelism and extension work, education, legislation, and the welfare of negroes, and adopted already existing bodies like the American Friends' Board of Mission (1894), the Associated Executive Committee on Indian Affairs (1869) and the Peace Association of Friends in America (1867).

The Richmond Declaration found its home as one of the pillars of faith on which the Five Years' Meeting rested but its exact status has always been a matter of controversy. For a while, the Gurneyite branch of Quakerism settled down and the new century found it as optimistic and ambitious as its unrecognised relatives in the Hicksite branch of the family. There were many changes below the horizon, and it is a suitable caution for Friends who wish to speculate about the future to see what happened. London Yearly Meeting, the most influential Orthodox body of all, was going through a sea-change. In a very short time the new mood of liberalism captured it as rapidly as evangelicalism had done. The twentieth century was to add a piece to the jigsaw puzzle which reveals that English Friends, for all their quiet demeanour and sweet reasonableness, are only happy at the extremes, and seem prone, theologically, to what amounts to violent reversals of opinion.

Ohio Yearly Meeting continued to thrive and was probably the yearly meeting most influenced by the holiness revivals, though even then it did not become a fully blown holiness church. By the early twentieth century the Pentecostal movement had made its appearance and Friends such as Seth Rees, Harry Hayes, A. J. Tomlinson and Susan Fitkin came out and took positions in such bodies as the Churches of God and the Nazarenes. Perhaps the most influential Ohio Friends of all were Emma and Walter Malone (1859–1924 and 1857–1935 respectively).

Under the Malones' guidance, the Friends Church in Cleveland became a pioneering institution in both education and social action. These were changing times, and the Malones looked at society from the bottom up. It has been argued that these strict evangelicals had views on race, poverty, economics and imperialism which were more progressive than those of many more theologically liberal Friends, for example taking the side of the union in the great Pullman railcar strike in 1894, which brought Clarence Darrow into prominence. Cleveland Bible Institute, now Malone College, opened in 1892. It was not interested in the secular elite and 'modern thought'. It was against smoking, dancing, alcohol and tobacco, and its emphasis was on practical help to people at street level. It did not campaign. Its focus was on the quality of life of the urban poor. Now Evangelical Friends Church, Eastern Region, the old Ohio YM remains one of the two largest yearly meetings in the United States. It numbers about ten per cent of the total number of Friends in the country, and is the driving force behind the Evangelical Friends International.

Idealism, Mysticism and Modernity

T HE RAW MATERIALS OF HISTORY LIE CLEARLY IN THE PUBLIC
domain. They include the personalities and events, movements
and influences which produce change with the passing of time. No
attempt to understand ourselves can avoid the fact that we are the product of these things. But the past is not wholly a matter of our collective
experiences. If we want to get to the humanity behind the inscriptions
and memorials, chronicles and monuments, there is another road open
to us. It is held by many that poetry, by its intimacy and freedom, can
come closer to the spirit of an age than historical scholarship ever can.

The state of religion on the eve of the twentieth century illustrates
this point. In the pause between the lightning of evolution and the
thunder of psychoanalysis, many found that belief was deserting
them. Matthew Arnold, looking down on Dover Beach, heard in the
grating pebbles and the roar of the undertow the draining away of
faith. Thomas Hardy, comfortable in his chair by the fire, was sure that
the cattle were all on their knees, but did not go to find out because
nobody invited him to, and in any case, they might not have been.
This rueful indifference was given a sharp focus by another strand of
sensibility. For Francis Thompson, the divine reality was not fading
into inconsequence or extinction. Though he fled in fear from the
Hound of Heaven, he found no escape. Agnosticism was ultimately
intolerable.

On the other hand, faith of a traditional kind had been stopped
in its tracks by scientific secularism. Doubts had been nourished by
philosophy and scientific enquiry before, but in a piecemeal way. Now

the churches were faced with a comprehensive world-view which provided a satisfactory explanation of the whole of reality without the hypothesis of 'God'. Truth was ascertainable, measurable and predictable. Moreover, the economic and technical developments based on science produced steadily rising prosperity. In 1900, Europe was optimistic about the future, confident of its calling as tutor to the world, and satisfied that it was being carried along on a rising wave of continuous enlightenment by a force called 'progress'.

So where were religious people to turn for a way of preserving their intellectual integrity as well as their faith? It is possible to argue that faced with a serious challenge, believers in any faith will respond in one of three ways. First, there is the impulse to get back to basics. This is a continuing part of Christianity and its usual expression is some form of fundamentalism. Second, there is the reaction of tightening the grip on tradition, to trust the faith of the forefathers to pull one through. Third, there is the attempt to preserve what is understood to be the core of inherited truth while being prepared to let go that which is believed to be outdated.

Each of these elements was present in the Society of Friends at the turn of the century, and it is to them that we must now turn, for we are only now taking leave of the youngest members of the generation which faced that challenge. While waning in influence, evangelical principles were still widely held in London Yearly Meeting. Simultaneously, though, there were signs of a move to rediscover and reinterpret the original Quakerism of the seventeenth century that had been overlaid by quietism and evangelicalism. In addition, the religious outlook known broadly as 'Liberal Protestantism' became the almost universal idiom of theological discourse among Friends outside the old Orthodox yearly meetings.

One figure, whose life reflects these cross-currents well, is the chocolate manufacturer, George Cadbury (1839–1922). He and his brother Richard took over an ailing business employing about a dozen people in the centre of Birmingham in 1861. Such was their managerial skill that, by 1900, their new factory at Bournville, on the outskirts of the city, had a payroll that ran into thousands, and Cadbury was the first name in chocolate throughout the British Empire. The wealth and influence that came with this success enabled George Cadbury to pursue a life of unremitting social service, which he saw as inseparable from the gospel. He was closely in touch with social conditions, for he was an adult school class teacher all his life. He was keenly aware of the privations of poor housing and exploitation. Being of a practical turn of mind he spent his life devising schemes for the betterment of his fellows: he received the mantle of William Allen.

Teaching was probably his greatest interest, for he was a passionate believer in the power of education to change people for the better. He was no paternalist, though, and ran his factory on enlightened principles to which the workforce responded. He set up Bournville village, which is one of the springs of the modern town planning movement, because he believed in a clean and healthy environment. He also knew that neither private philanthropy nor purely personal effort could cure deep-seated social ills. In politics, he was committed to the Liberal Party in its most radical citadel, in the days of John Bright and Joseph Chamberlain.

Underlying all these activities were George Cadbury's religious convictions. He was of the first Quaker generation to reach adulthood after the relaxation of the Discipline had swept away so many restrictions, and his biographer remarks that his freedom from sectarian bitterness was one of his most notable characteristics. He knew Cardinal Newman, Bishop Charles Gore, and William Booth, the General of the Salvation Army. He provided land for the Anglican parish church at Bournville, and in the meeting house there he installed its unique feature among English meeting houses – an organ loft. He was actively engaged in setting up the body which became the Free Church Federal Council. For many years he was a leading contributor to the Friends' Foreign Mission Association and the China Inland Mission. His undogmatic, practical Christianity was an inspiration to thousands.

George Cadbury's influence on London Yearly Meeting extends far beyond his own particular concerns, for he was one of a circle of forward-looking Friends who sensed, in the years around 1900, that the Society would be unable to live much longer on its past glories. So, together, out of common interest rather than concerted design, they began a movement for renewal which provided the Society with the intellectual and spiritual direction which it needed and at the time appeared to lack. The movement emerged at the Manchester Conference of 1895, consolidated with the foundation of Woodbrooke Settlement in 1902, and came to fruition with the setting up of the Friends' Ambulance Unit in 1914.

Renewal, Liberalism and the Manchester Conference, 1895

We have seen that in 1887 London Yearly Meeting had been represented at the Richmond conference, but had found itself unable to endorse the Richmond Declaration. This refusal is significant, for it shows that opinion within the yearly meeting was on the move, and significant numbers of Friends were uneasy at the tendency of the Orthodox bodies to formalise and systematise the Quaker faith. There was a feeling that this line of development would hinder rather than assist the process of coming to terms with the contemporary world. Though it might be squared with both scriptural teaching and the writings of early Friends, some felt that it had squeezed the essential ingredient out of Quakerism, tilted the balance between corporate commitment and personal conviction too far the wrong way, and that the emphasis on formal belief would lead to a weakening of personal faith.

In 1895 the opportunity arrived to articulate these feelings and to put them to constructive use. The Home Mission Committee asked the yearly meeting to hold a special conference to discuss the life and work of the Society. In the short space of six months, preparations were made, and in the November of that year over a thousand Friends gathered in Manchester with the future of British Quakerism in their hands. They were certainly thorough. Seven topics were placed on the agenda covering the whole range of Quaker concern. A glance at the report will show a concern for roots, for organisation and for outreach, and the matters discussed there remain on the agenda for today.

The opening session was entitled 'Early Quakerism, its Spirit and Power', and was followed by a session which asked, one hopes rhetorically, 'Has Quakerism a Message for the World today?' Next, Friends turned their attention to the relations between adult schools, mission meetings and the organisation of the Society, following this up later with sessions on 'The Vitalising of our Meetings for Worship' and 'The more effective Presentation of Spiritual Truth'. Looking beyond the Society in a practical way, the conference also turned its attention to the attitudes of the Society to social questions and 'modern thought'. It concluded with an inspirational address by Thomas Hodgkin entitled 'The Message of Christianity to the World'.

Many things were said at the Manchester Conference that released clouds of relief, as many respected Friends, often with influence and reputation outside the Society, rose to testify to the hope that was in them. It was asserted roundly that modern thought, far from being evil, was largely a blessing to be accepted and used, and not forlornly to be opposed. Included in this was the principle of evolution, which need by no means be regarded as subversive of religious belief. On the theological level, it was argued that the doctrine of total depravity was no part of Quakerism, and the shades of Abraham Shackleton and Hannah Barnard might have beamed to hear it said that there was 'no need to accept Hebrew cosmogony or chronology as a necessary part of an all-round and infallible word of God'.

The enthusiasm released by the Manchester Conference found immediate expression in the summer school movement. The first summer school was held at Scarborough in 1897 and an eminent panel of speakers was assembled including Rufus Jones, Rendel Harris, T. R. Glover and H. G. Wood, and over 650 people attended. A chord had obviously been struck. There was a great demand for this kind of continuing religious education and the best Quaker minds of the day were clearly committed to its success. The task was to release the talents of the Society and to show that modern scriptural knowledge and biblical criticism could be used to enhance and not hinder faith.

Perhaps the organisers were surprised at the response. But they must have been overjoyed; it was proof positive that the Manchester Conference had read the signs of the times correctly. So a Summer Schools Continuation Committee came into existence. In 1899 the school met in Birmingham, in 1900 at Windermere, and again at Scarborough in 1901. Summer schools acted as a leaven. A number of quarterly and monthly meetings arranged similar lecture courses and study circles, provided loan boxes of books and began to design suitable courses of study to support personal concerns and interests.

A key figure in this period was John Wilhelm Rowntree (1868–1905), a man who had come through a searching period of agnosticism and doubt to a serene and genial faith which enabled him to meet the personal tragedy of deafness and impending blindness with the assurance and courage that marked so many of the early Friends who were such an inspiration to him. His early death was a tragedy for the Society, but the effects of the Manchester Conference are a fitting memorial to him. He left only a few addresses and two volumes, but shining through them come confidence and optimism, and a challenge to the Society of Friends that it still needs to take seriously.

Aware of the American developments, he asked whether it was possible for the Society of Friends to continue as a society of lay people, all having some responsibility for the ministry of the word, or must it follow the American example by adopting the pastoral system? He pointed out that it was becoming increasingly difficult in modern business or professional life for people to give the same attention to the requirements of ministry that previous generations felt able to give. His words must have struck home with some degree of sharpness: 'Our present deficiencies cannot be overcome by reserving for the ministry the lees of our energy and the fag-ends of our time . . . the dread of the human element has encouraged a spirit of indolence, and lulled Friends into a belief that the minister need set no time apart for study or definite meditation.'

He pleaded for a teaching ministry and stated his view that there should be placed before any Friend who felt called, the opportunity for further equipment and closer study. He therefore proposed the creation of a 'Quaker settlement', which would have the form of a permanent summer school, a Bible school of sorts rather than a theological college. It was not to be a seminary for the training of ministers, but a 'wayside inn, where a traveller might temporarily find refreshment and repose'. His concern was not only for teachers and ministers, but for a wider circle of Friends too.

George Cadbury put the same point more bluntly: 'We have had the theory that every man and woman is to be a priest, and yet we have done nothing to train them for that office.' The great cocoa magnate did not make his fortune by tolerating unnecessary delay. He recalled his part in the burgeoning movement for renewal: 'One morning, while taking my usual ride on horseback before breakfast, it was strongly impressed upon my mind that the house and gardens of Woodbrooke should be handed over to the Society of Friends as a college for men and women.' This was a reference to his family home at the foot of Griffin's Hill, Selly Oak, Birmingham, at that time unoccupied. He called together a group of Friends and laid his proposal before them. In 1903 the college opened its doors. It was not to be a Quaker ghetto but part of the liberal Christian think-tank.

Quakers tend to be introspective, and they sometimes fail to appreciate the ways in which they are affected by ideas arising outside their own religious tradition. The Manchester Conference, the summer school movement, the principles and curriculum of Woodbrooke were all optimistic, idealistic and immensely compassionate. They truly reflected the values of Friends at the time. Yet the principles on which these attitudes were based were sharply at variance with those of the Quakers who adopted the Richmond Declaration, and raised the same question: how far were their principles Quakerly and how far did they arise from some other influence? The basic principles of Quaker renewal in Britain early in the twentieth century have a family resemblance to what is known as 'liberal theology', the first conscious attempt to come to terms with modern secular thought.

The clearest difference between liberalism and evangelicalism lies in its attitude towards the Bible. Throughout the nineteenth century, a considerable body of critical scholarship had been built up to show that the Bible should not be taken at face value. Parts of it were simply incredible. It contained proven inaccuracies and inconsistencies. Some of the books could not have been written by the people to whom they were attributed. Scripture was found to contain a wide variety of literary forms, some elevated, some crude. Archaeology began to show how there was a cultural assimilation from non-Hebrew societies, and marked parallels were noticed between many biblical narratives such as the Flood story and the literatures of other near-eastern civilisations. So, many convinced Christians came to the conclusion that if the Bible were authoritative, its authority lay elsewhere than in its infallible text. This is very close to one of the traditional Quaker positions, so it is easy to see why Friends proved particularly receptive to the principles of liberal theology.

Throughout the nineteenth century there developed a movement among New Testament scholars that has come to be called 'The Quest for the Historical Jesus'. In many ways this was the keystone of the liberals' endeavours. It was an attempt to assess the value of the different sources that make up the Gospels of Mark, Matthew and Luke and sift out the historically reliable features of these accounts of the life and work of Christ, and to put on one side whatever material was thought to represent misunderstanding, superstition, errors and special pleading. There is a long tradition among Christians, as we have seen earlier, of arguing that the early Church corrupted Jesus' message, and Quakerism itself was born out of one such version of this idea.

Applied to the text of the New Testament, this sort of analysis allowed people to say that the religion of Jesus had been changed, for no very good reason, into a religion about Jesus. Some commentators had reservations about the miracle stories. Questions were raised about the authenticity of the Virgin Birth, the Transfiguration, the Resurrection.

Some considered that alien ideas derived from the Greek mystery religions had been superimposed on Jesus' simple ethical monotheism. Yet others looked at what they took to be a marked difference in atmosphere and teaching between the Gospels and the Epistles, and reached the uncomfortable conclusion that, so far from deserving admiration as the bringer of good news to the gentiles, the Apostle Paul was in fact a corrupter of the original Christian message. Only the real radicals were as blunt as this, but to many it seemed a logical inference to draw.

This meant a marked shift of emphasis in devotional practice. If Jesus were no longer to be understood primarily as the divine, pre-existing Son of God, what sort of phenomenon was he? In a period interested in history, possessed of high ideals and considerable seriousness of mind, Jesus appeared to be the supreme ethical teacher. To be sure, his manner of life and death were most powerful examples of his devotion to God, and therefore an inspiration to us, but he stood in the line of the prophets. No matter what spiritual solace we may derive from the story of his life and actions, what he was concerned to do was to teach us the will of God for our lives. The corollary of a confession of God as our father was the practice in our lives of that brotherhood which this relationship automatically involves.

Accordingly, the social applications of Christianity came to occupy an increasing place in liberal concerns. Plainly, if brotherhood lies at the heart of the gospel, and reconciliation is the task of Christ's servants on earth, these things must be realised within what was an acquisitive and sometimes brutalising social system. Not all Christians of this persuasion felt that socialism was a sign of the Kingdom of Heaven on Earth, but some brave spirits did. Many more put ideals of personal service into practice in the settlement movement, which was influenced in some degree by the Quaker adult schools, going to live and work among the poor of the great industrial cities of Britain. George Bernard Shaw gives a not unsympathetic account of such a spirit in the character of the East End clergyman James Mavor Morell in his play, *Candida*.

Such ways of thinking left their mark on the more abstruse departments of theology also. If there was reason to take the reported words of Jesus and Paul with some caution, the way was open to avoid two of the more unattractive positions taken by evangelicalism. Liberalism in fact engaged a far wider range of emotions and impulses and saw the faith in practical, ethical terms rather than in doctrinal, confessional ones, also a strong point of correspondence with early Quakerism.

Salvation was by no means rejected as the promise of the gospel, but a different meaning was given to it. It could not be made to depend entirely either on the correct formulation of belief or a once for all acceptance of the benefits won by Christ on the cross. Liberals felt that the development of social science and psychology were beginning to show that the simple biblical account of 'sin' was seriously defective, for conduct and attitudes were frequently not a matter of choice, but were unconsciously imposed by cultural factors. So pessimism about human nature was out of tune with the optimism of the age. A doctrine of personal salvation based on a conviction of sin left out a whole dimension of human experience, and strict evangelicalism was less than the whole truth about Christianity.

This sketch of some of the more characteristic liberal positions has portrayed the movement as more cohesive and iconoclastic than it really was. It had no manifesto, organisation or set of accepted principles. The outward statements and vocabulary of liberal theologians were little different from those not of their persuasion. It was a matter of how beliefs were held rather than what they contained. It was no part of the liberals' intention to cast doubt on the Christian revelation. They were in search of an expression of it more adequate to the idiom of their times.

As the first wave of investigation into Quaker origins got under way in the early years of the century, Friends discovered that much in liberal theology could be harmonised with original Quakerism. Unconsciously the two were assimilated in many minds. It came as rather a shock when the second generation of the century's Quaker researchers considered the differences to be as significant as the similarities, and suggested, by implication, that the Quakers had more to say than the liberals.

The Christian faith as taught by liberalism was one of inward transformation. In the life of Christ, the will of God is made manifest. The obedience, the gentleness, the self-sacrifice, the self-emptying love are part of a pattern of revelation which culminates in the death on the cross. This, they said, is the way God saves. By taking human form he showed humanity its true potential, and broke down for ever the obstacles of doubt, fear and sin that keep it bound to earthly things. Reconciliation takes place in the heart when the individual, moved by the example of Christ, through the preaching of the gospel or reading the New Testament, finds in the Christ-life the meaning of his or her own life.

Though seemingly modern, much of liberalism was enshrined in the traditions of the past, notably this 'moral', or 'subjective', theory of the atonement, as it is called. No Church Council has ever laid down a dogmatic statement about how this mystery is to be understood, so Christians have always differed about it among themselves. The liberals actually added their own dynamic to the theory in addition to its medieval devotional aspects. If you put together faith in progress and faith in Christ, you have an unstoppable combination. The earthly powers of tyranny and exploitation and the spiritual powers of ignorance and paganism were doomed, as the message of history was that the world would be won for Christ from its civilised parts. In one form or another, mission was the thing.

Winning the World for Christ

We know with hindsight that this ideal was not to be realised. The dream was generous and compassionate, the dreamers committed and skilled in the useful arts. They went out and won souls; they brought hospitals and schools to places benighted by superstition and disease; they raised irrevocably the consciousness of the third world to the possibilities that lay before it. Unhappily they were also the prisoners of their time. The modern Protestant missions reached Africa and Asia on the coat-tails of imperialism. In the years between 1890 and 1914 they were at the height of their influence, but the ground on which they were standing was beginning to move.

The early Quakers had been totally committed to mission. They sought to convert the Jews, the Pope, the Caliph, Prester John, the Emperor of China and everybody else. Religious plurality was not a part of their scheme. When they withdrew from the world in the eighteenth century, they were far more concerned to preserve their own purity than to convert people, desirable though that might be in theory. Such endeavours would have involved them in the creaturely activity of giving forethought to religious projects, which was taboo. It would also have compromised their testimony against association with hireling ministry. Since all the other denominations had a hireling ministry, the scope for co-operative missionary enterprise was nil.

Evangelicalism came as a breath of fresh air in this stifling atmosphere, and in parallelism with the relief work that it promoted among Friends there grew a concern to preach the word. In 1868 the Friends Foreign Mission Association came into being '. . . to aid the spread of the Gospel of our Lord Jesus Christ and Mission work abroad, chiefly by assisting such members of the Society of Friends, or those in profession with them, as are believed to be called of the Lord to this service.' This concern was also shared by many of those Friends moving out of evangelicalism to a more contemporary form of theology.

The Friends Foreign Mission Association was representative of a number of unofficial groups, the history of which is typical of the Society of Friends of the period. The FFMA and its companion bodies were loose organisations that worked with considerable flexibility, and pursued their concerns in advance of the thinking of the yearly meeting, which only later came to adopt and assimilate them. It took five years for the existence of the FFMA to be acknowledged. In 1881 it first submitted its report to Yearly Meeting, but by the turn of the century it could not be ignored.

In 1899 it had thirty-eight missionaries in the field and this figure had risen to ninety-three in 1902. By the First World War the number had climbed to over a hundred, and in 1917 the work of the Association was formally taken over by London Yearly Meeting, which then acquired direct responsibility for work being carried on in Madagascar, India, Ceylon and China.

The Quaker presence in Madagascar dates from 1867, when Joseph S. Sewell went out to take up educational work in company with Louis and Sarah Street of Richmond, Indiana. The interdenominational London Missionary Society had pioneered the work and the churches on the island were run in an ecumenical spirit, Friends contributing largely to the setting up of the printing press on which the first Malagasy translation of the New Testament was printed. The official Quaker ambivalence towards mission was well illustrated when, a week before departure, Meeting for Sufferings withdrew its endorsement from Joseph Sewell's concern. He had stated clearly that his intention in going to Madagascar was to be useful and not divisive. If he felt it appropriate to take part in the Lord's Supper, he would do so. Meeting for Sufferings' fears were misplaced. He never did, and his position was respected by his fellow missionaries.

The turmoil created by the scramble for Africa washed over this missionary outpost. In the midst of civil disorder in 1895, a number of mission staff lost their lives, including William and Lucy Johnson and their little daughter Blossom. Sitting down to breakfast in the mission station at Arivonimamo, they were set upon and killed. They had been warned of the danger. They knew its seriousness. They were prepared to witness not only with their lips but with their lives. A century later the indigenous United Protestant Church of Madagascar has grown out of these traumatic times. The Society of Friends does not now exist there as a separate entity, but has amalgamated with this body.

The first Quaker missionary in India was Rachel Metcalfe, who originally went out to help teach sewing at Benares but who ended up at Hoshangabad in the Central Provinces, now Madhya Pradesh. Despite chronic rheumatism which rendered her almost helpless towards the end of her life, she mothered a small family of orphans for whom a home was subsequently opened. As the vocation of Friends in Madagascar had been education and ecumenical reconciliation, so in India circumstances turned them to schemes of relief.

The great famines of 1895–6 and 1899–1900 were of exceptional severity. The British Raj was unable to cope. Served by dedicated and experienced administrators, it nevertheless found the needs of India beyond both its vision and its control. In the Hoshangabad district, in a different continent, but not perhaps such a different age, Friends took up once more the problems they had encountered in Ireland. They gave relief and support to eleven thousand people. They resettled villages, they administered emergency funds, cajoling, educating, reforming. They distributed seeds, built roads and dug wells. Though their faith brought them to India, it is for their works that we remember them – and the bridge they built for themselves to cross over safely to the inter-war period, which was to be dominated, for them, by the personality of Gandhi.

China was another main field of Quaker mission work in the years leading up to the First World War. Indeed, if the nineties witnessed a great expansion of work in India, China was the growth area in the first decade and a half of the twentieth century, the number of missionaries on station rising from thirteen in 1901 to thirty-nine in 1916. Friends Foreign Mission Association originally worked in co-operation with the West China Mission in Szechwan Province around Chungking, motivated perhaps by a feeling of guilt for Britain's part in the Opium Wars which had taken place earlier in the century.

In the confused period following the Boxer Rising in 1900, Quakers continued their work, creating schools and hospitals. The International Friends' Institute at Chungking, part adult school, part recreation centre, part cultural agency, part meeting place for different communities, foreshadowed the development of similar centres in Europe after the war. The West China Union University, also founded in 1910 at Chengtu – Christian, interdenominational, independent – struggled in difficult times to establish itself, to grow and to find the contribution it might ultimately make to Chinese life. Henry T. Hodgkin (1877–1933), who left his stamp on the university, was for many years secretary to the Foreign Mission Association and a China hand of great experience.

At this time American Orthodox Friends were also rapidly expanding their missionary efforts, some in collaboration with London Yearly Meeting Friends, some separately. As one would expect, they heeded the call to labour in their own hemisphere and various yearly meetings gave support. We have seen how Louis and Sarah Street joined J. S. Sewell in Madagascar in 1869, and in 1871 Indiana Yearly Meeting sent Samuel A. Purdy to begin Friends' mission work in Mexico. Iowa chose to work in Jamaica, now one of the constituents of Friends United Meeting, and by 1914 there were well over a thousand Quakers on the island.

The Alaska Territory was ceded to the United States in 1869 and the story of California Yearly Meeting's mission to the Eskimos is one of the most touching and beautiful episodes in Quaker history. The yearly meetings then called Kansas and Oregon (now Mid-America and Northwest) gave support. The Atlantic Quaker community circled the globe the other way. In India and China, London Friends found colleagues from Ohio, while any intrepid soul reaching as far as Japan would have found representatives from Philadelphia. They were there unofficially, for, like London, that yearly meeting was still too timid to take up the Great Commission on its own account.

Friends' witness still continues in the turmoil of the Middle East as a direct consequence of the Syrian Mission, started in the days of the Ottoman Empire, independently of any of the Associations of Yearly Meetings. Various Quaker groups in Britain and the United States began to raise money for the development of village schools. Following the ministry of Eli and Sybil Jones of New England Yearly Meeting and their convert, the Swiss Theophilus Waldmeier, support became concentrated mainly on a hospital, the High School at Brummana, now closed, and a similar institution at Ramallah, on the West Bank of the Jordan.

East Africa Yearly Meeting

East Africa Yearly Meeting, which has recently fragmented into many parts, was for several decades the largest yearly meeting in the world. In 1902, three American Friends, two from Ohio and one from Iowa, landed at Mombasa and trekked up to the highlands of the interior of Kenya. They had come to found the Friends' Africa Industrial Mission, and made their centre at Kaimosi, a 'place of God's choosing'. Though Kenya was a British colony, London Friends were often unaware of the success of the mission there. After the Second World War, however, a strong tradition grew up for teachers from London to spend time in Kenya and it is now one of the main fields of endeavour for service workers. East Africa Friends are members of Friends United Meeting.

In the years before 1914 there was a movement to rationalise and systematise mission work. In Britain it was coming to be felt that the relationship between the yearly meeting and the Foreign Mission Association should be made clearer, particularly in view of the immense support the Association enjoyed. Money had to be raised and opinion educated at home. There were problems in the field – of missionaries' health, their tendency to overwork, their need for leave, the demands the service made on their families, the need to educate their children.

In 1906 the Association's training school was removed to Kingsmead College, just up the hill from Woodbrooke in Birmingham, to be run jointly with the Methodists. In 1910 the World Missionary Conference at Edinburgh, which set off the modern movements for church unity and a mission of witness and dialogue, highlighted the growing co-operation within the Protestant missions, with all the difficulties that entailed for Friends. Work was expanding rapidly and there was difficulty in finding suitable personnel. In the United States, where the Five Years' Meeting was well placed to play a co-ordinating role, the American Friends' Board of Missions came into existence. Founded in 1902, it had come by 1912 to manage practically all the mission work of the Gurneyite tradition with certain exceptions that will appear in due course. This task is now carried on by the Wider Ministries Commission of Friends United Meeting.

To set the Quaker missions in perspective, we must look behind them to the crisis of identity that the non-evangelical wing of the Society was going through at the time. The missions were primarily an expression of the Orthodox tradition of Quakerism. Opportunities for the rather self-effacing 'service' more congenial to the non-Orthodox were largely non-existent in the period before 1914. In fact, the non-Orthodox were going through a period of introspection which was destined to make them the challenging and progressive force in twentieth-century Quaker life that the Orthodox had been in the nineteenth.

Reconciliation in America

The group which has come to be called 'liberal' was more diverse than the simplicity of the label will allow. It included the successors of the Hicksites, theological liberals proper, the remaining traditionalists, and possibly the most important sub-group of all, the Young Turks of London Yearly Meeting. While much of its strength came from the old Hicksite yearly meetings, it was also strong in London and Philadelphia, the premier Orthodox yearly meetings of the nineteenth century. It was weakest, but by no means as insignificant as one might expect, in the by now largely pastoral yearly meetings of the Gurneyite, Five Years' Meeting tradition. Two factors which encouraged the spread of liberal values in the Society of Friends were the reconciliation of Orthodox and Hicksite in Philadelphia, and the strong links between that city and London. Additionally there was the recognition of the Hicksites by London Yearly Meeting, and the life and work of one of the most influential Friends, Rufus M. Jones, Professor of Philosophy at Haverford College.

In Philadelphia, Arch Street (Orthodox) and Race Street (Hicksite) meeting houses are about a mile apart. For most of the nineteenth century they might as well have been at opposite poles of the earth, so deeply did the antagonisms of 1827 run. But as the twentieth century approached and the grandchildren of the separation slipped into unobtrusive old age, a new spirit was abroad. Joint meetings were held for social and educational purposes, common peace work was undertaken, Young Friends met together and in 1916, for the first time in ninety years, Joseph Elkinton travelled the mile from Arch to Race with the olive branch of a letter of goodwill. It would take until 1955 for a formal reunion of the two bodies, but in 1900 the artificiality of the division was already showing up.

During the nineteenth century, London Yearly Meeting had refused to recognise the Hicksite 'other branch'. It neither sent epistles to their yearly meetings nor accepted them. Its correspondents in the Orthodox bodies sent advance information about forthcoming visits by ministers, but Hicksite ministers were unwelcome and unrecognised. It was highly suspicious of books, however good, emanating from the wrong quarter, and probably found the whole American scene quite, quite tiresome.

Then opinion changed. As travel to North America became easier, personal contact with Hicksite Friends opened up, and they were found not to conform at all to the character the received wisdom said they ought to have. This put London in a quandary. As Hicksite Friends started to visit Britain and to take as full a part in Quaker life as any other sort of visiting Friend, so the oddness, indeed the wrongness, of the official policy became increasingly obvious. Things were said, minutes agreed, proposals made, pressure brought. Eventually, in 1908 the opposition of the older, Orthodox-inclined Friends was overcome, and a London Yearly Meeting Epistle was sent to the Hicksite yearly meetings. The wall of Jericho remained securely in place.

The Renaissance of Quaker History

Crucial to the whole renaissance of liberal Quakerism is the friendship of a small number of influential men. Principally, there is John Wilhelm Rowntree, whom we have met as a leading member of the Manchester Conference of 1895 and the summer school movement that resulted from it. Prominent among John Wilhelm's concerns was the deepening of Friends' ministry and in 1895 he made an extensive study tour among American Friends. His interest in mysticism had already drawn him to an examination of early Quakerism and in 1897, when on a walking tour of Switzerland, he had met Rufus M. Jones in the company of a mutual Friend, J. Rendel Harris.

Harris was a distinguished figure who had taught at Cambridge, Johns Hopkins and Haverford, and was destined to become the first Director of Studies at Woodbrooke. He was the link between the two sides of the Atlantic, and by introducing John Wilhelm Rowntree to Rufus Jones he encouraged a friendship that had far-reaching effects. Out of their association came the plan to produce a definitive history of Quakerism that would show how George Fox and the early Friends stood in a long line of mystics and spiritual reformers. Tragically, John Wilhelm's eyesight finally failed him, and in 1905, while travelling to America to consult a specialist, he contracted pneumonia and died.

William Charles Braithwaite, lawyer, banker and historian, was the son of Joseph Bevan Braithwaite who is thought to have penned the Richmond Declaration. But the two were of different ways of thinking, and on the death of John Wilhelm, William Charles took up the task of writing the first volumes in what are now known as the 'Rowntree' histories, the solid, blue-bound books to be found in so many meeting houses round the world and which remain to this day the classical narratives of Quaker history.

The project took just over a decade to complete. William Charles dealt with the origins, and his *Beginnings of Quakerism* appeared in 1912, followed by *The Second Period of Quakerism* in 1919. Rufus Jones continued the story from the quietist period onwards, and the two volume result, *The Later Periods of Quakerism*, completed the historical sequence in 1921. (His *Quakers in the American Colonies* had already appeared in 1911.) True to the original intention, Rufus Jones provided a longer perspective on the phenomenon of Quakerism in his *Spiritual Reformers of the Sixteenth and Seventeenth Centuries* in 1914, and his famous *Studies in Mystical Religion* in 1923.

Underlying these impressive contributions to scholarship is the first level of the liberals' self-discovery. They were not content with a scriptural interpretation of Quakerism of the Richmond Declaration variety, for they did not accept the datum of biblical literalism. So where was the foundation of their faith? Where did they belong? Where were their roots?

It has already been suggested that religion at the turn of the twentieth century was under great critical pressure from modern scientific enquiry, and that liberalism was the response that took both religion and science seriously. But liberalism contained dangers for Quakerism because it arraigned traditional religion at the bar of reason and expediency. It would not allow the sacrosanct as a religious category.

Yet denominations live by sacrosanctity. They come into existence as an act of protest, and to assert that changed circumstances have now rendered the original protest outdated is to strike at the very reason for their existence. This is thinking the unthinkable, and in serious cases it can lead to virulent ecumenism. So certain Quaker dogmas had to be excluded from scrutiny. Silence was silence. Free ministry meant no leadership. No sacraments meant no compromise.

Friends were, therefore, challenged to show why their traditional peculiarities still mattered. It was no good being defensive, for liberal Christians from other folds simply said that the church was no longer what it had been in the seventeenth century, and much contemporary Quaker argumentation was simply tilting at windmills. So where were they to turn? There were two immediately available courses open to them as we have suggested. They could take the fundamentalist option and justify their position solely by reference to the Bible. That was out of the question for it meant solving the difficulty of modern thought by avoiding it. The alternative was a return to the security of the traditions of the Fathers. The clue to Quaker identity would be found in Quaker history. and this is where the non-Orthodox started to look.

If this analysis is anywhere near correct, Quaker liberalism of the period was not a true liberalism – it proceeded not from a resolutely open mind but from the desire to preserve Quakerism. In spite of appearances there were certain no-go areas. But then, that was the epitaph on the whole of liberal theology anyway. As Friends discovered it and began to use it, it was already past its prime. The men of the future, such as Albert Schweitzer and Karl Barth, were bidding it goodbye.

There was a prodigious revival of Quaker historical scholarship in Britain at this time, but it was rather different from that earlier in the nineteenth century, which was little more than a cull of the early writings to provide texts to support the evangelical interpretation of Quakerism. In some ways the new research reflected the emergence of the Society into the world. It was painstaking, objective, and concerned to see the Society against the general background of English religious history. There are certain leading figures of this movement but it is noteworthy that it also captured the imagination of many obscure Friends who made solid contributions to research. One of the most noteworthy of Quaker historians was Norman Penney, of Bishop Auckland, Co. Durham. A birthright Friend, he was educated at Ackworth School, at Minden and then at Nîmes, and gained considerable experience of his father's printing business. He felt a definite call to religious work and for sixteen years prior to 1900 he was a missioner for the Friends' Home Mission Committee. He was a man of deep but nevertheless eirenic convictions, having a concern for the reconciliation of the divided factions of Quakerism while at the same time periodically attending the Keswick Conventions, a personal holiness movement among English evangelicals with strong similarities to the positions adopted by the American Quakers David Updegraff and Dougan Clark.

In 1900, Norman Penney became Librarian to the Society of Friends and began his work as an editor of early Quaker texts. The first issue of the *Journal* of the Friends' Historical Society in November 1903 expressed the view that there was a need for a body to undertake research into the Quaker past because a considerable amount of information was becoming available through government publications, the work of voluntary bodies and local historical and archaeological associations. The *Journal* remarked that there was considerable archive material in the stores at Devonshire House (where the offices of the Society were then located), in the British Museum, in the care of local meetings and in the hands of private individuals. This material needed proper care and investigation and it was to promote this concern that the Historical Society came into existence.

Almost immediately the *Journal* began to publish supplements, and the first collection, under the title *The First Publishers of Truth*, came out in one volume in 1907 under Norman Penney's editorship. It appeared that between 1676 and 1704, four separate attempts had been made to get Friends in the counties to send in a summary of the manner in which Public Friends (i.e. the travelling ministers and evangelists) first came among them, what success and opposition they had encountered, and what meetings they settled. The replies had gathered dust for two centuries, but now Friends had almost contemporary documentary evidence about how their Society came into being. The impact of the book is still staggering.

By 1911 Norman Penney was a Fellow of the Society of Antiquaries, a mark of his distinction, and in that year he brought out his transcription of the Spence Manuscript. This is George Fox's account of his life and times, thought to have been dictated during or shortly after his imprisonment at Worcester in 1674 to his step son-in-law, Thomas Lower, in whose handwriting it mainly is. Thus it was possible to establish the bulk of the text on which Thomas Ellwood based the great 1694 edition, and to see where the circumstances of the time had required editorial emendations or omissions. The Spence MS is partly dependent on an earlier document, the 'Short Journal' dating from the Lancaster imprisonment of 1664. With the encouragement of the Friends' Historical Association of Philadelphia, this was also transcribed *literatim* and seen through the press in 1925 by Norman Penney.

The fourth work of importance from Penney was the *Extracts from State Papers relating to Friends 1642–1672*, listing all the occasions between these dates when Quakers had got into the hair of the authorities, as revealed in the files from the period now lodged in the Public Record Office in London. It contains lists, inventories, instructions, petitions, legal documents, papers of all kinds that were the normal fodder of the bureaucrats of the time.

The *Journal* of the Friends' Historical Society more than justified the hopes of the first editorial. There can now be few meetings of any antiquity that cannot show a lovingly compiled history. There can be few clerks who now do not understand the importance of preserving records. There are few County Record Offices that do not have cordial relations with the provincial Society of Friends. So successful has the preservation of records been, with original documents spread out among institutions, that the detailed comparative statistical work that is often now required can be prohibitively expensive.

Places as well as documents can assume importance. In 1912, Swarthmoor Hall came on to the market and was purchased for London Yearly Meeting subject to an arrangement with one of the descendants of Margaret Fell who had herself hoped to purchase and restore the building. Shortly thereafter a plaque appeared on 'Fox's Pulpit', the rock on Firbank Fell where George Fox is supposed to have preached to about a thousand people. Cheap rail travel, the bicycle and the growing popularity of hiking all combined to create new tourist attractions. If walkers from the mill towns of Lancashire climbed Pendle because of its associations with witches, the Quakers were going to do it because of George Fox. Out of all this ultimately came the circuit of Quaker sites in the north-west, visited by Friends from all over the world. Officially it is the '1652 Tour'. To the pious it is the 'Quaker Pilgrimage'. The irreverent call it the 'Fox-trot'.

It is instructive to pause and consider why these rocks and burial grounds and old meeting houses exert such a fascination. It was not always so. A comparison of the Quaker history books in the nineteenth and twentieth centuries will show up marked differences. The modern works place great emphasis on George Fox's experience on Pendle Hill, when he reports that he saw a great people waiting to be gathered. By and large, the nineteenth-century accounts do not.

It seems that the older writers discerned a common theme throughout the pages of Fox's *Journal*, and that was his activity as an evangelist. That suited their theological predilections, and his life was presented rather like the Acts of the Apostles – the interest in the story was the way people of all kinds responded to the message. The more modern writers present us with the earlier parts of the book as a sort of *preparatio evangelii*, rather than the record of Fox's conversion. On Pendle Hill, Fox receives the premonition that he is now to gather a community, and in due course, in Westmorland and the Furness district around Swarthmoor, the community appears. There is a gospel, but care must be taken not to confuse it with the gospel as understood by non-Quakers. The rest of the story of Fox's life is the record of how a community was built up that accepted this gospel with a sense of joyous release, and went out to proclaim the possibility of similar release to the religiously disinherited.

The liberals reached the second level of their quest for identity at this point. They sensed that the secret of maintaining faith in a sceptical age was to be found somewhere in their heritage, so they went back and repossessed it through their historical scholarship. If they could find a non-evangelical form of Christianity they could preserve their intellectual integrity. If they could find a justification for such a faith that went beyond the principles of liberal theology, they might find that their Quaker peculiarities were rationally defensible. But they had to solve both problems together. The man who handed them the key was Rufus M. Jones, father of the mystical interpretation of Quakerism.

Rufus Jones and Mystical Quakerism

Rufus M. Jones (1863–1948) was a down east Yankee, born in the small town of South China, Maine. Though he achieved eminence as a scholar, his early life on the farm gave him such a vivid sense of the glory in everyday things that he got on as well with corn-belt Quakers as he did with the college campus variety among whom he spent his professional life. Capable of writing prose of high refinement and nice distinction, he nevertheless retained the common touch, and for this he was loved. By common consent he was one of the most influential Quakers of all time. He was from New England Yearly Meeting, which was in the Orthodox tradition, never having experienced a Hicksite separation, though driving the Wilburites from its benches in 1845. New England was not on the frontier of enthusiasm and revival in the way Ohio was, and the balanced and comprehensive Quakerism expressed by Rufus Jones is in part a tribute to his origins.

Passing through Harvard College at one of its greatest periods, Rufus Jones was appointed instructor in Philosophy (afterwards Professor) at Haverford College, Philadelphia, in 1893, simultaneously becoming editor of a journal that subsequently became the *American Friend*. Haverford (where Jones had been an undergraduate) is one of the few citadels of cricket in the United States. Nobody has ever managed to win the prize put up by Rufus Jones for a six-hit that would lift the ball on to the veranda of his house, which is on the boundary of the green where the great game is played. He travelled widely, speaking and lecturing. After much heart searching in 1903, he decided to decline the invitation to become the first Director of Studies at Woodbrooke, and, with hindsight, that was probably the right decision for the Society; he was needed where he was.

Apart from his books, Rufus Jones has two memorials of continuing vitality. In 1917 the American Friends Service Committee came into being on the basis of some existing work instigated by him. He died thirty-one years after its foundation, and for twenty of those years, he was its chairman. Quaker service bodies in modern times have attracted many people who, while at one with Quaker values, and wishing to be associated with Friends, nevertheless do not wish, for various reasons, to be in membership. Aware of this, Rufus Jones proposed that there should be some way for the Society of Friends to express its appreciation of such feelings while respecting the independence of those having them. Accordingly, in 1936, the Wider Quaker Fellowship came into being.

Apart from the personal inspiration he gave the many Friends who knew him, he is best known for an interpretation of Quakerism that captured a whole generation of the silent tradition. It gave such a stamp to the vocabulary, the personal devotion and the self-awareness of such Friends that criticism of the positions he took is often more hurtful than it would have been had his words seemed less self-evidently true.

Rufus Jones' central conviction was about the nature of the human relation to the divine. In his beautiful book *The Trail of Life in the Middle Years*, he writes: 'And the deepest thing about man is the fact that he is self-conscious spirit – made in the image of the divine Spirit – in reality unsundered from God as the stream is unsundered from the fountain which is its source, and that true "life" begins when man finds that eternal Reality to which he "belongs". This inward junction of the soul with God, Fox, and the Quakers after him called "the Light within," "the seed of God," "something of God in man." If it is true, it is universally true.'

Almost by definition, therefore, religion must be a matter of personal experience, and to this kind of experience Rufus Jones attached the word 'mystical'. Hence, mysticism becomes a constant theme in his writings and he offers a number of definitions of it. We can see him striving for clarity of expression, but it is a mistake to look for too great a precision, for his understanding, like the phenomenon itself, was alive and growing and not really the sort of subject suitable for abstract formulae. In *The Flowering of Mysticism* he puts it this way: 'Mysticism is an immediate, intuitive, experimental knowledge of God, or one might say it is consciousness of a Beyond or of transcendent Reality or of Divine Presence.' He goes on, '. . . but the phrase will mean much or little or nothing as it wakens or does not waken in consciousness some memory of high-tide moments when the Spirit flooded in and changed the old levels of life.'

As a result of his historical studies, Rufus Jones was convinced that early Quakerism was this high-tide, spirit-flooding kind of religious experience and that it had lineal ancestors among the mystics of medieval and early modern Europe. But there are various forms of mysticism and he was concerned to be accurate. The kind of mysticism of which Quakerism was an example was positive and life-affirming rather than being a discipline of self-denial. Its fruit was an abiding sense of the divine presence rather than a periodic and hard-won experience of ecstasy. Its best expression came in social awareness and concern rather than in intense devotional life. It therefore led to the 'group mysticism' of the silent meeting and the Quaker business method.

This attitude to religion rests on the assumption that the human and the divine are in some way parts of a single continuum. It is therefore artificial to conceive the human being as a creature, not naturally endowed with a measure of divinity. Without gainsaying its capacity for evil, human nature must include some component that is either divine of itself, or else gives the life of the soul access to the divine. If the soul is to transcend its limitations, be redeemed from its imperfections, be saved from its moral transgressions, it must find and submit itself to the divine principle within. It must adopt the path of the mystics.

It is easy to see the appeal that this sort of reasoning has in its own right. It is equally clear that such views answered the needs of the silent tradition in Quakerism at a critical point in its history. Quakers are always in need of respectable reasons for being different. The Orthodox could always use scriptural arguments, however specious, but for the non-Orthodox moving towards theological liberalism, some rationale for the continued avoidance of sacraments, the preservation of silent worship and the avoidance of paid ministry was imperative. An enlightened and liberal age would never succumb to the dangers of idolatry, sacerdotalism and lip-service in religion, so what justification was there for Friends to preserve their peculiarities? Tradition could not answer the rational religion of the early twentieth century, but Rufus Jones could, and the mystical basis of Quakerism was his answer.

Central to his thought is an identification of what Quaker tradition has called the 'inward light' and what the wider mystical tradition has recognised as that of God within the soul. This can be expressed in a variety of ways, but it is certainly consonant with the early Quaker insistence on the possibility of direct and unmediated experience of God. If that is not mystical, nothing is. As he put the point in one of his magazine articles, 'No philosophy can remake men and fill them with power. Theology which deals with dead systems is not creative or re-creative. It is the direct contact of a living Christ with the soul of man that effects the change.'

Rufus Jones was far more interested in incarnation than atonement, for he saw Christ as a revelation of a way of life rather than the key figure in some cosmic sacrificial drama that alters our lives over our heads. It was this view, combined with his understanding of mystical experience, that produced his distinctive interpretation of Quakerism. The golden cord of shared mystical experience that is the life of the meeting is made up of many individual strands of discipleship. Fundamentally, liberalism was just another theology. Its insights were valuable, but if it had any sort of unity it came from its critical and intellectual principles. You could use it well, but you couldn't base your life on it. Mysticism was not like that. It was not thinking. It was fundamental religious experience.

Granted all this, a picture emerges of original Quakerism as an outcrop of the mystical tradition at a time of rigid religious formality. It was, therefore, in sharp contrast to its competitors. The inward light was an expression of an experience rather than teaching, and carried with it a freedom denied to others whose more rigid or intellectual faith could not convey the same power. So Quakerism was not a denomination or a sect – it was a spiritual movement. It had great power to change people, and it could have again.

This is the understanding of Quakerism that developed in the silent tradition in the first part of the twentieth century. It was articulated and vindicated by Rufus Jones. Though he caught perfectly the mood of others and was one of a group of like-minded souls, all of whom breathed the same religious atmosphere, it is not going too far to describe him as the founder of modern mystical Quakerism. He was well placed for this role – his personal influence and prestige, his professorship at Haverford and the editorship of the *American Friend*, his travelling ministry and the fifty-four books he published all combined to set an indelible and unmistakable seal on the Society of Friends.

The London Yearly Meeting of 1914 came at a time when opinion had swung over decisively to this new understanding. At the level of personal faith it reflected the confidence and optimism of society at large. The changes in the Discipline of forty years before had worked through the Society, which was now, through its wealth and influence, a respectable and respected part of the establishment. George Cadbury, Seebohm Rowntree, T. Edmund Harvey and others sought to influence national policy in a progressive direction. A long political liaison between Quakers and the state was beginning. As so often appears in Quaker history, undercurrents flow in opposition to surface currents. The Somme, Ypres and Passchendaele posed questions about both human nature and human societies to which optimism had no convincing answer, and in the long run would lead to a new movement that would question the adequacy of the mystical interpretation of Quakerism.

Peace Witness in the First World War

Part of the shock of the First World War was its scale. Though idealists had seen prosperity and technical change as symptoms of advancing civilisation, they had overlooked the parallel increase in the power of states to organise for destructive purposes, as farms, factories, railways, docks, capital markets and labour movements were controlled and directed towards participation in total war. The conflict was not that of armies alone. Whole societies were now joined in mortal combat.

The contemporary peace movement was a response to this process and represented a coalition of interests. The Quakers were obviously the group with the longest-standing organisational commitment to pacifism, though there were growing pacifist groups in the other churches too. Radicals and rationalists of all kinds have traditionally seen war as futile, and their voices were added to the choir of protest. Often overlapping with this group were the socialists, some of whom objected to the war because it was a capitalist war, others of whom objected to all wars as a denial of brotherhood. Then there were the many thousands of men and women who simply viewed killing with repugnance and wanted to do something about it.

The Quaker peace testimony, venerable though it was, took the form of a personal reservation rather than a political claim. During the nineteenth century, war-resisters had concentrated most of their efforts on promoting schemes for international negotiation and arbitration, like the International Court of Justice which was later born out of the Hague Conventions of 1899 and 1907. This attitude was no longer sufficient. New forms of witness were required. The closely-integrated societies of the twentieth century, which conscripted people, property and money indiscriminately into the war effort, evoked new forms of protest. Freedom of individual conscience was held to entail the right to refuse military service. The maintenance of freedom of speech required the refusal to acquiesce in the government's control and manipulation of the media of communication. The price of both these freedoms was enacted during the First World War; the Friends were among those who had to pay.

Compulsory military service for adult males was introduced into Britain for the first time by the Military Service Act 1916. Conscription had been strongly opposed, but to no avail. Pressure by a number of Members of Parliament, including the Quaker T. Edmund Harvey, caused the insertion of a conscience clause into the bill. Local tribunals were set up before whom all those claiming a conscientious reason for not entering the armed forces were required to appear for examination. There was considerable criticism of the way in which many of these tribunals functioned, and many hearings were a travesty of justice. There was also ambivalence towards them from war-resisters. Some were prepared to accept the alternative forms of service provided for, such as hospital or farm work, but some were absolutists, refusing concessions and insisting on total exemption from participation in the war. Over a thousand young Quakers applied for exemption to tribunals, and so sharp were their disagreements with the way they were treated that a quarter of the number were forced to continue their witness through imprisonment.

They were not the worst treated, though. A number of conscientious objectors unlucky enough to appear before the wrong tribunals were refused exemption and drafted into the forces against their will. There then followed the macabre and spiteful process of transporting thirty-four of them (including three Friends) to the front so that, if they continued to bear their testimony there, they could be shot as deserters. This was a step too far, and public pressure obtained their return. The bogus crime remained on the record but the sentence was commuted to ten years in gaol. Those otherwise in military hands were often treated with great brutality. The return of sanity after 1918 eventually secured the release of these great men.

Friends also played their part in the battle to maintain free speech during the war and were involved in two notable trials in the City of London. The curtain raiser, held at the Mansion House in 1916, concerned proceedings brought against the No Conscription Fellowship. This body, not a Quaker enterprise though supported by Friends, opposed the Military Service Act and brought out a leaflet calling for its repeal. With the exception of the chairman, its whole executive committee was prosecuted. Among their number was a sixty-two-year-old man who knew he was in breach of the law but was willing to take the consequences. Edward Grubb (1854–1939) used his trial to make an inspiring apologia for the action the Fellowship had taken. He was fined, but five members of the committee, including a Friend, Alfred Barratt Brown, refused payment and left the court for prison.

Edward Grubb was one of the leaders of his generation. He was a schoolmaster and private tutor, and came to a deep faith of a different variety after the collapse of his earlier evangelical beliefs. His Christianity had a strong social dimension and he was deeply involved in the transition of London Yearly Meeting to a liberal outlook. He opposed the adoption of the Richmond Declaration and published a number of books interpreting Quakerism in a liberal vein. Closely associated with John Wilhelm Rowntree and his circle, he became the first secretary of the summer schools movement that preceded the setting up of Woodbrooke, thereafter editing the *British Friend* and acting as secretary of the John Howard League for Penal Reform.

The more celebrated of the two trials was held at Guildhall in May 1918 when the chairman and two secretaries of the wartime Friends Service Committee were charged with publishing a leaflet entitled *A Challenge to Militarism*, without submitting it to the censor. The trial was listed while Yearly Meeting was in session, and destiny arrived for her appointment with the clerk, John H. Barlow. He vacated the table to go to court, leaving Mary Jane Godlee in his stead as the first woman ever to preside over London Yearly Meeting. When the magistrate retired to consider his verdict, John Barlow invited the many Friends present to unite in what must have been one of the most impressive meetings for worship ever. Ultimately, all three Friends served terms of imprisonment, but they were no more defeated than William Meade and William Penn had been before them.

The official response of British Quakers to the war had been prompt. Faced with the likelihood of an outbreak of mass hysteria and mob violence directed against enemy aliens, the Emergency Committee was set up in August 1914 to give help to thousands of Germans, Austrians, Hungarians and others who lived or worked in Britain or were simply stranded. By November 1914 a policy of internment was in operation and Friends became involved for the duration in helping to provide work and entertainment for the twenty-three thousand people interned on the Isle of Man.

This was not the sum total, of course. Friends were to be found in all sorts of places where work suitable to their own ages and aptitudes needed to be done, and where the object was the relief of suffering and not the promotion of the war. The Society of Friends is good at mobilising its resources in support of members who feel called on to do pioneering work. They attract an aura of romance and turn it into inspiration, returning it to the ordinary Friends in the meetings, whose own great service is usually unsung.

For work abroad, the Friends War Victims Relief Committee was revived, building in many ways on the experience of 1870–1. The Committee was an official body of London Yearly Meeting. It did much of its work in France. Women were prominent in it and it gladly accepted service from non-Friends. Medical and relief schemes were immediately needed, but reconstruction and development projects followed. On the eastern front, FWVRC workers found themselves in Serbia, Poland and Russia, where their presence survived the Revolution and Civil War, and in 1921 they were still struggling with the results of poor harvests, finally leaving the Soviet Union in 1926.

On the other hand, the Friends' Ambulance Unit was an unofficial, and predominantly male body and it also had a sizeable proportion of non-Quaker pacifists in its ranks. It came into being with a training camp at Jordans in 1914, at the instigation of a committee and under the leadership of a young man later to achieve fame as the Nobel laureate Philip Noel-Baker (1892–1982). This vigorous young Friend and athletics blue, Olympic medallist and President of the Cambridge Union, later became a socialist politician, peer of the realm and lifelong campaigner for disarmament. He began his public career at the head of a group of men who disowned war, but wished to serve peace on the battlefield, where those with different scruples were already willingly accepting death.

The French were more amenable to what the Unit wished to do than the British High Command, who would not allow these unpaid volunteers near the front. So they had to content themselves with the evacuation of the wounded, to which end they ran trains, drove lorries, organised hospitals and assisted on hospital ships. They also undertook civilian medical work, notably the control of the epidemics that usually follow the dislocation of war.

Life was not easy for them, and there were tensions, miscalculations and mistakes. The FAU was even disowned by the Friends Service Committee in 1916. However, the work was carried on, and with the entry of Italy into the war in 1915, a number of FAU people, seeking the opportunity to witness in the midst of danger, turned up in the Anglo-Italian Ambulance Unit, which saw a lot more action. The Friends' Ambulance Unit was laid down in 1919. It had been served by well over a thousand people in Britain and abroad, and like the nation at large, it had its roll of honour. Twenty-one of its members died on active service.

Peace Work between the Wars

An event which was to have far-reaching effects on European Quakerism between the wars took place in 1916, when Kingston Monthly Meeting admitted Carl Heath (1869–1950) into membership of the Society of Friends. Of Huguenot and English dissenting descent, Carl Heath was educated for a while in Paris and also spent time in both Belgium and Sweden while training to be a teacher. When he was forty he became secretary of the National Peace Council. His association with Friends antedated his membership by some years, but he was already involved with both the Emergency Committee and the Friends War Victims Relief Committee. In 1917 he attended an unofficial conference of Friends at Skipton in Yorkshire and floated his suggestion for a series of 'Quaker embassies' to be set up in every European capital after the war. His feeling for peace, his concern for Europe and his understanding of the Society of Friends from the outside made his proposals for an unofficial diplomatic service to assist in conflict resolution appear both realistic and viable.

In due course his ideas appeared in pamphlet form and Quaker heavyweights such as Henry T. Hodgkin came to his support. Yearly Meeting approved the plan and it became part of Friends' official thinking. A convenient way opened in 1918 when there was a reorganisation at Friends House, and the Council for International Service came into existence. One group of Friends now took over responsibility for what work remained from the FWVRC and the other wartime committees and also the interests of the Continental Committee, which had been founded in 1817. Thereafter this body maintained contacts with autonomous Quaker groups in Europe.

A new creative period was beginning, and London often worked in tandem with the American Friends Service Committee. The word 'embassies' was soon dropped and 'centres' substituted. Carl Heath's drive was such that his proposal was given high priority and he became chairman of the new Council. Centres were set up in London, Berlin, Vienna, Paris and other places. The present Quaker offices at the United Nations in New York and Geneva and at the headquarters of the European Union in Brussels are an extension of Carl Heath's vision.

Among the responsibilities of the new Council for International Service was the maintenance of the foreign membership list. Over the years, Quaker activity in Continental Europe had resulted in the setting up of occasional meetings and the appearance of isolated individuals who wished to join the Society. To place their membership on a proper footing, it became the practice for such Friends to be registered as members of London Yearly Meeting. The list was (and is) available to any Friend resident abroad in an area where there is no other yearly meeting. The arrangement applies mainly in the sphere of influence of British Quakerism in Europe and the smaller territories of the Commonwealth.

In fact, there was already a tradition of Quakerism in Europe. In a number of places there were small groups of people whose outlook was similar to the Friends, and there still remained sometimes sizeable churches such as the Mennonites, and perhaps the Dutch Remonstrants, whose roots went back to the same stock as English Quakerism. In Norway, a Quaker movement grew up as the result of the convincement of some prisoners during the Napoleonic Wars, and it became an autonomous yearly meeting in 1846. Denmark Yearly Meeting was set up in 1875 after encouragement from London for an indigenous revival movement. Friends had been strong in the Netherlands at the beginning, but the meetings there gradually died out in the eighteenth century.

In the twentieth century the pattern changed although the number of clearly identifiable Friends probably remained pretty constant.

Because of admiration for relief work, respect for the peace testimony, association with the Quaker centres or inspired just by the friendship of Friends, people began to seek membership, and the flow of Continental students to Woodbrooke began. Germany Yearly Meeting was set up in 1925, followed by Netherlands in 1931, France in 1933, Sweden in 1935 and Switzerland in 1946.

Probably the greatest Friend to seek admission through the foreign membership list procedure was Pierre Ceresole (1879–1945), the son of a former President of Switzerland, who spent only the last nine years of his stirring life as a Quaker. When he finished training as an engineer, he spent five years travelling round the world doing a number of tough, physically demanding jobs. He began to practise his profession in Japan and then returned to Switzerland, but in 1917 made a celebrated declaration against war in the French church at Zurich. He was imprisoned several times for his pacifist convictions and he became the founder of what is now International Voluntary Service; this work camps movement, adopted by the American Friends Service Committee and many other bodies, has now spread round the world. Illustrative of his spirit and daring was his witness of entry both to the Kaiser's and Hitler's Germany without papers, to bring a message of peace.

The inter-war years saw a deepening of the vocation of the Society of Friends to organised social and international service. There was a change of mood and a subtle alteration in attitudes took place. Many idealists in the years before 1914 felt confident that the mechanism of progress was more or less self-regulating. Effective social action was part of the machinery of improvement. As domestic prosperity and reform reduced social antagonisms, so the pressure to settle international disputes by force would diminish. But the ideal was not to be fulfilled. In the cold disillusioned years of the Versailles Treaty, the world was running nonchalantly towards the great crash and the rise of fascism. The determination to strive for effective change was there, but it was not automatically optimistic.

The destructiveness of the Great War had given many people a glimpse of Armageddon, and their overriding principle was, it must not happen again. One senses a much deeper awareness of personal spiritual responsibility to work for change – not a knight errant idealism but what has come to be called an existential commitment. The alternative to war was not inaction or sole reliance on politics – it involved constructive direct action.

The clearest illustration of this is the development of the American Friends Service Committee. At first, AFSC was set up for the duration, which for the Americans proved to be about a year. With typical Yankee efficiency they had over a hundred men and women in France within six months of the entry of the United States into the war, and when it finished they were left with personnel, organisation, finance and supporters, but no war to go to. There was plenty to do, but it was no longer on the Western Front. So expansion and permanence became possibilities. A social order committee began to examine American society and to look for a Quaker attitude towards it, studying labour conditions and the causes of poverty, the democratisation of industry, the distribution of wealth and, finally, simplicity. The data for future action were in this way gathered in.

In 1924 a permanent organisation came into existence with four separate sections – foreign service, home service, inter-racial work and peace work. The first item on this list involved close co-operation with the Council for International Service in London, though the AFSC was entirely independent, and under the executive secretaryship of Clarence Pickett (1925–50) its activities spread world-wide. During the Great Depression of 1929–31 and its aftermath, AFSC fed the children of starving miners, organised craft training and co-operatives for share-croppers, opened up contacts for collaboration with similar groups such as the Mennonites, and began a dialogue aimed at promoting unity and greater social concern among the traditional peace churches.

There was a similar awareness in Britain and comparable activities were undertaken, though in different circumstances. London Yearly Meeting worked closely with AFSC, notably in the Quaker Centres. In 1927 the Friends Foreign Mission Association merged with the Council for International Service to form the Friends Service Council, the official body responsible for all London's relief and development work abroad until a further reorganisation in 1978.

Quaker involvement in social reconstruction between the wars was by no means confined to providing support for the official projects of the Society. While there is a corporate commitment to political activity in its widest sense, London Yearly Meeting only undertakes it as an adjunct to its religious concerns. Politics as a way of operating often involves compromises that Friends are temperamentally unsuited to make. There is also considerable disagreement among Friends on basic political questions, so there is never any suggestion of endorsing one party at the expense of others.

This state of affairs creates two distinct patterns of unofficial involvement in politics among Friends. Many have strong party affiliations and enter public life or the business of local electioneering with enthusiasm. Others are more committed to direct action of a non-party kind, such as one-issue pressure group agitation, seeking to influence opinion and bring pressure to bear on governments and elected representatives.

The clearest example of the latter attitude is in the peace movement. In Britain the two main pacifist bodies are the Fellowship of Reconciliation, an interdenominational religious association formed in 1915 and the Peace Pledge Union, which was created after the war and attempted to mobilise public opinion for disarmament. While Friends were individually involved with both, the nineteenth-century tradition of the Peace Congresses was carried on by those who joined in the activities of the League of Nations Union, to give support to the first international organisation (almost) representative of the world community.

CHAPTER TEN

The Later Twentieth Century

IN 1918, LONDON YEARLY MEETING COMPLETED THREE YEARS' exercise of mind and produced, in eight points, a manifesto for the peace entitled *The Foundations of a True Social Order*. The statement begins with an assertion that the fatherhood of God as revealed by Jesus Christ implies a human brotherhood that is unrestricted by race, sex or social class. It makes the claim that this relationship should express itself in a social order directed beyond the satisfaction of material needs to the full growth of the personality of each of its members, who should be free of unjust conditions and economic pressures. The statement shows its Quaker pedigree by balancing sufficiency with simplicity, warning by implication of the dangers of bondage to material things. It then asserts the power of an appeal to the best in people and advocates co-operation and goodwill as the means to solve industrial problems. It finally teeters on the edge of the great debate of the period and draws back, saying, not that the means of production should be owned in common but only that they should be 'so regulated as best to minister to the need and development of man'.

This statement has the nature of a working document rather than a permanently inspirational piece which engages the heart through its literary qualities. It is based on a Christian theological premise about the origin of human solidarity, and leans heavily on the particular Quaker application of these principles usually associated with John Woolman. It sees an appeal to the best in human nature as a sufficient sanction for the adoption of its principles, but goes into no detail as to how they can be carried out. After the lapse of almost a century it is possible to see the weaknesses of the statement as well as its strengths, but in the period under discussion it represented the thinking of London Yearly Meeting, and asserted, as it probably still asserts, the values Friends try to carry into their social lives.

British Friends and Social Reconstruction

While this document was in preparation, the political ground was moving in the United Kingdom. The Liberalism of the nineteenth century, based on free trade, British mercantile supremacy and the nonconformist conscience, was giving way to forces released by compulsory schooling, increasingly powerful trade unions and the sense of solidarity engendered by the pattern of working-class life in the great industrial cities. The constitution of the Labour Party, adopted in the same year as *The Foundations of a True Social Order*, went further than London Yearly Meeting and said that fraternity would not come until the goods of the earth were communally owned. For many Quakers this was a challenge to their sincerity and they turned with enthusiasm to socialism as the logical outcome of Quaker social principles. There is no index of Quaker political attitudes, of course, but one indication of the strength of feeling on this issue during the twentieth century is that in 1945 the number of Quakers standing for Parliament in the Labour interest outnumbered the rest by two to one. That figure had fallen back to less than half by 1983.

Another response to the post-war world was to go into the poorer parts of the big cities to work, in whatever capacity one could, to bring about an improvement in social conditions directly. Two notable examples of this come from the London dockland. Mary Hughes, daughter of Tom Hughes, judge, Christian Socialist and author of *Tom Brown's Schooldays*, went to live in Whitechapel to identify her life with the East End poor, and joined Friends in 1918. Alfred Salter chose Bermondsey, one of the capital's most deprived boroughs, in which to practise his profession. Though he later became a respected Labour MP, it was primarily for his idealism and dedication as a doctor that he was remembered.

Friends were already a part of the settlement movement which derived from the same impulse. As the nineteenth century drew to a close, many public schools, Oxford and Cambridge colleges, individual philanthropists and trusts built or took premises in poorer districts to carry out social service. Education was a priority and work done was often similar to the adult schools. There were sports, youth clubs, provident schemes, handicrafts, music and other activities designed to develop character and repair some of the damage to physique and imagination that poverty inflicted.

Toynbee Hall in Whitechapel and the Birmingham Settlement are perhaps the most well known institutions, but Friends worked in London with the settlements of the Bedford Institute Association, whose hall in Hoxton is the oldest remaining mid-Victorian music hall, with wrought iron gallery rails and an exceptionally high stage. Elsewhere, in Quaker-inspired settlements and others, many Friends sought to come to terms with the price of the educational and social privileges into which so many of them had been born.

In similar circumstances in Chicago, the Hicksite Friend Jane Addams founded the pioneer settlement of Hull House, possibly the best-known American example of the movement. Active in many causes, Jane Addams was one of the founders of the Women's International League for Peace and Freedom. It was the silent meeting attached to the settlement which joined with Chicago Friends Church in 1931 to form the 57th Street Meeting, one of the first, if not *the* first, meeting to have a dual affiliation through the appropriate yearly meetings to both Friends General Conference and Friends United Meeting.

There is a strong Quaker educational tradition, and from the earliest times the Friends took great pains to provide schooling and proper vocational training for their children. During the quietist period this was one of the ways of maintaining the peculiarities of the Society also, and was undertaken less out of philanthropy than the need to preserve a way of life. As we have seen, the evangelical revival broke down the fear of creaturely activity and by the twentieth century Friends valued education for its own sake. Reasoning that education is the best antidote to prejudice, many Friends began to enter the teaching profession. Again, no statistics are available, but for many young men and women who had grown up in the war years looking for a constructive way of life, the attractions of the classroom were obvious.

The Foundations of a True Social Order was a generous and idealistic document which enshrined Quaker values. However, it overlooked certain significant political forces that came to the fore in the inter-war period – the influence of Marxism in its widest sense following the success of the Russian Revolution of 1917, and the European nationalism which the British experienced in its Irish form, which eventually led to the setting up of the Free State in 1922.

To be sure, social stability rests on shared assumptions and values, and benevolent and tolerant values will produce a similar kind of society. But how are values acquired? It may be vitally important for Quakers to proclaim that 'the spiritual force of righteousness, loving-kindness and trust is mighty because of the appeal it makes to the best in every man . . .' Nevertheless, it is naive to place too much faith in the operation of these virtues in the short run. If different classes have different interests and different values because of their relationship to the means of production, and the interests of employers and employed can be shown to be fundamentally opposed, it is socialist politics, not just good will that will have to be employed to establish justice. It would be silly to criticise the statement for not realising this, but it has to be said that the Quakers, who like to see themselves as pioneers, missed, at this juncture, the signpost to liberation theology that others, later, found.

The second force released by the Versailles settlement in 1919 was nationalism, which in spite of its ideals usually works against the values of fraternity that Quakers have. Democracy was put under intolerable strain in many parts of post-war Europe by the well-meaning attempt to give effect to the legitimate aspirations to statehood of many nations, who ended up with their own territory and constitutions, but also an endemic minority of a different language and culture which felt threatened under the new arrangements. The rise of fascism was partly a combination of these forces, which was used by unscrupulous politicians who saw an opportunity in times of economic stress. The evil that was Nazi Germany was the result. The holocaust is the acid test of Quaker social theory.

In the twenties, Quakerism was making headway in Germany. The relief work undertaken in Berlin, Frankfurt, the Ruhr and other places attracted a number of people, and meetings began to grow. Summer schools were held from 1920 onwards and in 1925 the yearly meeting was set up. The old meeting house at Bad Pyrmont was rebuilt and the Berlin Centre's activities were in full swing. The outlook was bright, until the coming of the New Order in 1933.

Friends, both British and German, were as undecided as anybody else about the true nature of what they were up against in Hitler, and were, of course, denied the analysis available to those whose ideology told them what was going to happen. They therefore approached the new regime with caution, and tried as best they could to carry on with their work and life. They sought to assist the victims of the anti-Jewish laws, which also restricted the civil rights of those with a partly Jewish ancestry. They maintained a rest home at Falkenstein and gave what support they could to those who were coming under persecution. A deputation visited Hitler. Others visited concentration camps and brought to bear what pressure they could to ameliorate conditions there. Information was sent back to London and contacts maintained with the authorities, but both the British representative at the Berlin Centre and the leading German Friend were arrested and questioned. One was released with a charge hanging over him and the other imprisoned for a month on a charge that clearly warranted a much more severe sentence.

With this sort of subtlety, the Gestapo made it clear that critical outside attention to what was going on in the Reich was not welcome. If continued, it would result in the rapid termination of what constructive work the Quakers were doing. So the discreet path was chosen, and silence was part of the cross Friends had to bear, as well as the fearful personal danger in which many of them moved. In 1945 the Epistle of London Yearly Meeting recorded, 'In Europe unmasked we see the evidences of demonic evil.'

On the other side of the world, 1947 saw the end of the British Raj in India and the death of Gandhi. Events in Europe were a marked challenge to Quaker ideas of peacefulness, but the place of non-violent resistance in the successful campaign for Indian Independence somewhat redressed the balance. Numbers of Friends were associated with the Mahatma and his work, both visiting India and giving what support they could in Britain. He had come to Friends' notice during his earlier struggles in South Africa, but the connections had grown so close that at the beginning of the salt tax campaign in 1930, Gandhi sent a British Friend, Reginald Reynolds, to the Viceroy with a message that the symbolic act of disobedience was about to begin. When Gandhi came to London for the second Round Table Conference in 1931 he spent much time among Friends, often attending meeting and ministering. There are close similarities between some Gandhian and Quaker ideas. It is perhaps not going too far to suggest that there is a peculiarly Gandhian form of Quakerism.

Changes in London Yearly Meeting

In the inter-war years the Society of Friends finally emerged from its traditional seclusion into full participation in the life of the world. London Yearly Meeting had never adopted a pastoral system. Though Friends usually gave sound Quakerly reasons for this, the sceptical modern Quaker might remark that it had been so well endowed with educated, comfortably-off Friends with time to spare for the Society's service that it hardly needed to. There were still members of the old Quaker clans in London (and Ireland) Yearly Meetings, but the Society as a whole was now far more democratic and its membership comprised large numbers of people who wanted to support all kinds of Quaker witness that their circumstances prevented them from undertaking personally. What had happened to the joint-stock company now happened to the Quakers – influence shifted from the owners to the managers.

The Great Fire of London in 1666 had destroyed Friends' London headquarters at the Bull and Mouth tavern in Aldersgate. Three years thereafter they acquired Devonshire House, an old mansion in Bishopsgate, and, with additions and alterations of various kinds, these premises remained adequate for their needs for the next two hundred years or so. The atmosphere of the place was surely captured well by Charles Lamb in his essay *A Quakers' Meeting*. But such was the business the Society needed to transact that by 1925 the old place was quite inadequate for its purpose and the central offices were moved out of the City, with all its traditional associations, to a new building opposite Euston Station that was mercifully to be preserved from destruction in the blitz.

The long-term benefits of earlier reforms now began to work through the organisational system, and though the Society now had a large secretariat serving its standing committees, the centre was clearly accountable to the constituents. Since 1857, Yearly Meeting itself had been open to all Friends, not just the duly appointed representatives of monthly and quarterly meetings. This widening of the Quaker franchise was somewhat limited, for there was still a select Yearly Meeting on Ministry and Oversight with its own prerogatives and responsibilities that were not within the province of the Yearly Meeting proper. This body was the senate of Quaker worthies who had earlier exercised such power. In 1906 they were turned out to grass.

Other historical relics were disposed of also. The Morning Meeting, the hallowed body that antedated Sufferings, the library and censorship committee of former times, disappeared in 1901. In 1880, the separate Men's and Women's Yearly Meetings met in joint session for the first time and in 1896 women were made a constituent part of Yearly Meeting and at last became eligible for appointment to Meeting for Sufferings.

By the thirties, therefore, the organisation of London Yearly Meeting was clearly recognisable in its modern form. One development which may not have been as successful as these structural changes was the decision in 1924 to cease the practice of recording ministers. It was felt that this practice tended to discourage ministry from many who might otherwise feel moved to offer it, and gave undue prominence to the ministry of a restricted body of Friends who appeared to have some sort of 'official' approval. Disquiet at the state of ministry was one of the concerns behind the summer school movement and the foundation of Woodbrooke.

The abolition was not lightly undertaken by Yearly Meeting and it was coupled with the placing of responsibility on monthly meetings to encourage ministry. Traditionally, ministers were Friends who felt a sense of vocation to the task, and were willing to dedicate time for the study and meditation which it required. As Friends entered an outward-looking rather than an inward-looking period, this commitment was perhaps undervalued and the advantages of spontaneous ministry were not sufficiently counterbalanced by depth. Preparation does not necessarily entail premeditation.

Changes Elsewhere

Other changes were taking place within world Quakerism and there were signs of new life all around. In the United States, Friends had always been involved in higher education, running their own colleges and being instrumental in the foundation of others. They were not always as good at providing theological education. Evangelical Friends had the benefit of several Bible schools to choose from, of which the best known was probably Cleveland Bible College, now Malone College, Canton, Ohio. Five Years' Meeting Friends who did not opt for a stricter evangelical school tended to go outside the Society to one of the larger interdenominational seminaries.

For Friends of both branches in the silent tradition in the East, an attempt had been made to emulate Woodbrooke by the foundation of a similar institution called Woolman School at Swarthmore, Pennsylvania, in 1917. This initiative from the Hicksite group started encouragingly but was closed ten years later. In 1930, however, it was succeeded by Pendle Hill, an educational community set in the leafy grounds of an old dairy farm at nearby Wallingford. Under the care of friends of both branches and the encouragement of scholars such as

Henry J. Cadbury, Rufus Jones, Howard Brinton and Douglas Steere, it has become one of the most influential institutions in the silent tradition. As at Woodbrooke, there are no examinations or qualifications, but through its programme and its publications it nevertheless maintains high spiritual and intellectual standards.

Evangelical Friends were experiencing challenging times too, poised at one end of the Quaker spectrum, with many connections in kindred circles beyond the Society. One of the strengths of evangelicalism is that its loyalty to Christ always outweighs its denominational affiliations. This does tend to make for a more difficult time than a more relaxed theological outlook usually enjoys, but it does keep other people on their toes. If the Five Years' Meeting had difficulties with the Hicksite tradition, it certainly had them with its evangelical outriders too.

In 1926 Oregon Yearly Meeting resolved to send no more representatives to the Five Years' Meeting until the leadership of that body conformed more closely to its own ideas of Orthodoxy. It was unhappy at liberal tendencies, symbolised by Rufus Jones' membership of the Five Years' Meeting, it was disturbed at the tone of the mission work and it was also exercised over recondite points in the theology of salvation and personal holiness. The following year a small meeting took place at Cheyenne, Wyoming, attended by Friends from Oregon, Kansas, California and Ohio, the already independent yearly meeting that had not joined the Five Years' Meeting in the first place. This was the beginning of a movement that would result in further secessions but which would consolidate and give confidence to the avowedly evangelical wing of the Society of Friends. Against all the expectations, evangelical Friends were to play an important part in the movement for renewal and reconciliation that gathered increasing force later in the century. The Cheyenne conference of about a dozen people was the point from which they began.

Throughout the twenties and thirties the mood of rapprochement grew in the Society, fostered, no doubt, by the wartime experiences of Friends from widely different backgrounds working amicably together. A conference took place in London in 1920 at the suggestion of New England and the invitation of London, at which it was proposed to consider the implications of the peace testimony. More than a thousand Friends attended, representing all the traditions, but in the relief and confusion after the war, very little of a formal nature was accomplished. But it was a start. This was the first ever conference of the whole of the Society of Friends.

The initiative then passed to the service bodies and at Philadelphia in 1937 the Second Friends' World Conference was held with an altogether more practical programme. Many people felt that there was need for a body able to represent the whole Society in a world where international organisations such as the League of Nations were becoming increasingly important. Also, new Quaker meetings were appearing independently of the historic groupings and some way had to be found to recognise and care for them. The outcome was a permanent body – the Friends World Committee for Consultation.

When the Second World War broke out in 1939 the mood of the British nation and the Society of Friends was chastened. Those who supported the war effort knew the real nature of Nazism, and their willingness to take part stemmed from something much deeper than a facile patriotic fervour. Friends, likewise, were faced with the real consequences of their peace testimony. The question was whether it would stand up against an enemy more evil than war itself. Winston Churchill spoke in the House of Commons in June 1940 of '. . . the abyss of a new Dark Age, made more sinister, and perhaps more protracted, by the lights of perverted science.' Warriors and pacifists alike had to live with that possibility.

Paradoxically, it was easier to oppose the war in those years, for the battles won by the conscientious objectors of 1916–19 had been consolidated. The tribunal procedures were fairer and the willingness of objectors to undertake dangerous non-combatant service was accepted. On the other hand, the moral stand was often far more difficult, both because of the nature of the enemy, and the fact that the population was conscripted into industrial work, fire-watching, civil defence, the Home Guard, the Women's Land Army and numerous other schemes. Much nicer distinctions had to be drawn between what was a tolerable involvement in the conflict and what was not – and this applied to people of all ages, not just the young men of service age, as had been the case in 1916.

The Friends' Ambulance Unit was reconstituted and so was the Friends War Victims Relief Committee. With widespread bombing and the evacuation of children, new forms of service developed. As always, as battle receded, Quaker relief workers moved in. They served in Finland, Egypt, Syria, Ethiopia, Burma, China, India and elsewhere. They went back to France, Greece, Italy and Germany itself. They struggled to help displaced persons, collaborators, refugees, the destitute, the handicapped, the diseased and the starving. They were a small part of the total effort of the relief services, but they were distinctive. In 1947, through its representative bodies, the American Friends Service Committee and the Friends Service Council of London, the Society of Friends was awarded the Nobel Peace Prize.

Shortly after the United States entered the war, a meeting had been held at Quaker Hill, Richmond, Indiana, at which eleven Quaker organisations and twenty-four out of thirty-one yearly meetings had been represented. From this gathering in 1943 emerged the Friends' Committee on National Legislation, a registered lobby on Capitol Hill in Washington, which was originally concerned with conscientious objector legislation, but later widened its scope. In London, the departments of Friends House have all kinds of informal links with government departments, but under the American system the Congressional lobby is the best channel for exerting influence.

The FCNL maintains a small office, and its job is to know what is happening in Congress, to keep Friends informed, and to keep congressmen informed of Friends' concerns. Its method of working is to review its *Statement of Legislative Points* every five years and, from this broad statement of objectives, to select its *Legislative Points* for concerted attention at the beginning of each congressional session. It has been very influential in stimulating the efforts of others to lobby for progressive causes, quite apart from its own achievements. By its methods it has enhanced the public reputation of Friends for integrity.

The Second Renaissance in Quaker History

In the years around the Second World War, theology underwent a sea-change as circumstances forced a re-examination of liberalism. It is one of the curiosities of history that the theology of Karl Barth never caught the imagination of Friends. Barth's disillusion with liberal theology reached its turning point in 1914, when he saw, to his dismay, the enlightened German theological establishment throwing the weight of its prestige behind the war. This seemed to him to be unchristian, and he began to appraise the nature of faith that could tolerate the barbarities of trench and submarine warfare. That was his beginning. His output and his scholarship was immense. He quarrelled with some of his theological supporters, and by the 1950s it was clear that he was destined to represent an influence rather than a movement.

Barth took issue with liberalism at this strongest point, the assimilation of the results and processes of modern science to the Christian faith, the sufficiency of psychology and mysticism as accounts of religious experience, the welcoming acceptance of secular culture and an involvement in social and political life resting on the belief that progress and the Kingdom of God were the same thing. Brought up a liberal in theology, remaining a socialist in politics, Barth sat out the First War and wondered how it could be that such an outwardly genial faith could collapse so completely at the sound of a drum. So he went back to first principles, to the leaders of the Reformation.

Under Barth's influence, certain themes that had been muted in liberalism reasserted themselves, notably the sovereignty and otherness of God as the basis for our relations with him. For Barth and those who thought like him, the First World War severed the automatic connection between human endeavour and divine purpose which the liberals took as axiomatic. God was not the unrecognised inspirer of secular culture; he was its judge, for it was found to be not an expression of improving humanity, but the flawed expression of a flawed being. Sin and the need for a personal salvation were re-established as proper concepts quite independently of the continuous evangelical tradition, from which Barth's theology must always be very sharply distinguished.

This analysis provided very little room for natural theology – the discoveries humanity is able to make about God without revelation – so that the weight of emphasis falls even more solidly on Jesus Christ as God's sole revelation of himself. This is our only source of grace, and the cultural achievements which we think express our search for God are worthless. Out of such strivings come 'religion', doctrines and theological systems by which the human mind seeks to render God intelligible. They are totally misguided. The narrow gate through which we all must enter is the revelation of Christ witnessed to by the Church and attested in scripture.

The strong influence of this kind of thinking surfaced dramatically in 1934 in the Barmen Declaration, in which the Confessing Church in Germany stood out against the Nazis. It asserted that the basis of the Church's existence was the revelation of God in Christ, not any subordinate revelation in history or nature. This principle provided a protection from political blandishments of all kinds, thus sidestepping the need to engage German fascism on its own ground, and preserving the gospel as the essence of Christianity. Dietrich Bonhoeffer, who was martyred later in the war was deeply influenced by the movement and was one of the founders of the Confessing Church. His ideas about 'religionless' Christianity, which became widely known after his death, find their origins in this 'crisis' or 'dialectical' theology.

These developments occurred at the same time as other trends more directly associated with Quaker thinking than the general mood of the period. There was a revival of Puritan studies, which was in itself part of a new approach to seventeenth-century history. The political and religious climate was right for a reappraisal of the period and the Calvinism of people such as Barth played its part in generating such interest. It then began to be suggested that perhaps the Quakers should really be regarded as a species of Puritan. A new, second generation of historians of Quakerism went back to the sources and discovered a great deal to be said for this proposition. There were significant differences, naturally, but the received view of the Quakers as optimistic, untheological, mystically-inclined seekers was no longer tenable.

In many ways, the true originality of Quakerism was rediscovered in the extreme difficulty of making it correspond to any of the various models suggested for it. If it had Puritan features, it was also spiritual. If it was mystical it was also highly biblical. If liberal, it was also evangelical. It was both conservative and progressive, simultaneously libertarian and theocratic. It was said of one great German theologian that he looked down the well of two thousand years of Christian history and what he saw gazing up at him was not Christ but the visage of twentieth-century liberalism. If that was true of liberalism, it was also true of the shallower well of Quaker history. It raised the question of Quaker identity for the twentieth century in such a way that this time it could be constructively answered.

The "Tradition" was something that was lived in the quietist period, and was sufficient for most Quakers' needs. It could not withstand the influence of religious changes outside the Society, however, and as factions developed in the nineteenth century, each sought to justify its particular position by claiming the mantle of the first Friends. The question of the true nature of Quaker origins was overlaid by factional argument and the result was the divisions. After 1945 it became increasingly clear that the factional perspectives were inaccurate, so that in theory it ought to be possible to describe a distinctive original Quakerism and to show how its values came to be expressed in various theological forms. If this programme were successful, the way would be clear for closer association without the fear of losing the distinctiveness of the particular traditions. Instrumental in this process has been the work of such scholars and teachers as Hugh Barbour, Arthur Roberts, Wilmer Cooper, T. Canby Jones and Maurice Creasey. The course of the dialogue can be followed in the pages of the journal *Quaker Religious Thought*.

An extremely important influence in this process was the New Jersey Friend Lewis Benson, who devoted his life to the study of the original message of George Fox. There is no interpretation of Quaker origins nowadays that can avoid taking account of what Lewis Benson has to say. The New Foundation Fellowship is a network, mainly at the moment in the English speaking part of the Society of Friends, which is exploring and publicising what it believes to be the truest understanding of the Christian revelation and the most complete expression of the Christian faith since the apostolic age. Many who do not share its views *in toto* have nevertheless been influenced by it and believe its activities to be very important in the quest for Quaker renewal.

Renewal among American Friends

Perhaps the most sensitive group in this respect were the evangelicals. Not all of them belonged to independent yearly meetings but they tended to feel isolated and outside the mainstream of Quaker life. In 1947 they met in conference at Colorado Springs and articulated a position that was soundly evangelical but also firmly based on traditional statements of Quaker principle. Further conferences followed at frequent intervals as the evangelical position was clarified, and in 1956 the Association of Evangelical Friends was formed. It comprised Friends from across the range of pastoral yearly meetings and existed to promote evangelical causes.

Parallel to this, a firmer evangelical grouping of yearly meetings was in course of development. In 1937 Kansas had followed Oregon out of the Five Years' Meeting and in 1957 the bulk of Nebraska Yearly Meeting seceded to set up the new Rocky Mountain Yearly Meeting. So, with Ohio, there were now four strong independent yearly meetings with a similar outlook, not affiliated to either of the associations. There were obviously sound reasons for closer co-operation in the fields of education and publications, mission and revival, and in 1965 the constituents gave full approval to the foundation of the Evangelical Friends' Alliance.

In due course the EFA incorporated many yearly meetings that were originally its mission fields and in 1989 matured into the Evangelical

Friends International, the second largest – and most internation-al – grouping in the Quaker world. It has churches in, among other places, Ireland, Romania, the UK, Hungary, Burundi, Rwanda, Congo, Cambodia, India, Indonesia, Nepal, Philippines, Taiwan, Mexico, Guatemala, El Salvador, Honduras, Nicaragua, Cuba, Bolivia and Peru.

Relations between the Five Years' Meeting and the avowedly evan-gelical yearly meetings were cool at the official level. If they had not been, the secessions would not have occurred. But against that must be set the connections formed at grassroots level by pastors moving back-wards and forwards between groups to positions in equally congenial Quaker congregations. To draw a naughty parallel, there were (and are) conforming and non-conforming Puritans among American Friends. On its other wing, the Five Years' Meeting still contained silent meet-ings of the Orthodox persuasion and a considerable number of liberal or mystical Friends who also sought to influence its nature, but in a non-evangelical direction.

Five Years' Meeting also felt the breeze of renewal and in 1960 it completed a thorough overhaul of its organisation and finances, as a result of which it presented a new face to the world. The biggest change was that it henceforth proposed to meet triennially. This meant that the old name was inappropriate and it became Friends United Meeting. The publications were amalgamated into one journal and the old *American Friend* that had been edited with such distinction by Rufus Jones be-came one part of the new *Quaker Life*. With the largest single number of both affiliated yearly meetings and Friends in membership, Friends United Meeting is the largest Quaker group in the world. On the basis of numbers it obviously represents the majority. Whether it represents the mainstream is another question.

One of the difficulties of the programmed tradition was that the number of pastoral vacancies in meetings and Friends' churches did not necessarily correspond with the number of Quakers coming forward. Hence, if no Friend were available, it was the practice to call a pastor who might be personally highly acceptable, but who was quite unsea-soned in Friends' ways. Over a period, this trend began to dilute certain cardinal Quaker principles such as the right holding of business meet-ings. So it became clear that the Society of Friends should have its own seminary institution at which men and women intending to offer them-selves for Quaker service, not just as pastors in the pastoral meetings, might receive an adequate grounding in the skills they would need.

In 1960, a graduate school of religion was opened for an experimental period at Earlham College, Richmond, Indiana, under the guidance of Wilmer A. Cooper. It prospered, and soon opened an undergraduate programme with a strong emphasis on equipping students for ministry. At the same time it maintained a rigorous academic standard and soon attracted students from outside Quaker circles, too. The existence of Quaker pastors should not be allowed to conceal the fact that in the silent tradition there is also a need for well-trained personnel. Silent Friends need their secretaries, superintendents, finance wizards, experts in religious education and journalism, social and relief workers and so forth, and the greatest success of the Earlham School of Religion might prove to be its contribution to building up in the next generation of Quaker leaders an understanding of their faith that does not rely on the conflicts of the past, because its student body transcends them.

The need for trained personnel at all levels of church life exists throughout the Quaker world. When the Earlham School of Religion came on the scene there were already institutions in existence serving Friends. Haviland Bible Institute and Cleveland Bible Institute (now Barclay College and Malone College respectively) began by providing pastoral and Christian education training for meetings, and have now established themselves as distinguished Christian colleges with a much wider curriculum. Friends can now train at Houston Graduate School of Theology, George Fox Evangelical Seminary, the Haggard School of Theology at Azusa Pacific University, and Carolina Evangelical Divinity School. At each institution there are special Quaker-related courses within the wider seminary training on offer. Elsewhere the Great Lakes School of Theology has joined Friends Bible Institute, Kaimosi, providing training throughout the East African Quaker community. In Latin America institutions that are Quaker or have Quaker connections include Berea Theological Seminary at Chiquimula, Guatemala, Bolivian Evangelical Seminary, and Colegio Emma Canaday at La Paz and Colegio Jorge Fox at Ilave, Peru.

In the Friends General Conference, the changes coming over the Society were as real, but not as plain to see. The old opponents of Orthodoxy had a conception of Quaker church order as a decentralised network of units, each with considerable autonomy. Thus, their successors were more comfortable with a Conference than the greater formality of a delegate body like Friends United Meeting. Like the evangelicals on the other wing, the Hicksite Friends experienced growth while the centre held steady or declined.

The 1960s were years when social taboos of all kinds were relaxed and the young were emancipated from many conventional restrictions. The decade (and its generation) was characterised by the intense pursuit of self-awareness and personal spiritual fulfilment and the mood was expressed to perfection by the music and career of the Beatles. There was a great revival of interest in mysticism and eastern faiths, and many people, religious, but not satisfied with conventional Christianity, turned to Quakerism with what they saw as its foundation in silent meditation. The period saw the often spontaneous growth of new meetings, particularly on college campuses, and Friends enjoyed a refreshing transfusion of the young and the new.

Actually, it was no longer appropriate to talk loosely of 'Hicksites' to describe the more individualist and libertarian kind of Quakerism. The movement to reunion we have seen at work in Philadelphia was actually anticipated in New England Yearly Meeting, which reunited in 1945, followed in the next decade by both Baltimore and New York. These three new combinations decided that they would have dual affiliation to Friends General Conference and Friends United Meeting. Thus it came about that in the historic eastern yearly meetings it is possible to find a very wide variety of Quaker thought and expression. Whether this variety represents the essence of Quakerism is, again, another matter.

The characteristics of these eastern Quakers are repeated in the nonpastoral meetings elsewhere in the United States. Some are affiliated to Friends General Conference alone, such as Illinois, Lake Erie, Ohio Valley and South Central, whereas Southeastern is affiliated to both. There are other important yearly meetings which are very similar to these, but retain their independence and face considerable difficulty because of their remoteness and the wide areas they cover, like Central Alaska Friends' Conference. Intermountain, Pacific and North Pacific were once united, and took for their bailiwick the whole of the West. They have divided not so much because of geography, but because growing numbers made them each a viable size for a separate yearly meeting. In the Midwest there are the Missouri Valley Conference of Friends, Northern, which lies on the western margins of the Great Lakes, and finally Southern Appalachian Yearly Meeting and Association. In spite of their number and variety, British Friends are able to follow the doings of these sister yearly meetings, for their epistles appear annually in the Report of Britain Yearly Meeting.

While many of these groups are small and are spread out over a wide area, their members are active in the usual Quaker concerns, notably peace work and lending support to enterprises such as the American Friends Service Committee and the Friends' Committee on National Legislation. This, it could be said, is the counterpart of support for mission work which takes up a good deal of time and effort in the programmed tradition, where there is a big investment in church extension in the third world and the developing countries. This is gradually altering the balance and outlook of the Society in the world and may prove to be the strongest long-term influence at work in it.

In 1978 the evangelical yearly meetings, now called Eastern Region of Friends' Church (Ohio), Mid-America (Kansas), Rocky Mountain (Nebraska), and Northwest (Oregon), formed the Evangelical Friends Mission – a representative body to co-ordinate and assist their various mission enterprises. In its own capacity, EFM has begun mission work in Mexico City and is taking part in the formation of a university at Vera Cruz, Bolivia, with other evangelical societies to train Latin American church leaders. It is estimated that in Bolivia and Peru there are some eighteen thousand members and adherents of Friends' Church, many among the Aymara Indians. In 1977, Amos Redhair at Rough Rock, Arizona, became the first Navajo recorded minister among Friends. It is not known whether he is the first Indian to be called to this service, but without doubt the future will place him at the beginning of a long line.

Most Latin American Friends are of what the British would recognise as the evangelical persuasion. In Guatemala, Honduras and El Salvador, Central America Yearly Meeting of Friends, with over a hundred and fifty meetings, has close contact with Southwest Yearly Meeting, and there are Friends in other places also, both north and south of Panama. This is not the whole story, by any means, for in Mexico, Colombia, Brazil, Argentina and also in areas where the missions are active, there are groups of Friends worshipping in silence and following the liberal Quaker tradition.

We have seen that the First World Conference of Friends occurred in 1920, and the second in 1937. At a roughly similar interval, Friends gathered at Oxford in 1952 and again at Guilford, North Carolina, in 1967 for a fourth conference, in the shadow of the Vietnam war. This conference was a watershed in many ways and was the most representative so far. By this time the Friends World Committee for Consultation was making its mark as an indispensable part of the Society over and above its various national and sectional loyalties. The mood of the conference was practical and determined. From it came a concern that world Quakerism should become more vocal and influential at the United Nations (whose Secretary-General, U Thant had addressed the conference), that the right sharing of world resources should be a Quaker priority, and that mission and service, so often seen as alternatives or opposites, should be more closely harmonised. In keeping with these concerns, the decision was taken in 1982 not to call another World Conference for the time being, but to limit effort and expenditure to the regular triennial gatherings around the world and to the regional conferences that were beginning to be held.

Reconciliation among American Friends

Though it was not the first of its kind, the conference that was held at St Louis, Missouri, in 1970 to consider the future of Friends in the United States probably marks the end of a beginning. For some time, Friends from the different traditions had worked together through the Friends World Committee for Consultation Section of the Americas and in the periodic gatherings of the yearly meeting superintendents and secretaries of other Quaker bodies. The leaders of the Society were therefore in a position to match what their opposite numbers were feeling with the mood in their constituent bodies.

The decision to meet formally could not have been taken in the absence of a substantial desire for such a conference in the whole of the Society. The initiative came from a group of evangelical Friends from both EFA and FUM who had called themselves 'The Committee of Concerned Friends for Renewal'. They invited up to five representatives from each yearly meeting and asked that the delegations should include at least two non-ministers and one young Friend as well as the superintendent, secretary or presiding clerk. In the event, twenty-eight yearly meetings responded. Though the conference may have originated in a concern for evangelism and religious revival, it was a clear indication of the desire to heal the breaches of fellowship that had occurred between 1827 and 1845.

As Jack Willcuts of Oregon wrote in the London *Friend*, 'As discussion groups and brief plenary sessions continued, certain erroneous generalisations were exposed, such as that evangelical Friends were concerned only with vertical relationship to God and liberal Friends . . . with horizontal relationships with the world. It became apparent that most Friends were interested in both, while expressing these interests in different ways.'

The only specific decision of the conference was to ask the Friends World Committee for Consultation to continue the initiative by calling further regional conferences to explore the common purpose and inspiration of the Society. A few were held, and proved to be a turning point in the lives of many of the participants. Better known is the series of studies which emerged and eventually gave rise to the 'Faith and Life' movement. These books, by single authors or several, sought to relate the religious issues in contemporary Quakerism to a common tradition. In 1976 *New Call to Peacemaking* appeared and this examination of the basis and consequences of the Quaker peace testimony had consequences beyond the Society. It led to interdenominational contacts with the other peace churches such as the Mennonites and an outreach of Friends, through their evangelical wing, to Bible-Christian pacifists in other mainline churches.

Parallel to these developments in the wider life of the Society, there was a growing intellectual consensus, fostered in part by the influence of a periodical. In the United States in 1957 a number of Quakers from across the Society's divides, scholars and practical people, came together to set up the Quaker Theological Discussion Group. It was not a campaigning organisation but a forum at which the co-operative task of thinking through the renewal of the Society of Friends could be undertaken. At its annual gatherings and in the pages of the many issues of *Quaker Religious Thought*, the dialogue between Friends has been continued. Most shades of opinion have been expressed, and through it one can come to grips with the constructive thinking of nearly all the finest Quaker minds of the period. The statement of principle said that the group had no intention of formulating a creed but wished to explore more fully the meaning and implications of Quaker faith and experience by both historical and contemporary approaches.

Friends of the silent tradition, both in Britain and America, are used to having large residential conferences for all comers and all ages. These events are usually held in the summer months and frequently in beautiful settings. Britain Yearly Meeting Summer Gathering has been held every four years since 1991, though the Friends General

Conference Gathering in America has been an annual fixture for much longer. Business is kept to a bare minimum on these occasions, to leave plenty of time for speakers, workshops, worship in many different styles, children's and young people's activities, music, art, drama and many other things besides. Such gatherings are market places, fairs, revival meetings, family reunions, holiday camps, theatres, studios, and places of very deep spiritual refreshment. The Summer Gathering and the General Conference Gathering have much the same atmosphere, and if one is at home in one, one will almost certainly be at home in the other.

At Wichita, Kansas, in June 1977, nearly one thousand Friends of all traditions came from everywhere between Alaska and Argentina to join a 'Conference of Friends in the Americas' on the theme 'Living in the Spirit'. The conference aroused great enthusiasm, but had no specific outcome, like the earlier St Louis gathering. It meant a great deal to the participants, for whom it provided a place of meeting, challenge and a sense of wider Quaker community. These participants were mainly ordinary Friends who went back home to their meetings to give reports and impressions, and doubtless to show slides, but how far those meetings were affected is difficult to say. Probably the cumulative effect of such encounters will show itself in due course in ways that are not immediately obvious.

There was, nevertheless, one development that will be watched with great care. Part of the conference was the Mesa Redonda (Round Table) – the gathering of Latin-American Friends conducted in Spanish. Since that time the links between Friends in North and South America have strengthened and proliferated. The yearly meetings in South and Central America are all autonomous, and among the fastest growing Quaker communities in the world. Most are affiliated to Evangelical Friends International and enjoy considerable support from that body, notably in technical know-how for things like development work, evangelism and religious education. There are moves to increase the supply of classical Quaker literature in Spanish.

The process of rapprochement in general may be coming to an end, however. The older generation of Friends which established links between the branches is now passing away. Each of the branches seems quite content with its own identity, and certain strains have emerged in the attempt by FUM to maintain a central position among Friends. The dually affiliated yearly meetings in the east – New York, New England,

Baltimore and Southeastern – are actually predominantly liberal in theology and find themselves able to prevent FUM taking many positions which its evangelical members would prefer to adopt. Shortly after the formation of the North American section of EFI, proposals were made for a realignment of FUM, whereby the eastern yearly meetings would recognise the reality and leave, and the remaining yearly meetings would join EFI, in which, it was argued, they would be more at home. The realignment controversy subsided fairly quickly, but the issues it raised have not gone away.

Friends and the Ecumenical Movement

Quakers tend to be introspective and sometimes fail to see that what happens to them is actually part of a wider historical process. Large bodies of people change slowly, and the average Friend is probably not over-concerned with the changes we have been describing, if, indeed, he or she knows about them. The liberal or evangelical Friends on the back benches of the meeting house or Friends' church still think of each other in the old stereotypes, and thus justify them. There are still leading Friends who secretly wish the new complexities would go away so that they can carry on with the comfortable attitudes they have always had. But that is not possible. The world is changing and Friends have to change. Within the Christian Church the divisions of the Reformation – strangely paralleled in later, Quaker history – are being reversed. If divided Friends are talking to one another again, so are divided Christians of other persuasions, and the Society has a part in that dialogue too.

The pattern of Quaker membership of the World Council of Churches is uneven. Very roughly, evangelicals tend to think of it as unsound, and the silent tradition is suspicious that its basis of membership constitutes a credal statement. There was a strong component of liberal theology in the moves to set up the Council, and perhaps this aspect of its existence caused difficulty, for the silent tradition, while decidedly liberal, is also highly denominational and jealous of its Quaker peculiarities.

In 1938, when the formula, 'a fellowship of Churches which accept our Lord Jesus Christ as God and Saviour' was agreed as the basis for the forthcoming World Council, London Yearly Meeting took the credal point and declined membership. Five Years Meeting accepted, however, on the basis that this was an affirmation of faith and not a creed. Friends General Conference would have preferred the declaration to include bodies which did not require acceptance of a formula from their members, but recognised that 'that the essentials of unity are the love of God and the love of man conceived and practised in the spirit of Christ.' and were thereby willing to remain in membership. Though a constituent part of the then Five Years Meeting, Canada accepted and still receives invitations to send observers to some World Council gatherings.

In 1965, when the British Council of Churches (to which London Yearly Meeting belonged) altered its basis of membership in line with the rather fuller 'New Delhi' basis of the World Council, Friends were unable to concur. Life without the Quakers being unthinkable, the British Council promptly invented associate membership so Friends could stay in. They paid their dues and got full privileges except the right to vote on changes to the constitution. Their consciences were not offended by this arrangement.

While the world Protestant community continued its slow progress towards unity, the Roman Catholic Church made a sudden leap out of its defensive, post-Tridentine isolation with amazing speed. The Second Vatican Council met in Rome between 1962 and 1965, and although the proportion of Catholics to Quakers in the world is of the order of two thousand to one, a place was reserved for the Friends World Committee for Consultation among the corps of observers, and throughout the sessions, Friends were represented by four individuals with wide experience of ecumenical contacts. One of the most interesting features of late twentieth-century Quakerism was the rapport so many Friends felt with the mystical tradition in Roman Catholic spirituality and its contemporary practitioners. The complementary influences of Thomas Merton and Daniel Berrigan on Friends of a certain age should not pass unnoticed.

However, the nature of ecumenical co-operation in the British Isles changed significantly in 1990 when the Council of Churches for Britain and Ireland was created, with a slightly different set-up to reflect the different religious circumstances in each of the home nations, though with a general assembly for the body as a whole. Whereas Friends were associate members of the British Council of Churches, they became full members of what is now Churches Together in Britain and Ireland. CTBI specifically allows for the membership of churches which on principle have no credal statements (by no means all of a liberal theological outlook), and are willing to accept any church which subscribes to its

'Basis', namely that such a church '. . . manifests faith in Christ as witnessed to in the Scriptures and is committed to the aims and purposes of the new ecumenical body, and . . . will work in the spirit of the Basis.' Britain Yearly Meeting has so far found these terms acceptable.

On the other hand, there are many who are no longer comfortable with Christian orthodoxy. A century ago, liberal theology released many Friends from reliance on the literal meaning of the Bible, doctrines their intellects could not accept, and a sense of sin they did not feel. But as the twentieth century developed, questions arose for those who desired a Christianity without the divinity of Christ. The way of life Jesus exemplified was available on other religious foundations too. Thus, the view began to gain ground among theologically liberal Friends that though it was historically rooted in Christianity, what was distinctive and valuable in Quakerism actually went beyond it.

There were many components of this view. The Seekers of the seventeenth century were singled out as the characteristic recruits of the early Quaker movement. The studied lack of evangelism in the quietist period was seen as a classical expression of the true Quaker temperament. The points of difference between Friends and the Church were interpreted as an intrinsic heretical tendency, notably the lack of concern with the life and work of the historical Jesus. Added to this was the insistence on spiritual experience as the supreme good in religion and the marked similarities between the classical Quaker writers and the mystics of other faiths.

Ideas such as these helped to complete the swing from liberalism to mysticism among non-evangelical Friends. In the second half of the twentieth century there grew up a form of Quakerism which laid primary emphasis on the symbolic and psychological process of religion rather than its doctrinal content, often finding resources for this viewpoint in the world-views and ways of life of eastern faiths like Buddhism, Hinduism and the Tao. What is called 'Universalism' is in fact a complex phenomenon with a number of sources and concerns, but its broad character is that it claims that no religion can have a monopoly of the truth and there is truth in all religions. Expressed in various ways this is now the dominant theology among the liberal, unprogrammed meetings in Britain, the United States and elsewhere.

The problem of ending a story that comes right up to the present is slightly comical. Like Jerry, the cartoon mouse, desperately scampering away from the enormous figure of the pussycat Tom, the historian of

Quakerism looks desperately for a hole to disappear into. Shall it be a fixed date one or two years ago? That seems to avoid the responsibility of drawing some conclusions about the future. Shall it be now? That is the least satisfactory get-out, for tomorrow, today is yesterday, which is an untidy solution. The only possible course is to look into the future and take the consequences of conjecture, that the writer may be wrong, or that he will unconsciously betray whatever personal preferences he has not already disclosed in the narrative.

Conjectures and Speculations

The Society of Friends began as a revolutionary new religious movement in seventeenth-century England, and failed signally in its initial endeavour to supplant all the old churches and usher in a new age of inward, spiritual Christianity. It then withdrew from the world and developed a characteristic set of institutions and a way of life which became widely admired but not widely adopted. With the passage of time, social pressures of various kinds brought Friends into increasingly close contact with the rest of society and new ways had to be found of preserving what was valuable in the past, but at the same time accepting what was valuable in the surrounding religious culture. This is the story I have tried to tell.

While the history and theology of Friends are interesting in themselves, we should also take account of the wider cultural movements in which Quakers have been involved. What I have tried to portray here is the emergence of a small and fairly exclusive sect into a much broader engagement with the religious tradition of which they are a part. Such developments are usually portrayed as the gradual mellowing of a sect into a denomination, and there is much that can be learnt, as we have seen, from taking that point of view. Denominations gradually take on the colouring of their surroundings, and the wider community in turn sometimes receives great benefit from what the denominational tradition has to say. There is a bargain, in fact, and often continuing debate within the denomination as to whether it has been struck in the right place. The question also arises as to how many of a denomination's principles are unique to it, and how much in fact reflects the wider realities of the religious world.

As we have seen, the two main branches of Friends have struck the balance in different places. The evangelical, or programmed branch of Friends takes its basic character from the way Friends on the American frontier adjusted themselves to the quite new society beginning to emerge in the nineteenth century, and reflects much of the character of rural America. In Britain, and the eastern cities of the United States, the liberal, or unprogrammed branch used liberal theological principles to provide a new rationale for many of the traditional ways and values. What has emerged is a kind of Quakerism which reflects the values and interests of the progressive urban middle classes from which, on both sides of the Atlantic, most unprogrammed Friends now come.

So it would seem that with different histories, the two main branches of Friends now have different concerns. These need to be seen against their cultural background, because divergent values and principles may simply reflect circumstances and not how well a particular yearly meeting has preserved the original deposit of the Quaker faith. As we have seen, sociology can perhaps be more illuminating than theology in this respect. So to understand a particular religious body it helps first to have some idea of what is happening to religion in general. At this point, we should move beyond the particular concerns of Friends to see what is happening in the Christian world at large, and what responses evangelical and liberal churches might be called upon to make.

There is a widespread idea in Europe that Christianity is in rapid, possibly terminal decline. There is no doubt that the churches of that continent have suffered a catastrophic loss of membership over the last half century, but the reasons for this are not as clear as may be thought. In the United States and elsewhere in the world, churches are thriving, and the suggestion has been made that Europe is simply a special case and not an example of a general rule. In early modern times the European churches were allied closely with the state, so that political liberalism almost necessarily involved anticlericalism and the rise of the social democratic state has meant a fatal weakening of religious commitment. British Quakers, while part of the religious segment of society, were also in the anti-clerical camp. Historically they have always had the status of a minority having to assert and define itself against a much larger majority tradition.

None of these conditions applies in the United States, where there is a traditional separation of church and state and a free market in religion. In these circumstances, the testimonies of Friends operate differently because they originated in another country and another time. The circumstances that created them have no embodiment in the institutions of state, which specifically provide for religious liberty. On the contrary, religious equality was established by the constitution and no longer needed to be argued, leaving citizens free to think about other things. This is of course why such large numbers of religious refugees came to America from Continental Europe, where persecution was far harsher. Friends' history in this respect is not particularly distinctive, as a comparison of Besse's *Sufferings*, and the Anabaptist *Martyrs Mirror* will show. The hedge is easy to maintain in a highly stratified society. In a more open society, the reasons for maintaining it are correspondingly weaker. The United States was a vehicle for religious freedom and not an obstacle to it; America never needed anticlericalism because it never had a religious establishment.

The other reason usually advanced to account for the alleged decline of religion is the idea of secularisation. On this view, a process is at work in modern societies whereby it is becoming increasingly difficult to maintain that the significance of human life rests on the existence of a transcendent deity. So what is that process? Plainly a major part of it is the way scientific discoveries displace traditional explanations of the workings of the world, for example in the diagnosis and treatment of disease. This leads naturally to the devaluation of religious beliefs and symbols and their disregard by individuals who find the answers to ultimate questions without reference to supra-sensible reality. In Max Weber's term, we see the disenchantment of the world.

But this is not the script the world seems to be following. In all the major religious traditions of the world there are movements towards the recovery of traditional sources of authority led by members of the educated urban classes, the sort of people the theory envisages as exemplars of the secularisation process. It is entirely inappropriate to lump all these things together under the general term, 'fundamentalism', as if it is nothing more than a defensive or reactionary response. Perhaps the reverse is true, for across the Anglo-American world it is the churches that have sought an accommodation with the forces of modernism and secularisation that are in apparently terminal decline.

This seems to me to be the widest frame of reference in which to look at the future of Friends. What happens in each of the Quaker traditions will depend on the accommodation each makes with what it has inherited and the challenges of this kind of world. I have suggested that after the emergence from sectarian seclusion, each branch of the Society of Friends found a distinctive way of relating to the wider religious community based on its own particular circumstances. This was the denominational move. However, history moves on, and it may be the case that denominations are less a permanent part of Christianity than one of the by-products of the Reformation. If that is so, one of the surprises in store could be a revival of sectarian values as a consequence of the return to traditional values that we have just noticed.

And so I reach my bolt-hole. My sense is that each of the major branches of Friends will go the way of the larger group with which they have chosen to be affiliated. The fate of liberal Friends is bound up with the future of liberal religion, the evangelicals with evangelicalism. That is why I have tried to sketch the main features of the contemporary religious landscape, because it is the hills and valleys, watercourses and heathlands of this landscape that will determine the route the Quaker movement takes. Broadly, one can say that Quakerism came into existence as the Enlightenment was dawning, and in one sense, its story is about coming to terms with that way of viewing the world. But the principles of the Enlightenment are now being questioned, and there is a widespread sense that something new is coming into being. Friends are a traditional people, but have learned to use their tradition not as a refuge from reality, but a way to negotiate it successfully and generously. This, if their past is anything to go by, is what they will continue vigorously to do.

Bibliography

Though no footnotes have been used in this book, a large number of works have been consulted during its preparation. This bibliography therefore includes titles which should be acknowledged as sources of information, particularly those by non-Quaker scholars, and also those which may be consulted by readers wishing to follow up topics referred to in the text. The list is select.

Ayoub, Raymond, and David Roeltgen. 'Lexical Agraphia in the Writing of George Fox'. *Quaker History*, vol 87, no. 2, Fall 1998.

Bacon, Margaret Hope, ed. *Wilt Thou Go On My Errand? Three 18th-Century Journals of Quaker Women Ministers*. Wallingford, PA: Pendle Hill, 1994.

Baker, Frank. *The Relations between the Society of Friends and Early Methodism*. London: Epworth Press, 1949.

Barbour, Hugh. *The Quakers in Puritan England*. New Haven, CT: Yale University Press, 1964.

Barbour, Hugh, and Arthur O. Roberts, eds. *Early Quaker Writings 1650–1700*. Grand Rapids, MI: Eerdman, 1973.

Barclay, Robert. *Truth Triumphant (Collected Works)*. Philadelphia, PA: Benjamin Stanton, 1831, 3 vols.

Barclay, Robert. *The Inner Life of the Religious Societies of the Commonwealth*. London: Hodder, 1876.

Bittle, William G. *James Nayler 1618–1660: A Quaker Indicted by Parliament*. York: Sessions, 1986.

Bradley, Ian. *Call to Seriousness*. London: Cape, 1976.

Brailsford, H. N. *The Levellers and the English Revolution*. London: Cresset Press, 1961.

Braithwaite, W. C. *The Beginnings of Quakerism*. Macmillan, 1912; 2nd edn. prep. by Henry J. Cadbury, Cambridge Univ. Press, 1955; reprinted York: Sessions, 1970.

Braithwaite, W. C. *The Second Period of Quakerism*. Macmillan, 1919; 2nd edn. prep. by Henry J. Cadbury, Cambridge Univ. Press, 1961; reprinted York: Sessions, 1979.

Brayshaw, A. Neave. *The Personality of George Fox*. London: Allenson, 1933.

Bronner, Edwin B. 'The Other Branch: London Yearly Meeting and the Hicksites'. *Jnl. of Friends Historical Society Supp.* 34, 1975.

Capp, B. S. *The Fifth Monarchy Men: a study in seventeenth-century millenarianism*. London: Faber, 1972.

Clarke, George, ed. *John Bellers, His Life, Times and Writings*. London: Routledge & Kegan Paul, 1987.

Cole, W. Alan. 'The Social Origins of the Early Friends'. *Jnl. of Friends Historical Society*, vol. 48, no. 3, Spring 1957.

Comfort, W. W. *William Penn 1644–1718: a tercentenary estimate*. Philadelphia, PA: University of Pennsylvania Press, 1944.

Coward, B. *The Stuart Age: a history of England 1603–1714*. London: Longmans, 1980.

Crawford, Patricia. *Women and Religion in England 1500–1720*. London: Routledge, 1993.

Creasey, M.A. '"Inward and Outward": a study in early Quaker language'. *Jnl. of Friends Historical Society Supp.* 30, 1962.

Damrosch, Leo. *The Sorrows of the Quaker Jesus*. Cambridge, MA: Harvard University Press, 1996.

Dandelion, Ben Pink. *A Sociological Analysis of the Theology of Quakers*. Lewiston, Queenston, Lampeter: Mellen, 1996.

Dandelion, Ben Pink, Douglas Gwyn and Timothy Peat. *Heaven on Earth: Quakers and the Second Coming*. Birmingham: Woodbrooke, 1998.

Davie, Martin. *British Quaker Theology since 1895*. Lewiston, Queenston, Lampeter: Mellen, 1997.

Davies, Adrian. *The Quakers in English Society 1655–1725*. Oxford: Clarendon Press, 2000.

Davies, Horton. *The English Free Churches*. London: Oxford University Press, 1952.

Davis, J. C. *Fear, Myth and History: The Ranters and the Historians*. Cambridge University Press, 2002.

Doncaster, L. Hugh. *Friends of Humanity with special reference to the Quaker William Allen 1770–1823*. London: Dr. Williams's Trust, 1965.

Doncaster, L. Hugh. *Quaker Organisation and Business Meetings*. London: Friends Home Service Committee, 1958.

Elliott, Errol T. *Quakers on the American Frontier*. Richmond, IN: Friends United Press, 1969.

Emden, Paul H. *Quakers in Commerce*. London: Sampson Low, 1939.

Endy, Melvin B. *William Penn and Early Quakerism*. Princeton, NJ: Princeton University Press, 1973.

Fox, George. *The Journal of George Fox*, ed. John L. Nickalls. London: Cambridge University Press, 1952; reprinted Philadelphia and London: Philadelphia and Britain Yearly Meetings of the Religious Society of Friends, 2005.

Fox, R. Hingston. *Dr. John Fothergill and his Friends*. London: Macmillan, 1919.

Furcha, E. J. and F. L. Battles, eds. *Selected Writings of Hans Denck*. Philadelphia, PA: Pickwick Press, 1975.

Gardiner, A. G. *Life of George Cadbury*. London: Cassell, 1923.

Garman, Mary, Judith Applegate, Margaret Benefiel and Dortha Meredith, eds. *Hidden in Plain Sight: Quaker Women's Writings 1650–1700*. Wallingford, PA: Pendle Hill, 1996.

Greenwood, J. Ormerod. *Quaker Encounters*. York: Sessions 1975–8, 3 vols.

Grubb, Edward. 'The Evangelical Movement and its Impact on the Society of Friends'. *Friends' Quarterly Examiner*, January 1924.

Grubb, Isabel. *Quakerism and Industry before 1800*. London: Williams & Norgate, 1930.

Grubb, Isabel. *Quakers in Ireland 1654–1900*. London: Swarthmore Press, 1927.

Gwyn, Douglas. *Apocalypse of the Word: the Life and Message of George Fox*. Richmond, IN: Friends United Press, 1986.

Gwyn, Douglas. *The Covenant Crucified: Quakers and the Rise of Capitalism*. Wallingford, PA: Pendle Hill, 1995; reprinted London: Quaker Books, 2006.

Gwyn, Douglas. *Seekers Found: Atonement in Early Quaker Experience*. Wallingford, PA: Pendle Hill, 2000.

Hamm, Thomas D. *The Transformation of American Quakerism: Orthodox Friends 1800–1907*. Bloomington: Indiana University Press, 1988.

Hancock, Thomas. *The Peculium*. London: Smith, Elder & Co, 1859.

Hershberger, G. F., ed. *The Recovery of the Anabaptist Vision*. Scottdale, PA: Herald Press, 1957.

Hill, Christopher. *Puritanism and Revolution: studies in interpretation of the English revolution of the 17th century*. London: Cresset Press, 1958.

Hill, Christopher. *The World Turned Upside Down: radical ideas during the English revolution*. Harmondsworth: Penguin Books, 1975.

Hill, Michael. *A Sociology of Religion*. London: Heinemann, 1973.

Hinshaw, David. *Rufus Jones: Master Quaker*. New York: Putnam, 1951.

Hirst, Margaret E. *The Quakers in Peace and War*. London: Swarthmore Press, 1923.

Hodgkin, Henry T. *Friends beyond the Seas*. London: Headley, 1916.

Hodgson, William. *The Society of Friends in the Nineteenth Century*. Philadelphia, PA: Smith, Elder & Co, 1875–6, 2 vols.

Horle, Craig W. *The Quakers and the English Legal System 1660–1688*. Philadelphia, PA: University of Pennsylvania Press, 1988.

Hunt, N. C. *Two Early Political Associations: The Quakers and the Dissenting Deputies in the Age of Sir Robert Walpole*. Oxford: Clarendon Press, 1961.

Ingle, H. Larry. *First Among Friends: George Fox and the Creation of Quakerism*. Oxford University Press, 1994.

Ingle, H. Larry. *Quakers in Conflict: The Hicksite Reformation*. Knoxville, TN: University of Tennessee Press, 1986.

Isichei, Elizabeth. *Victorian Quakers*. Oxford University Press, 1970.

Janney, Samuel M. *History of the Religious Society of Friends*. Philadelphia, PA: Hayes & Zell, 2nd edn., 1860, 4 vols.

Janney, Samuel M. *Examination of the Causes of the Separation of Friends in America*. Philadelphia, PA: Ellwood Zell, 1868.

Jones, Rufus M. *The Later Periods of Quakerism*. London: Macmillan, 1921, 2 vols.

Jones, Rufus M. *The Quakers in the American Colonies*. London: Macmillan, 1911.

Jones, Rufus M. *The Trail of Life in the Middle Years*. New York: Macmillan, 1934.

Kennedy, Thomas C. *British Quakerism 1860–1920: The Transformation of a Religious Community*. Oxford University Press, 2001.

King, Rachel H. *George Fox and the Light Within 1650–60*. Philadelphia, PA: Friends Book Store, 1940.

Leadbeater, Mary. *The Leadbeater Papers*. London: Bell & Daldy, 1862, 2 vols.

Littell, Franklin H. *The Origins of Sectarian Protestantism*. New York: Macmillan, rev. edn., 1964.

Lloyd, W. Arnold. *Quaker Social History 1669–1738*. London: Longmans, 1950.

Mack, Phyllis. *Visionary Women: Ecstatic Prophecy in Seventeenth Century England*. Berkeley and Los Angeles: University of California Press, 1992.

Marietta, Jack D. *The Reformation of American Quakerism 1748–1783.* Philadelphia, PA: University of Pennsylvania Press, 1984.

Milligan, Edward H. *The Past is Prologue: 100 Years of Quaker Overseas Work 1868–1968.* London: Friends Service Council, 1968.

Moore, John M., ed. *Friends in the Delaware Valley: Philadelphia Yearly Meeting 1681–1981.* Haverford, PA: Friends Historical Association, 1981.

Moore, Rosemary. *The Light in their Consciences: the Early Quakers in Britain 1646–1660.* Pennsylvania State University Press, 2000.

Morton, A. L. *The World of the Ranters: religious radicalism in the English revolution.* London: Lawrence & Wishart, 1970.

Moulton, Phillips P., ed. *The Journal and Major Essays of John Woolman.* New York: Oxford University Press, 1971.

Nuttall, Geoffrey F. *The Holy Spirit in Puritan Faith and Experience.* Oxford: Blackwell, 1946.

Oliver, John. *Walter Malone: The Autobiography of an Evangelical Quaker.* Lanham, MD: University Press of America, 1993.

Penn, William. *Select Works of William Penn.* London: James Phillips, 3rd edn., 1782, 5 vols.

Penney, Norman, ed. *The First Publishers of Truth.* London: Headley, 1907.

Penney, Norman, ed. *Extracts from State Papers relating to Friends 1654–72.* London: Headley, 1913.

Pickvance, T. Joseph. *George Fox and the Purefeys: a study of the Puritan background in Fenny Drayton in the 16th and 17th centuries.* London: Friends Historical Society, 1976.

Raistrick, Arthur. *Quakers in Science and Industry.* London: Bannisdale Press, 1950; Newton Abbot: David & Charles, reprinted 1968.

Rathbone, W. *Narrative of Events in Ireland.* London: J. Johnson, 1804.

Reay, Barry. *The Quakers and the English Revolution.* London: Temple Smith, 1985.

Robbins, Keith. *John Bright.* London: Routledge, 1979.

Roberts, A. O. *The Association of Evangelical Friends.* Newberg, OR: Barclay Press, 1975.

Rose, June. *Elizabeth Fry.* London: Macmillan, 1980.

Ross, Isabel. *Margaret Fell. Mother of Quakerism.* London: Longmans, 1949; York: Sessions, reprinted 1984.

Rowntree, John S. *Quakerism Past and Present.* London: Smith, Elder & Co. 1859.

Rowntree, John S. 'The Friends' Book of Discipline'. *Friends' Quarterly Examiner*, October 1898.

Russell, Elbert. *History of Quakerism*. New York: Macmillan, 1942; Richmond, IN: Friends United Press, reprinted 1979.

Shaw, Howard. *The Levellers*. London: Longmans, 1968.

Shaw, W. A. *The History of the English Church during the Civil War and under the Commonwealth*. London: Longmans, 1900, 2 vols.

Soderlund, Jean R. *Quakers and Slavery: A Divided Spirit*. Princeton, NJ: Princeton University Press, 1985.

Tallack, W. *George Fox, the Friends and the Early Baptists*. London: Partridge, 1868.

Taylor, Ernest E. *The Valiant Sixty*. London: Bannisdale Press, 1947.

Terrell, C. Clayton. *Quaker Migration to South-Western Ohio*, 1967. (Privately published.)

Thomas, Allen C. and H. Richard. *History of the Society of Friends in America*. London: Edward Hicks, 1895.

Trevelyan, G. M. *History of England*. London: Longmans, 1926.

Trevett, Christine. *Women in Quakerism in the 17th Century*. York: Sessions, 1991.

Trueblood, D. Elton. *Robert Barclay*. New York: Harper, 1968.

Vann, R. T. *The Social Development of Early Quakerism 1655–1755*. Cambridge, MA: Harvard University Press, 1969.

Vipont, Elfrida. *The Story of Quakerism through three centuries*. London: Bannisdale Press, 2nd edn., 1960; Richmond, IN: Friends United Press, 3rd edn., 1977.

Watts, Michael R. *The Dissenters, Vol. 1 From the Reformation to the French Revolution*. Oxford: Clarendon Press, 1978.

Williams, G. H. *The Radical Reformation*. London: Weidenfeld & Nicolson, and Philadelphia, PA: Westminster Press, 1962.

Williams, G. H., ed. *Spiritual and Anabaptist Writers* (Library of Christian Classics, vol. xxv). London: SCM Press, 1957.

Wilson, Bryan, ed. *Patterns of Sectarianism: organisation and ideology in social and religious movements*. London: Heinemann, 1968.

Wood, Richard. 'The Emergence of Revivalist Pastoral Quakerism in Midwestern America 1850–90'. (Unpublished paper.)

Woolrych, Austin. *Britain in Revolution 1625–1660*. Oxford University Press, 2002.

Index

Lightning Source UK Ltd.
Milton Keynes UK
UKOW04f1240140716

278388UK00001B/93/P